God Shall Grow Up

Body, Soul & Earth Evolving Together

by Wayne Bloomquist, Ph.D.

God Shall Grow Up

Pondy Publishing
2868 Vista Blvd. #124
PMB #200
Sparks, NV 89434

www.pondypub.com
email: waynebloomquist@sbcglobal.net

ISBN 0-9759755-0-1

Library of Congress Control Number: 2004096246

First Printing 2005
Printed in the United States of America

Cover Design by Robert Howard
Fort Collins, Colorado

Book Design by Casa Graphics, Inc.
Burbank, California

Printed by Central Plains Book Manufacturing
Winfield, Kansas

To Surama

Acknowledgments

For inspiration and/or guidance:
Sri Aurobindo, the Mother, Nolini Kanta Gupta, Haridas
Chaudhuri, Mona Sarkar, Arabinda Basu, Udar Pinto, Judith
Tyberg (Jyoti Priya), V. Madhusudan Reddy, Joseph Martinez,
Jack Schwarz.

For professional help:
Dan Poynter—Self-Publishing guidance, Ernie and Patty
Weckbaugh—book design, Robert Howard—cover design,
Rick Lipschutz—reviewer, Bob and Sunjoy of Ashram's
Archives Department for suggestions for Chapters 4 and 5.

A few shall see what none yet understands;
God shall grow up while the wise men talk and sleep;
For man shall not know the coming till its hour
And belief shall be not till the work is done.

—Sri Aurobindo, *Savitri*, I.IV.55

The Sri Aurobindo Ashram Trust Copyright Department, Pondicherry 605002 India, has given permission to use the quotations of Sri Aurobindo and the Mother.

The Mira Aditi Centre 62 'Sriranga 2nd Main 1st Cross T.K. Layout Saraswatipuram Mysore - 570009 India has given permission to use the quotations from Mother's Agenda.

The Author is grateful to both institutions for allowing the use of extensive quotations.

Contents

Introduction
God Is Somewhere Else

The media have become obsessed with instant worldwide news. Startling breakthroughs in medical and computer technology seem to occur weekly. Many people are communicating daily on the Internet with newfound friends in every corner of the country to form a new connectedness.

We are indeed a nation in change. A dynamic energy is at play that is unprecedented, partly because we are a melting pot without the historical baggage that other countries carry. The family ties and traditions that give strength, permanence, and security in other parts of the world are not present in America. This places us in a very vulnerable and precarious position, but it also gives us unlimited possibilities for unfettered growth, not only in science but in consciousness. In fact, the external is a reflection of the internal activity in our consciousness, invisible to our senses for the moment. In the twentieth century, we witnessed some radical breakthroughs in physics, especially in relativity and quantum mechanics. How does this affect our worldview?

Along with the startling emergence of global communications, the computer has spawned incredible inroads into space travel and medical biology. Unyielding and immovable governments have broken down as in the Soviet Union after seventy years. Women and minorities are demanding either equal rights or at least a voice that can be heard.

New Consciousness—Old Body

In spite of all the tumultuous change in the world, we seem to be stuck with the same body and consciousness that have existed for millennia. If our consciousness is to change radically, our body must change to contain it.

Where is spirituality in this milieu? Will not our concept of spirituality have to change, both in the East and West? Are we Americans up to the task?

At first glance, this question may appear strange, since we do not have significant spiritual roots, as the people do, for example, in India. In this realm, we are like naive babes in the woods—open, trusting, sincere, and receptive. In short, we Americans are highly suitable for embodying the new Truth Consciousness pioneered by two formidable spiritual figures in India: Sri Aurobindo (1872–1950) and the Mother (1878–1973).

Imagine a beautiful flock of white doves that has been nurtured and groomed for decades on the subcontinent of India. Suddenly, the cages are opened, and the birds fly to all parts of the globe. Sri Aurobindo and the Mother collaborated in this impossible odyssey to awaken humanity and embody spirit in matter. This idea is expressed in Sri Aurobindo's epic poem *Savitri*, which is a poetic account of his own personal experience and vision:

> There is a plan in the Mother's deep world-whim,
> A purpose in her vast and random game.
> This ever she meant since the first dawn of life,
> This constant will she covered with her sport,
> To evoke a person in the impersonal Void,
> With the Truth-Light strike earth's massive roots of trance,
> Wake a dumb self in the inconscient depths
> And raise a lost power from its python sleep
> That the eyes of the Timeless might look out from Time
> And the world manifest the unveiled Divine.[1]

The Mother

Many authors on spirituality are not only aware of the writings of Sri Aurobindo, which include thirty volumes in the 1972 centenary edition, but some, such as Ken Wilber and Michael Murphy, have acknowledged him as a source of inspiration for their own work. On the other hand, Sri Aurobindo's spiritual collaborator, the Mother, has been all but neglected and ignored. In this country, she is virtually unknown. That is indeed strange, because Sri Aurobindo and the Mother were one consciousness with one mission.

When Sri Aurobindo died in 1950, the Mother carried on both the inner and outer work until her own death in 1973. Much of this period is documented in *Mother's Agenda* and in *Collected Works of the Mother*.[2] Most of this material, especially that in

Mother's Agenda, cannot be adequately grasped by the mind. One has to experience it to understand what she is relating about the fourth dimension—beyond the space-time continuum. She delved into the land of quantum mechanics without calling it that.

When people first heard about Einstein's law of relativity, $E = mc^2$, did it have any significance for them? We have all heard about the hypothetical trip on which people can return from outer space years later and be younger than when they left. Can we really comprehend that? We have all heard about the unbelievable energy in the atom, as in the atomic and hydrogen bombs, but do we really understand it? When it was first discovered, electricity was a marvel, as were telephones, radios, and television sets.

Around 1944, my Dad and I took the train to his old homestead in Minnesota. There was gas rationing during World War II, which is why we didn't drive there. At the train station in Minneapolis–St. Paul, we saw our first TV set. Neither of us had heard about television yet, let alone seen it. We were mystified and looked around for the projector. How could a picture come from *inside* a box? That thought never occurred to us.

And so it is that we move from one marvel to another. After a while, we take the latest invention for granted and don't question how it works. We are at that state now with consciousness in matter. There are extensive writings about it, but can we really comprehend them? Perhaps not, but we can certainly understand general concepts: why it is necessary; why its time has come; what the outcome will be; how it will affect us and the planet; and what we can do to facilitate it.

Paradoxically, the most difficult aspect to understand is its simplicity in the midst of the enormous complexity of the process. But we could say the same thing about the enormous complexity of the human body: we don't really understand how it all works together, but we accept it. What else can we do?

This book is about what is happening in the world today that is bringing us to a new state of embodied consciousness not affiliated with any religion or other institution. It addresses the issue of what we can do to help bring about this new state of consciousness. The process is surprisingly simple because the

Divine (God, the Creator, the Absolute, the Supreme, and so on) is now taking an open and active part in it. We certainly cannot transform ourselves on our own. "Just try," the Mother said, and you will see that you can't. You simply collaborate by giving your consent. Perhaps it is not quite that easy, but that is only because habit, mind-set, and lack of adaptability create resistance.

It is obvious that one of the first obstacles we encounter, especially in the West, is the separation of spirit and matter. That is, God is somewhere else, certainly not here in matter, in the atom, in my house, writing this paragraph, located in the center of my body.

Death

What about death? Death, too, is a bad habit. It has served its function by allowing us to end one life episode and begin another. We are entering a stage in our evolution where death will no longer be necessary. What are the implications in the abolition of death, and how will it be possible? Is our present bodily make-up adequate to contain this new consciousness? Do we need a new model?

These are a few of the questions that I will explore, based on my personal experiences and the writings of Sri Aurobindo and the Mother. After long reflection, I came to the conclusion that this was the only way I could convey my message and demonstrate that the transformation of consciousness is an ongoing living truth and adventure. Everyone on Earth is invited,even urged, to participate.

Notes

[1]Sri Aurobindo, *Birth Centenary Library*, vol. 28: *Savitri* (Pondicherry, India: Sri Aurobindo Ashram Press, 1972), p. 72.

[2]The Mother, *Mother's Agenda: Agenda of the Supramental Action Upon Earth*, 13 vols., ed. by Satprem (New York: Institute for Evolutionary Research, 1979–2000); The Mother, *Collected Works of The Mother*, 17 vols. (Pondicherry, India: Sri Aurobindo Ashram Press, 1972–1987).

Part One

14 GOD SHALL GROW UP

1

A Gift to Humanity

There is a dark double of all the stars and a luminous double of all the planets. In the occult way, it is said that there is a luminous Earth.

—*The Mother*[1]

Years ago, I had a vision in meditation that bears some similarity to the Mother's remark. Suddenly I was in outer space, looking at the Earth, which was not much larger than a full moon. The planet was luminous: the upper half was mostly transparent; the lower portion had some shadings of silvery gray. All around the Earth for 360 degrees, brilliant lines radiated out, each one a different color. The lines were close together and pulsating as if the Earth were alive.

My interpretation of this vision is that I was seeing the Earth's soul and its essence. The Earth itself is nothing without all its life forms. This book is really about our Earth, its inhabitants, its spiritual nature, and how we can facilitate our evolutionary process. In earlier stages of the Earth's evolution, humans did not exist. First life and then mind emerged from matter. Who could have brought these forth other than the Supreme? At the present stage of our evolution, human beings have a highly developed mental capacity and are ready for the next stage, the Supramental. Our soul, representing the Divine in matter, will be the primary recipient of and instrument for this transformation.

The spiritual transformation of matter will occur and is now occurring, whether or not we want it. But the ease with which it will happen is up to us—whether the transformation will be relatively smooth or cataclysmic. It all depends on our receptivity. A luminous humanity must co-exist with this luminous Earth.

We all witnessed staggering medical advances in the twentieth century and appear to be at the forefront of similar advances in this century as we learn more and more about genes, DNA, and cells. A corresponding but relatively unknown development has been occurring in consciousness for nearly a century, which will lead eventually to a transformed Earth.

While people have adapted quickly to technological change, spiritual evolution is occurring at an even greater pace and will eventually overshadow all of the technological advances. Spirit and matter are one, and the space-time continuum is about to undergo a radical transformation in our consciousness.

I will describe the evolutionary process from my own experiences over the last thirty years and from the writings of Sri Aurobindo and the Mother. The beginning stages of this process have been revealed through a series of experiences— some internal and others external, some in a waking state and others in meditation, some while asleep and others while waking from sleep. I know with certainty that the transformation is happening. It will be consummated one way or another, and is open to all who have a sincere aspiration to know the truth.

Sri Aurobindo began his exploration into spiritual dimensions of matter around 1910 and systematically wrote about it between 1914 and 1921. He continued writing, but less systematically, until his death in 1950. The Mother made a personal effort at bodily transformation via Integral Yoga until her death in 1973. One object of Integral Yoga is to establish an equanimity in body and mind in order to contain the higher spiritual forces.

Sri Aurobindo and the Mother began to recognize, confront, and deal with the many parts of the being—including, to name only a few, the physical body, the vital-emotional being, the mental being, the psychic being (or soul), the intellectual mind, the sense mind, the emotional mind, the physical mind, the subconscient, the inconscient, and the superconscient. It is through the work of Sri Aurobindo and the Mother that we are able to move with some relative ease to transformation. My story and this book are about that process.

When my wife, Surama, and I were national distributors for the books of Integral Yoga from 1990 to 1996, it was thrilling for us to hear from Westerners who had just discovered Sri Aurobindo and the Mother. They could often barely contain themselves. But there were exceptions. The vision and profound writings of these two spiritual pioneers puzzled many people— not just beginners but often quite intelligent and knowledgeable people. The shift in vision was too great, too radical, and too utopian—or so they thought.

The New Consciousness

During gestation, the human embryo goes through successive states of pre-historic development. Nature has recognized and adapted to previous development so that human gestation has been accelerated and compressed into nine months. At one stage, the embryo has gills, but these later evolve into lungs. Similarly, Sri Aurobindo did not discard the traditional philosophies and yogic practices of Vedanta, Vaishnavism, and Tantra, but incorporated them into his own system and used them as a foundation for further development. He called the descent of a new consciousness the "Supermind" or the "Supramental" or "Truth Consciousness." This descent was the culmination of his work, and the Mother continued the experiment, partially transforming her own body. The inner work that she did until her passing was awe-inspiring, laying a foundation for development and exploration by others. It is not necessary, however, for us to go through all the trials and tribulations that she endured. Her spiritual journey was her gift to humanity. When a disciple once asked her if the Supramental process would involve a lot of suffering, she responded, "No, for those who have faith and open themselves in surrender, the work will be done automatically."[2]

Westerners have a great deal of difficulty comprehending and believing in the immaterial—that is, what is not readily apparent to the senses. Soon after I started my own spiritual journey in 1969, I came to understand how we are conditioned to see only what everyone else sees.

In 1970, I took a beginning class on metaphysics. At one point, the teacher talked about how to see auras. To demonstrate, he stood on a table in the room and told us to observe him. A few minutes later, he got down from the table and asked us what we had seen. There was complete silence for five or ten seconds until a man said, "You disappeared." I had also seen him disappear, with something like heat waves coming off a hot pavement where his body had been. But, because this was not within my belief system at the time, I immediately suppressed what I had seen— until the other man spoke. Then I wanted to say, "That's right! You *did* disappear!" The teacher confirmed his "disappearance," saying that he had transported himself to his house in Oregon.

I have never forgotten the contortions my mind went through to disavow that experience. My rational mind said that this could not happen. It was not possible. But my eyes said that it had *just happened*. I will talk more about this phenomenon later, because we must learn to see and experience in a different way as we shift to a New World order.

Alchemy
The idea for a transformation or transmutation has been with

us for thousands of years. It was perhaps first expressed in alchemy in the attempts to transmute base metals into gold. Many experiments over the centuries were conducted to transform matter, often at the risk of death. If one claimed to be an alchemist but could not perform, the authorities could put him to death as a charlatan. There have been other variations of this theme, some bordering on the magical—as in, for example, the pursuit of the Holy Grail or the fountain of youth. Carl Jung pursued the alchemical process from a psychological viewpoint. That is, he attempted to reconcile opposites in our being.

The universe was created on the principle of duality. For wholeness to be achieved, something has to be reconciled with something else. Duality has served its purpose of creating the play, the drama, but now something else is emerging that is whole within itself. Sri Aurobindo called this new principle the Supermind or Supramental Consciousness, which will transform life on Earth.

Christianity largely ignores Hinduism, which states that there have been six prior civilizations on this planet, all of which were destroyed. We are now in the seventh civilization, which Hindus—as well as Sri Aurobindo and the Mother—predict will survive. What is going to cause us to survive so that we are not destroyed as in the past?

Of course, none of this has much personal relevance if one does not believe in reincarnation. But what a cruel injustice it would be if we only lived on Earth once! At some point in our evolution, many of us begin to realize that we have lived countless times and perhaps even have memories of former lives. With this belief, realizing the ignorance of the ego-centered separated self, one can become a self-realized being, discarding the body and merging into the Supreme.

Since I began my own conscious spiritual quest, a significant change in awareness has occurred in America. Spiritual practices have become almost commonplace, at least on the West Coast, and may be on the verge of being in the mainstream of society.

In 1972, the Sri Aurobindo Ashram in Pondicherry, India, published a thirty-volume set of Sri Aurobindo's writings to celebrate the hundredth anniversary of his birth. In connection with this, Dr. Haridas Chaudhuri, founder of the California Institute of Asian Studies (now the California Institute of Integral Studies, or CIIS), convened a daylong conference on the centenary celebration. The well-attended event, held at Lone Mountain College, in San Francisco, included as presenters, among others, Alan Watts and a California state senator. By the 1980s, however, interest in Sri Aurobindo waned as the public's focus shifted to Indian gurus who came to America. Their message, however, was for a more traditional self-realization.

It is ironic that virtually all of the great spiritual masters have come from the East, and yet there is such ignorance regarding their teachings, with the exception of Jesus. Hinduism has had little impact in the West, although Buddhism is widely recognized. Through the churches, Christianity has usurped the power from the people to have an authentic inner experience of the Christ.

The Next Stage

Historically, there has been a strong tendency for each religion to claim exclusive truth and to disavow the significance of other religions. Organized religion has served a purpose, but the true Supreme Being has no name. All paths lead to the One without a name. Some call the Supreme Being simply "That." There is a unity of all religions. Sri Aurobindo and the Mother incarnated to tell us that life on Earth, as we know it, is not finished, is not complete, and not only showed us the way to the next stage but prepared it for us.

Sri Ramakrishna (1836–1886) was important in this context by reconciling seemingly divergent religious paths. Through his own *sadhana* (spiritual practice), he realized in himself the essence of Christianity, Islam, and Hinduism (Vedanta and Tantra). Humankind is still very slowly getting this message. The completion of Sri Ramakrishna's mission set the stage for the next step in evolution. Each *avatar* (a direct emanation of the

Supreme as manifested in a human) has a specific mission to fulfill.

Sri Aurobindo recognized the spiritual genius of both Sri Ramakrishna and his disciple Swami Vivekananda (1863–1902). He also acknowledged the teaching he received from them in 1909, many years after their physical demise.

By 1914, Sri Aurobindo was formulating his Integral Yoga, and concluded writing his major works by early 1921. He continued working on the Yoga of Transformation for the rest of his life. Although he died in 1950 and the Mother died in 1973, their work still continues. Nevertheless, the forthcoming changes will be so swift and radical that humankind cannot as yet readily understand them. It is not that we will be intellectually challenged, but there is no precedent to help our understanding. There are signs, however, of the transformation already occurring, which will be discussed in later chapters.

Who Am I?

Before we can comprehend the wholeness of spirit, we have to have some recognition and definition of who we are. For example, when I first started studying and working with my dreams in 1969, I discovered that there was much more occurring at night while I was asleep than what is commonly referred to as dreaming. My nights had become more interesting than my days. Many of my own spiritual experiences have occurred while I've been asleep. Why is this? At night, our egos and rational defense mechanisms diminish, allowing our receptivity to other dimensions of consciousness to increase. The same receptivity can be achieved during meditation, when we often go into an altered state of consciousness.

Here is a dream that I had in 1970:

> I am attending a class given by Dr. Chaudhuri. Another student asks him a question. Before answering, Dr. Chaudhuri looks intently at the student, especially below the knees. When I

> realize in the dream state that Dr. Chaudhuri is
> addressing the student's level of understanding
> before answering, my body is suddenly filled with
> light—the light that is understanding and bliss.
> But my awareness is now separated and outside
> my physical body, which I observe to be still
> asleep and breathing slowly and heavily.

I learned from this experience the great power and joy that we have locked up within us because of our unawareness and the "habit" we have of lumping so many parts of our being together. This is a significant defect of Western Civilization, which has conditioned us to be dominated by our senses and our environment. Before I had that dream, I already sensed that I was in a steel cage. The dream motivated me to spend much of my subsequent life getting out of that cage and into something that was permanent and transforming. I interpreted the dream experience as a separation of *purusha* and *prakriti*. In Sankhya (one of six orthodox schools of philosophy in India that teach the two eternal realities of Spirit and Substance), *purusha* is the basic consciousness or the Truth Being in whatever plane it manifests, and *prakriti* is the energy apart from consciousness. I learned through this dream and other sleep experiences that dreams can be much more than we think—even sublime and otherworldly happenings. But one can have similar otherworldly experiences while awake.

Once we recognize that we are comprised of many parts of consciousness that we have lumped together, it is possible for us to allow the Supreme to reorganize us—that is, if we become receptive to the changes, our rigidity and limitations are loosened. Unfortunately, we do not have the vocabulary in the English language to define all of these states. Sanskrit does allow us to express and explore consciousness much more deeply, but we are still left searching for proper descriptive terms. Sanskrit delineates different states of consciousness instead of simply using the term *God*.

Sri Aurobindo spoke about the need to be aware of the

purusha (spirit) in the heart, the mind, the vital, and above the head:

> The Purusha, the Spirit within, who is no larger than the finger of a man is seated for ever in the heart of creatures: one must separate Him with patience from one's own body as one separates from a blade of grass its main fibre. Thou shalt know Him for the Bright Immortal, yea, for the Bright Immortal.[3]

Notes

[1]The Mother, *Collected Works of The Mother*, vol. 5: *Questions and Answers, 1953* (Pondicherry, India: Sri Aurobindo Ashram Press, 1976), p. 276.

[2]The Mother, *Mother's Agenda*, vol. 4: *1963*, ed. by Satprem (New York: Institute for Evolutionary Research, 1987), p. 468.

[3]Sri Aurobindo, *Birth Centenary Library*, vol. 12: *The Upanishads: Texts, Translations, and Commentaries* (Pondicherry, India: Sri Aurobindo Ashram Press, 1972), p. 265.

2

To India

*True spirituality is not to
renounce life, but to make
life perfect with a Divine
Perfection.*

*This is what India must
show to the world now.*

—*The Mother*[1]

In 1970, the year after I first heard about Sri Aurobindo, I had unexpectedly lost my job as a real estate appraiser and had no money whatsoever except for my unemployment checks. While struggling to make ends meet, I made every effort to find another job, but nothing worked out. Finally, after three months, it dawned on me that I needed to make a commitment about priorities in my life. Until that point, I had always placed my job first. I had not been successful in my business career, but was still trying. At that moment, I decided to give first priority to my spiritual life in Integral Yoga. This would come first in whatever decision I would make in the future about a partner, career, and so on. After I made that decision, I felt ready to go back to work.

Nothing happened for another three months, even though I kept saying to the inner presence, "I'm ready. I'm ready." It was as though I needed that time to make sure I was sincere.

After six months of unemployment, I found a job doing the same type of work as before, but everything else in my life had changed for me. I had found a new spiritual direction—Integral Yoga—which I had studied at the Cultural Integration Fellowship (CIF) and the California Institute of Asian Studies (CIAS), which later became the California Institute of Integral Studies (CIIS), both of which had been founded and were still administered by Dr. Haridas Chaudhuri, who was a disciple of Sri Aurobindo.

At CIF, I met an Indian student from Madras, whose name was L. Muthulingam, who was also interested in Integral Yoga and, in fact, was planning to go to Pondicherry to become a member of the Sri Aurobindo Ashram. We were sitting in my living room in San Francisco when I asked him what I should do next to deepen my involvement with Integral Yoga. He suggested that I write a brief letter to the Mother, enclosing a photograph of myself, and asking for her guidance. As he said this, I saw a bright light in the center of his chest, right over his heart. At that time, I knew practically nothing about the Mother. Nevertheless, the next day, I wrote a letter to her, describing my interest in Integral Yoga and asking her what she thought I should do next.

The day after that, as I was meditating, she appeared to me. The vision began as a swirl of colors that suddenly coalesced into her face. After a few seconds, the image dissolved. I knew then that there was no separation between us and that she had acknowledged that contact between us had just been made.

After I had that vision, an indescribable internal process started. Something inside me began moving very fast, almost like a whirlwind. It continued for a week or so and then abruptly ceased. But a day or two later, it started again. This continued for a year, until I left for India. Meanwhile, I began reading aloud every evening a few pages from *Savitri* until my body filled up with energy. Then I would resume again the next evening.

At CIAS, in a class on Tibetan mythology, I put together a collage that depicted all the chaos, misery, and despair in life around a brilliant center. At each corner of the collage, I placed a picture of an illumined being. When I was done, I placed the collage on my mantle and called it "Samsara," which in Buddhism and Hinduism is the karmic wheel that we are all on until we achieve liberation. Almost immediately, I got a headache, which lasted for three days. Wondering if the headache was related to the collage, I removed it from the mantle, and the headache immediately ceased. I knew then that my life had somehow changed.

Soon after this, I attended a presentation on Auroville, the international city founded by the Mother on the outskirts of Pondicherry, which at that time was only three or four years old. When I came out of that presentation, I knew that I would soon be going to India. A few days later, I decided to write my doctoral dissertation on sleep and dreams, studying them from both a Western and an Eastern perspective—the latter shaped principally by Integral Yoga, which I would further study in India while I lived there. Originally, I intended to go alone, but soon I decided to take along my 17-year-old daughter, Cathi, who was going through a rebellious period in her life, and my fiancée, Jacqueline, who would later change her name to Surama. Before setting off, however, I spent several months researching my subject.

In late October 1973, the three of us flew to London, toured around for a week, and then went on to Paris, where we did some sightseeing for another week. Finally, on November 14, we flew into New Delhi. When we left the airport, the taxi driver got lost trying to find our guesthouse. When we eventually arrived, after what should have been a short ride, he asked us for double the amount indicated on the meter. I argued with him about this, but some people came out of the guesthouse and assured us that the custom was indeed to pay twice the amount on the meter, because there had been a lot of inflation since the meter was made. This was our introduction to India.

For the next few days, we toured New and Old Delhi. Then we drove to Agra to see the Taj Mahal, and on to the palaces at Jaipur—all of this with a guide named Ravi, who had found us on the street in New Delhi. In the late afternoon of November 18, Ravi showed me a newspaper with the Mother's picture on the front page. As I read the article, I was devastated. The Mother had died the day before.

I went to a nearby park to take a walk and collect my thoughts. I was upset and angry that we had come halfway around the world and had just missed meeting the Mother by days. (I didn't know at the time that she had been in seclusion for months because of her ill health, and we wouldn't have met her in any case.) Across the street from the park, workmen were constructing an office or apartment building. A small Indian woman was loading bricks on top of her head to carry to the men. The stack got so high that she had to get the last ones up with a toss, which she did with a giggle. Then she looked over at her baby, who was lying nearby on a blanket on the sidewalk. The workers, noticing me watching the woman with fascination, said something I couldn't understand, and laughed. There was something about this whole scene that made my feelings appear insignificant, and my mood immediately changed. I returned to the guesthouse, ready to move on.

The next day, we took a train to the beautiful city of Udaipur, where we stayed at the lake palace, which was totally surrounded by water and appeared to be floating on the surface. We learned that Jacqueline Kennedy had stayed here many years before, and had suggested that it be turned into a hotel. It is certainly one of the most beautiful places that I have ever seen in my life.

Two days later, we flew to Bombay. From the airport, we took a taxi directly to the home of a man named Bhagwandas Shah, whose name had been given to us by Balkrishna Poddar, a friend of ours who lived at the ashram in Pondicherry, but whom we had met in San Francisco. Mr. Shah ran the local Sri Aurobindo Society Center in his apartment, which was located in an area of the city called Churchgate. He turned out to be a very generous and helpful man, who immediately helped us to find a hotel a few minutes away from his apartment.

The next day, November 21, we walked around the city for a while, and then, around noon, went back to the hotel to rest. Between noon and 3:00 P.M., everything closes down in India anyway, and everyone goes home or shuts down shop for a siesta. Jacqueline had been feeling very hot, although the temperature was mild that day. When we got back to our room, I lay down to take a nap and immediately dozed off. Jacqueline turned on the overhead fan, but this didn't make her feel any cooler. As she lay on the bed, she felt even warmer, so she got up to see if the windows were open. They were. She went back to the bed and lay down. Immediately, with her eyes shut, she saw a woman dressed in white standing in front of the bed. From pictures that she had seen, she knew it was the Mother. The woman held out both hands to Jacqueline and said, "I had to go. It was time. I could not wait for you." Then the image faded. Jacqueline was so astounded that it was several minutes before she woke me to tell me what had happened.

Two days after this experience, on November 23, we flew to Madras and at the airport engaged a taxi to take us to Pondicherry, which was a three-hour drive to the south. The driver took us to the edge of the highway in front of the airport and got out, whereupon a new driver got in. He quoted us a new fare, much higher than what I had previously negotiated. After a brief argument, I told him to unload our luggage from the trunk and the top of the car. A few minutes later, all our bags were sitting out on the highway. When the driver saw that I meant business, he capitulated and reloaded the bags into and onto the car.

After we had been driving about forty-five minutes, the engine started knocking and got louder and louder. Finally, we coasted to the side of the road with a dead engine. It was getting dark, and we were still two hours from Pondicherry in the middle of nowhere. The driver asked to be paid off in full. I calculated that we owed him a third of the fare. Another argument ensued, and I was getting quite indignant. Soon village people appeared out of nowhere and surrounded us, listening very attentively.

A well-dressed Indian gentleman who was parked just behind us walked up and asked what the problem was. After listening to my story, he said he would handle the situation and began negotiating with the driver. Finally, he turned to us and said we should pay one-half of the total fare. He was so calm and polite and self-composed. It was one of my first lessons that it is a mistake to get angry in India, even more so than in America. One either sets off everyone else's hysteria, provoking their resistance, or else one totally loses their respect. In either case, nothing gets accomplished. Furthermore, one is operating out of his lower levels of consciousness, so anger is also self-defeating on a spiritual plane.

In any case, the gentleman said that he had seen us on the plane, and asked if we would like to ride with him to Pondicherry. Of course, we accepted. After driving for a while, we stopped to rest at a small roadside teashop. As we were sipping our tea, a woman with a small child came up to Jacqueline and handed the child to her. As Jacqueline played with the girl, the gentleman joked that she had better be careful, or she might end up with a new daughter!

That evening, around 9:00 o'clock, we arrived at Pondicherry and headed for our guesthouse at the ashram. When we arrived, we said goodbye to the Indian gentleman and gathered up our bags to take them inside. At that point, the driver got out of the car and asked me for an additional tip because we had been unexpected passengers. Just then, our friend Balkrishna showed up and argued with the driver, eventually sending him on his way. Balkrishna had made arrangements for us to stay at this guesthouse, which was managed by a man named Reggie, to whom Balkrishna immediately introduced us.

Reggie was a middle-aged Austrian with a drooping moustache. We learned later that before coming to the ashram he had been a pastry chef with the Hilton Hotel chain. I recognized him from *Phantom India*, the film by Louis Malle, which had included a segment with interviews of several ashramites.

As we stood on the verandah, Reggie looked at our passports, saw that Jacqueline and I had different last names, and asked if we were married. When I said no, he told us that Jacqueline and I could not stay in the same room, but that Jacqueline could stay with Cathi. Jacqueline didn't like that idea at all, and insisted on staying with me. Reggie accepted this arrangement on condition that we agreed to abstain from sex, and we consented.

Although we had been in northern India for over a week, I was in a daze and felt very disoriented. At this point, everything seemed to bother us: the food, the climate, the noise, the odors, and, more than anything else, the mosquitoes. After a few days, we decided to try a less expensive guesthouse, called Cottage. However, it was undergoing some noisy renovations, so we soon moved again, this time to a guesthouse called Seaside. The manager there had promised Jacqueline and me a well-appointed room with a large verandah overlooking the ocean. When we arrived, however, he said that the room, although vacant, was not available, and we would have to take a smaller room at the rear of the building, at least for a week.

Jacqueline was miserable and wanted to go home. I was in such a daze and so unsure of why I was even there that I was in no condition to work on my dissertation, to say the least. Cathi, who had her own room, was beginning to spend virtually all of her time with friends her own age whom she had met at the ashram. She had no interest whatsoever in the spiritual aspect of the ashram, but only focused on the social opportunities.

Not wanting to have to rely on wearing glasses, Jacqueline and I began to attend daily sessions at the School for Perfect Eyesight, whose theory was that poor eyesight is caused by stress. The exercises, which were designed to relax us, included palming our eyes, reading by candlelight, watching a bouncing tennis ball, and dilating our eyes with drops and then facing the sun with our eyes shut. We found these procedures very helpful in making the transition to life in the ashram.

Shortly after we moved to Seaside, in mid-December, I suddenly came down with a fever and went to bed. I perspired profusely for three days, feeling extremely hot. I had no appetite and was so weak that I did nothing but lay in bed all day and perspire. My bedroom was, in effect, a makeshift sweat lodge for purification.

On the third day of my fever, in the middle of the afternoon, an intense light suddenly filled my being. In fact, I had the sensation that I had *become* the light. After a few seconds, the light was gone, and I heard the words in my head, "Mother, I never knew I loved you so much." I immediately started to sob with the sweetest tears imaginable. I lay there for an hour or two, and then decided to get up. I felt fine now and had no symptoms of fever or weakness.

With that experience, my life took a 180-degree turn. My mood and perception changed, and my external life fell into place so that everything was harmonious. The same thing happened to Jacqueline. My euphoric state continued for our remaining months in India, and even when I returned to California in May 1974.

As I later reflected on my soul experience, I realized that I had spontaneously thought of the Mother because my consciousness was already turned toward her. A friend of mine who is also a devotee of the Mother had a similar soul-encounter, but with Krishna. A Christian mystic would likely have a similar experience with Jesus. God actually has no name, but we identify with him or her, depending on our religious or spiritual persuasion. The various spiritual personalities merge into one Godhead, just as all the divine qualities are fundamentally one, including love, knowledge, power, joy, and peace. The division is necessary for the play in our own evolution. The antithesis of true spirituality is excluding and denying the beliefs of others. We can impose no limitations on how the Godhead can present itself.

In any case, shortly after my soul experience, we moved to a house behind the Sri Aurobindo Library, and I started to write my dissertation. I set a goal for myself of writing five pages a day. Usually, I had accomplished this by noon. After a month, I had 150 pages.

Jacqueline and I adapted to life at the ashram very quickly. The compound was comprised of many different buildings scattered within one neighborhood of the city. There were no group meetings or classes for visitors, so it was rather difficult for newcomers to become oriented. One had to let go and allow people and events to happen. We could conduct our lives as we chose, and therefore proceeded at our own pace.

Western civilization is driven by a work ethic. We are taught not to be idle, but instead to have goals and to make something of ourselves. For this the ego takes control. All of this went out the window for us in India, although I had had a premonition of such a lifestyle during the time that I had been unemployed.

A reverse process to the Western work ethic prevails in India. Instead of planning, controlling, and organizing our lives, Jacqueline and I trusted and surrendered to a higher power, without becoming indifferent or apathetic. We could see the organizing power in our lives in retrospect, but if we hadn't let events unfold without our active intervention, we would have missed out on the divine beauty in store for us. The plan reveals itself after the fact and not before.

When we had been attending the School for Perfect Eyesight for a week, Jacqueline had an experience that had implications for the rest of her life. The two of us were in a dark room at the school with our eyes closed and had just finished our candle exercise. What happened next I asked Jacqueline to tell in her own words:

I was aware that someone else had entered the

room, but it was not until they turned on the light and I opened my eyes that I saw this luminous being sitting across from me. He was dressed in white and had long-flowing hair, and he gave me a smile as he rose to leave the room. I asked Wayne if that was Nolini, affectionately known as Nolini-da.* Wayne said yes, it *was*. I had wanted to meet Nolini ever since arriving at Pondicherry in November, for Wayne had given me a book about him as a birthday present the previous year.

Three days later, on January 13, one of the students at the school said that Nolini was giving blessings in the courtyard for his eighty-fifth birthday. Since my birthday was on the 16th of January, I thought this was a perfect birthday present for me, a blessing from Nolini! I went and stood in line with the others. To each, Nolini gave a blessing and a sweet. When I stood before him with my hands pressed together in greeting, he looked up and smiled, and I was so shaken by this gesture that I fell to my knees before him. He reached out and patted my head. Then I got up and went to find Wayne. After that day, I often saw Nolini walking outdoors or at the Samadhi, the courtyard where Sri Aurobindo and the Mother are buried.*

When we returned to America, I began to write him a series of letters about what I had gotten out of my visit to the ashram, what it meant for me to meet him, and I would ask him for advice on problems that were bothering me. He always answered each letter and often enclosed a blessing packet and once a photo, which he signed. At the request of a friend who was close to him, I enclosed a photo of myself, which I sent with a scarf for his birthday in 1975. In return, he sent me a beautiful birthday card, and enclosed a separate card with a new name for me— Surama—which is Sanskrit for "The Most

Pleasing Person." I've used that name ever since.

The last time I saw him, in 1982, he was in bed, fragile but still alert. I was allowed to see him and to receive his blessing, and again I was so overwhelmed that I knelt and touched his feet. I've never met anyone like this man, and I don't expect I ever will again.

After my fever and Jacqueline's contact with Nolini, we were becoming more and more relaxed. Several times a day, we would visit the Samadhi. My whole body-sense was changing. Often, as we sat there, time was suspended, and we neither moved nor wanted to move. Sometimes, two hours might pass without our even noticing it. My identity with my definitive heavy body was widening into a diffused consciousness. In the evenings, when we returned home from the Samadhi, my body would often seem to merge into the surrounding space and become an effortless vehicle. Sometimes, I literally could not feel my feet touching the ground.

Before long, I developed an inner dialogue with the Mother at the Samadhi. She seemed so close to me that when I asked for a particular response, I could usually feel it immediately. Her presence was so spontaneous that a constant truth-touch seemed always to be there.

The Samadhi is such a remarkable place that it is impossible to describe its full impact. Visually, it is very appealing. There is a beautiful sprawling tree, called the Service Tree, in the center of the courtyard, and a breathtakingly beautiful display of fresh-cut flowers placed on the marble tomb, newly designed each day. On the side of the tomb is the Mother's homage to Sri Aurobindo:

To Thee who hast been the material envelope of our Master, to Thee our infinite gratitude. Before Thee who has done so much for us, who hast worked, struggled, suffered, hoped, endured so much, before Thee who hast willed all, attempted

all, prepared, achieved all for us, before Thee we
bow down and implore that we may never forget,
even for a moment, all we owe to Thee.[2]

The ashramites who came there were serene, and time
seemed suspended. All desires, fears, and anxieties melted away.
One felt transported to another world. Yet, I don't want to give
the impression that the place was like a library. Quite the contrary,
it could buzz with activity. Several members of the ashram lived
and worked in rooms surrounding the courtyard. Around noon,
people would line up to file through Sri Aurobindo's room. At
any time of day, busloads of tourists might arrive to see the sights.

The women's saris were colorful and eye-catching. It was a
pleasure to see so many happy people whose tranquillity did
not seem forced. I was struck with the way many of the devotees
would come up to the Samadhi, kneel, and place their foreheads
on the marble tomb. After watching this for a few days, I got up
the courage to do it myself, although I felt somewhat self-
conscious. This feeling did not last long, however. As I placed
my forehead on the cool marble, I felt an intense vibration, as if
there were an earthquake. I lifted my head, and the vibration
immediately stopped. But I felt it again as soon as I touched my
head once more to the stone. Clearly, it was the force emanating
from below. The force in Pondicherry seems to emanate from
the Samadhi outward because of the intensity here.

As the days passed, I absorbed more and more of the energy
from the force abounding in the atmosphere. The force was
always strongest at the Samadhi, but the character of the force—
its flavor—always seemed to be changing. One evening, as we
were leaving the Samadhi, I remarked to Jacqueline how
"sweet" the feeling was. I knew of no other way to describe
it. There seemed to be an incredible play of sweetness moving
through the air.

Before long, Jacqueline and I were totally immersed in this
new consciousness. We had stopped structuring our activities,
and yet we had a certain routine. Jacqueline would go off to help

Balkrishna at SABDA, the Sri Aurobindo Book Distribution Agency, while I worked on my dissertation every morning. My head was so clear that I could easily write four or five pages a day within two or three hours without the slightest distraction. This was in total contrast to my experience when I first arrived at the ashram, when my mind was in such a fog that I couldn't focus on anything.

The carefree Indian style was very appealing to me now. I was learning to let things flow. If I tried to arrange something, it often wouldn't materialize. But things usually fell into place spontaneously when I simply allowed them to do so. In some people, this laissez-faire attitude could lead to total complacency and inertia—as can be seen in an encounter that Jacqueline had with a clerk at one of the local grocery stores. Occasionally, a delicious goat cheese would arrive from the Himalayas, the only cheese available. One day, after Jacqueline had been asking for days when the next shipment would arrive, the clerk responded, "Maybe today, maybe tomorrow, maybe never." On the other hand, when Jacqueline walked in there for the first time on our trip two years later, the same clerk immediately said to her, "Madam, we have cheese today!"

Pondicherry often appeared to me to be a psychological workshop. The force or Truth Consciousness at work there is relatively peaceful, but it can also have a surprisingly dynamic effect. Pondicherry is not a place for anyone who does not have a fair degree of emotional stability, for the force can loosen repressed feelings that may be overpowering.

One day, while I was waiting to pay for my fruits and vegetables at a small produce market, three or four of the clerks, who had been assisting a European woman, got in front of me on the line and, a moment later, let the woman join them. Immediately, out of all proportion to the incident, intense anger surged up in me. I could feel it rushing from my solar plexus to my head. I was too stunned to say anything, but the woman, sensing my fury, turned around and said sternly, with a slight German accent, "You should not get so angry!" Unless one learns to maintain an inner equanimity, one's emotions in Pondicherry are so volatile that a literal sea of emotions can toss one about like a cork.

Most of the time, I was peaceful in Pondicherry, but once in a while something would irritate me. I soon learned that the best solution was to walk over to the Samadhi, offer my problems to the Mother, and sit quietly for ten or fifteen minutes. Then I would walk away feeling so intoxicated with my inner strength that, more often than not, I would forget why I had even come there.

One learns in Pondicherry to become aware at all times. At home, I had had a tendency to rush—rush to get to work, rush to start work, rush to finish work, rush to get home. In Pondicherry, when I tried this, I would be exhausted before breakfast. The Conscious-Force there simply does not allow actions without equanimity. I soon realized that to live and work in the West, people build up a certain tenseness to withstand the shock. This abuses our bodies enormously and blocks our receptivity to the universal forces of peace, love, joy, and light. To be inwardly aware requires a critical balance. This is even truer today than it was then.

If one keeps the Western frenzy alive within oneself while in Pondicherry, the results can be very unpleasant. For example, Jacqueline would go over to the Sri Aurobindo Library to read the weekly international copy of *Time* magazine. Just then, Watergate was prominent in the news, so she would return agitated and depressed. Newspapers, television, excessive talk, aimless mental activity, and similar indulgences are extremely effective in lowering one's level of consciousness.

More than any other place I had ever been, Pondicherry showed me the play of mental projection. I already knew, of course, in an intellectual way, that everything I perceive is a projection of my own consciousness. But it is an entirely different matter to experience this firsthand. One moment, I might feel elated, and the next moment, without any apparent provocation, depressed. Then everything would bother me—the heat, the noise, the smells, the mosquitoes—and everything would look bleak and dingy. This negativity would subside after a while, usually during a visit to the Samadhi. This gave me dramatic proof of the play of the mind and how subtle negative forces can invade one's consciousness like a lethal ray.

By the end of January, it seemed we were both feeling so good that it was impossible to go any higher. We were both looking forward to darshan (from the Sanskrit word for "seeing"), a time when we disciples and devotees could "see" Sri Aurobindo and the Mother. Darshan was coming on February 21, the anniversary of the Mother's birthday.

During the first week of February, at least twice as many people as usual were at the Samadhi in the evening. The force was becoming much stronger with the approach of darshan. One evening, as I was leaving the Samadhi, I suddenly felt electricity running through my entire body. Jacqueline could feel the energy as much as six inches from my fingertips. At the same time, my consciousness had dispersed to a circumference around my head, approximately three feet away. Normally, our awareness, at least in Western culture, is focused in our head, in our thoughts. That center of thought now became insignificant, like a useless appendage. It was "out there" somewhere, but very small now. My main awareness was no longer within one internal place, but all around me. My thoughts had separated from my consciousness, while "I" had expanded beyond my physical body. A feeling of love, oneness, calmness, and vastness pervaded me. This experience lasted for three days and brought me great joy and a sense of freedom.

In my own way, I had experienced darshan with the Mother. As always, it had happened quite unexpectedly. After this experience, the designated darshan day proved to be anticlimactic. I had found that darshan could be any day and every day.

Notes

*Nolini Kanta Gupta (1889–1984), Sri Aurobindo's oldest disciple, was one of those jailed with the master in 1908.

*Samadhi, the Sanskrit word for enlightened self-realization, sometimes leading to trance, also refers to the burial place of a spiritual figure.

[1]Vijay Poddar, ed., *Sri Aurobindo and The Mother on India* (Pondicherry: Sri Aurobindo Society, 1973), p. 28.

[2]The Mother, *Collected Works of The Mother*, vol. 13: *Words of The Mother* (Pondicherry: Sri Aurobindo Ashram Press, 1976), p. 7.

3

East and West

Europeans throughout the centuries have practiced with success spiritual disciplines which were akin to oriental yoga and have followed, too, ways of the inner life which came to them from the East.... There is no essential difference between the spiritual life in the East and the spiritual life in the West.

—Sri Aurobindo[1]

Throughout the 1970s, Surama and I returned to Pondicherry every two or three years. In 1985, I went to India for the first time without her. When it was time to return home, the ashram car delivered me to the Madras airport, a three-hour drive from Pondicherry. No sooner had I sat down in the 737 and fastened my seat belt than, out of the blue, I began to sob. I suppressed it, but it started again, and then, a moment later, it started for the third time. Somewhat embarrassed as the flight attendant passed by, I realized how much I loved India—so much that I didn't want to leave.

Yes, India is different. There is a way of life and a sensibility that is extraordinary. But one cannot go there with a sense of judgment, or one will miss the wonder of it all. Sri Aurobindo said that India represented the soul of the Earth and hence its importance in the planet's evolution. After my first visit, from November 1973 to May 1974, my feeling was, "Thank God, there's an India!" Going there can be both a shock and a love affair. When Surama and I returned to the States in 1974, I was in for an even greater culture shock than the one I had just had in India. I could not get used to the alienation here. One simply had to look at the faces to see the prevalence of sadness and despair. Where were people's souls? Had I changed that much, or was I simply taking a more critical look at American life? The answer was *both*.

When I returned, I had no money, no job, no car, virtually no possessions, and no place to live. Yet, I was far happier than I had ever been before in my life. My experiences in India had been astounding. I had placed impossible expectations on my visit, and they had been *exceeded*. I was now in such a blissful state and my consciousness was so diffused that I could hardly focus on conversation with anyone. Although our bodies were weak and depleted, Surama and I had to find work. Because of my blissful state, I was not able to work for several months, but Surama found a secretarial position in a bank in San Francisco. By grace, even though I had quit my prior position, I was able to get unemployment benefits. A clerk at the state employment office had first told me that I was ineligible, but then advised me how I could claim benefits if I got a temporary job—which I was able to do in a few days.

I could never make sense of life here in the States because people seemed to have no purpose. There was no fundamental satisfaction. Just recently, Surama and I saw an interesting existential film called *The Ice Storm*, which was about profound alienation in an upscale Connecticut suburb. There was no meaningful communication among the family members. Despite ample material wealth, everyone was dispirited. Sexual fulfillment became the main pursuit, but the alienation carried over into the bedroom. The only show of real feelings came when the father lost his teenage son in a freak accident. Suffering had opened him up.

This kind of existential emptiness is with us today in spite of our affluence—or perhaps *because* of it. We use food, alcohol, drugs, sports, shopping, entertainment, the Internet, and sex for diversion from the futility of life. Even family life is often unfulfilling or a cause for suffering. Yet, we are considered the fortunate ones, while in other parts of the world there are mass killings, starvation, refugees, and natural disasters of every kind. Is life really an absurdity? Will we *ever* find happiness? What is the point of existence?

Without formulating these questions in words, finding the answer to them was really my quest in 1973 when I first went to India. I sought happiness and peace and meaning in life—and I found it! But how would I be able to sustain it? The obvious answer for me was to return to India. And so, two years later, in 1976, I began another odyssey. And that was soon followed by another, and then another. I knew that I was not meant to live in India permanently, even if it were financially feasible. But each time I returned, I felt that the gulf between alienation and ecstasy was shrinking.

I had run head-on into the two irreconcilable differences in life. One can withdraw into the inner condition of peace, freedom, and joy that normally leads to an ascetic withdrawal from life; or one can engage in an active business life that becomes financially rewarding and perhaps intellectually challenging, but stifles the inner life. Sri Aurobindo proclaimed, "All life is yoga," meaning that we can use everything in life to evolve.[2] But that is easier said than done, especially when we are virtually alone on our spiritual quest.

A long preparation is required for the body to be able to

receive and contain the Conscious-Force. My solution, awkward as it was to travel back and forth, was to return to India periodically to be recharged. I could have done retreats in the United States, but that would not have been the same. The spiritual atmosphere at the ashram in Pondicherry is magnificent, but it takes a certain attitude to open to it.

I believe that we automatically put up an invisible barrier around us in the States in order to survive. Without realizing it, we are constantly bombarded by other people's feelings of desire, anger, ill will, greed, anxiety, and unhappiness. We adopt a defense mechanism that becomes more pronounced in densely populated areas, the worst being New York City. We often recognize this as stress after we go on vacation to relax.

I have seen people wonderstruck by Pondicherry, and I have seen others who either had a "nice" visit or were bewildered or even got a headache. What's the problem? Some people are not able to let down that barrier and become receptive, which is a feminine quality. One has to become quiet, relaxed, and trusting, which is hard for many people to do, especially those immersed in materialism and consumerism.

Two Complementary Countries

The Mother said that both India and America will have significant roles in the ongoing spiritual evolution of the planet—India for its profound and sustained spirituality over the centuries, and America for its openness to change, its high energy, its freedom, and its mastery over the material domain. The negative side of the equation is that Indians have been drawn to asceticism, denial, and escape to the mystical heights, while neglecting the material aspect of life; whereas Americans have gone on a feeding frenzy, putting their hopes on material satisfaction while reaping alienation from their souls.

Spirit and matter need not be mutually exclusive—and, in fact, are inseparable. Because we now know that the core of matter is consciousness, we can begin to experience this and bring on a change of consciousness within our own bodies. When this change is permanent, we will be able to carry it within us wherever we are—whether in the city, the country, America, or India. We now have the capability to achieve "Heaven on Earth," which will eventually lead to a new species of humanity. This is the significance of the Supermind or Supramental descent.

How can we participate in this new consciousness? The answer is incredibly simple: by *aspiring* and *surrendering* to it. The process is long and requires a considerable amount of patience, but what could be more rewarding and fulfilling?

Abraham Maslow studied the lives of people who were successful in their field while also attaining spiritual growth. He called these individuals "self-actualized." To Maslow this was the best of all possible worlds—and, indeed, a step forward in evolution.

The Mother was also interested in self-mastery over one's emotions, thoughts, and relationships. That is, she wanted people to know the ways of the world, participate in them, and be able to survive, while at the same time putting foremost emphasis on one's own spiritual practice. She did not want people to be untempered by life.

It is surprising how many people who practice Integral Yoga have never held a job to support themselves, or had to work for another person they do not like or respect, or had to pay dearly for making business mistakes. Many of these people have schemes that have little chance of success. It is by paying our dues that we become balanced.

Self-actualization and self-realization are not the goals of Integral Yoga. They can be steps in the process, and everyone should be tested by "real life." But there are times when we need to retreat for a few days, weeks, or even months to let things develop. I believe I was able to achieve more in a few months in India in 1973–74 than I could have in thirty *years* in America.

Incidentally, every time I return to India, I make it a point to relax and let go of my Western ways. During my visit in 1975–76, however, when Surama and I were busy meeting people and setting up a business to export clothing to the United States, I never did make the transition. I could not successfully engage in the outer activity while fully immersing myself in the inner life.

Prior to becoming involved in my spiritual quest, I studied psychology in an attempt to understand myself. I was intrigued by my dreams and found a way to interpret them. I attended classes and workshops in which I learned techniques from Gestalt Psychology and Psychosynthesis. I also became involved with Rolfing, massage, acupressure, acupuncture, Feldenkrais, Rosen Body Work, journaling, dream analysis, imagery, inner dialogue, self-hypnosis, Vipassana, and translation—that is, writing mental exercises that translate appearances into essential truths. I did a great deal of spontaneous writing without thinking.

The most important thing is that I made some effort. I was ready to let go of my attachments to parents, siblings, and friends. I released old hurts and anger. My reactions in life gave me the best clues as to how well balanced I was or was not at any one time. I was learning to respond rather than react. Could I accept criticism and praise with equanimity? Had I confronted my fears? Was I comfortable with the issues of sex, money, and power? Did I have convictions but openness to others' views? I had to become an "individual" without rigidity, which is a delicate balance. My dreams indicated my progress. Soon I had fewer dreams of anxiety and more of a luminous kind, in which I felt touched by something special.

In the beginning of one's spiritual search, there will usually be a great disparity between the inner and the outer awareness. Our meditations and a certain detachment from our circumstances can give us freedom and joy. Through all of this, a considerable amount of patience is needed. Different parts of our being will proceed or lag at different speeds. If we try to rush our spiritual search, we ask for trouble. The watchword is sincerity—being as free as possible from ego and personal ambition. More and more, we have to trust and surrender to a higher power.

Eventually, we hope to integrate all the parts of our being—mental, emotional, and physical—around our soul, which becomes the dominant force in our life. We can become an integrated being rather than a dysfunctional collection of warring inner factions.

We are by no means alone in this process. In fact, we are *never* alone, although we may think so. There are an infinite number of beings ready to help us if we call on them. After a number of years on the path, we may see that a stream of continuity has been leading us toward our goal all along—a goal that was chosen by our soul before we took on a body in this incarnation. Our task is not to be sidetracked. A few side trips of limited duration might be all right, perhaps even helpful, but one has to be cautious. Once a particular action has been taken, we have to see it through to its conclusion. You might say that the action has a mind of its own. Acts of charity, help, and benevolence can themselves be sidetracks. However, service is generally of benefit on this path, for it helps us to transcend our narrow personal preoccupations. Service is not an end in itself, but a step on the way. This is all part of self-mastery.

Although service is not emphasized in Integral Yoga because we have a different goal—transformation—it is possible to combine a life of service with the practice of Integral Yoga. This was accomplished by, for example, Dr. Venkataswamy, an eye surgeon in Madurai, India, who is a longtime disciple of Sri Aurobindo and the Mother. Dr. Venkataswamy developed crippling arthritis while he was in the army in the 1940s and was bedridden for a year. Eventually, he overcame his disability to the point that he was able to perform one hundred cataract surgeries in one day. After he retired from the army, he opened a small clinic that has grown to become the largest center for sight restoration in the world. Blindness is an especially severe problem in India because if the breadwinner cannot work, the family may starve.

There are no hard-and-fast rules in Integral Yoga. Everyone is unique and has a vital role to play. But it is important to take care of the basics as soon as possible. We think that when we have reached the age of eighteen or twenty, we are individuals. But this is true only in the most superficial sense. We will find that we have very few, if any, original thoughts or feelings, but are connected to a gigantic milieu of crisscrossing waves of thoughts and emotions in the atmosphere. Our soul is hidden behind layers of obscurity. By and large, we live in a most superficial and self-gratifying way. While this may appear to be an overly bleak assessment, look around at the faces in society, and contrast these with the hopeful faces of young children. Rigidity sets in after a time if one is not open to progress.

When the Mother was in her nineties, she said "I am not old, I am younger than most of you." Aging is a matter of attitude. Once I attended a memorial service in San Francisco for a woman who had died in her nineties after decades of being a member of the Cultural Integration Fellowship. She had been one of the younger persons there in spirit because of her attitude: she was always learning, always trying to progress. During the service for her, we had a brief meditation, which turned out to be remarkable. I had never reached such spiritual heights before. Perhaps her spirit had rubbed off on me!

The New Child and Cells of Light

I have heard a number of gifted individuals say that children being born now are of a very special quality. In Pôrto Alegre, in southern Brazil near Argentina, there is a healer named Jussara, who has a special gift of seeing cells and has noticed a change in them in recent years—a change that confirms the supramentalization of matter:

> I do not know about the Mother's work. But I have strongly felt that the cells had their commitment to death. I used the psalms of the Bible to help me in my work. But nowadays, there is a change. The cells are stronger. It is as if they themselves say: "I no longer need to suffer. There is no need

to die." Nowadays, I find that more and more people, especially children, have lots of light, lots of these little lamps, more so than grown-ups. I believe that in the future, the human body will be fully lit up. But for that, there is a lot of work still to be done. I firmly believe that the healing capacity that I have today, the level at which I am working today, will soon be the property of all. A time will come when everybody will be able to work at the level of cellular awareness.[3]

Notes

[1] Sri Aurobindo, *Birth Centenary Library*, vol. 23: *Letters on Yoga* (Pondicherry, India: Sri Aurobindo Ashram Press, 1972), pp. 555–556.

[2] Sri Aurobindo, *Birth Centenary Library*, vol. 20: *The Synthesis of Yoga* (Pondicherry, India: Sri Aurobindo Ashram Press, 1972), p. 4.

[3] Interview, *Auroville Today* (October 1997), p. 3.

4

Sri Aurobindo

German metaphysics and most European philosophy since the Greeks seemed to me a mass of abstractions with nothing concrete or real that could be firmly grasped and written in a metaphysical jargon to which I had not the key....
As to Indian Philosophy, it was a little better, but not much.

—*Sri Aurobindo*[1]

Aurobindo Ghose was born in Calcutta on August 15, 1872, the third son to Kristo Dhan Ghose, a medical doctor who had an excessive admiration for the British. When the boy was seven, after two years at an Irish nuns' boarding school in Darjeeling, his father took him and his two older brothers to Manchester, England, and placed them in the care of the Rev. William H.

Drewett, an English clergyman, with instructions that the boys were to be forbidden all contact with Indians.

Nevertheless, by the time Aurobindo was eleven, although he was by nature a poet, he already had a strong impression that he was destined to play a part in the coming general upheaval in India. This impression had become a conviction by the time he was fifteen.

At St. Paul's School in London, where he mastered English, Latin, Greek, and French, and taught himself German, Italian, and Spanish, Aurobindo began to deliver revolutionary speeches and decided to devote his life to the service of India and its liberation from British rule. He also studied Sanskrit and Bengali.

After his return to India in 1893, at the age of twenty-one, he took up service with the Maharaja of Baroda, which he had secured while in England, preparing public speeches for him and assisting him with the writing of letters and other documents. Four years later, Aurobindo became a lecturer in French at Baroda College and subsequently was appointed Professor of English. After a time, he became the Vice-Principal, and then the acting Principal, of the college.

Aurobindo learned Hindi, Gujarati, and Marathi during this period, and began writing articles in Bengali for a weekly newspaper, the *Bande Mataram* ("Hail to the Motherland"). In his political writings, he urged his countrymen to awaken to the tyranny of their British oppressors. His main strategy at this time was to promote non-cooperation and passive resistance, but as a serious student of the American, French, and Italian revolutions, he was prepared to engage in open revolt only if necessary.

In 1900, he decided to marry. After receiving numerous offers, he selected a young girl, Mrinalini Bose, who was the daughter of Bhupal Chandra Bose of Calcutta. The marriage took place in April of the following year, when Mrinalini was fourteen and Aurobindo was twenty-eight. After a month's honeymoon in Naini Tal, the couple settled down in Baroda. However, Mrinalini soon found it uncomfortable to live in unfamiliar surroundings where no one spoke her native language, Bengali. When a famine and bubonic plague hit the area, she returned to Calcutta for the next year. Until Mrinalini's death in 1918, this was the pattern of their married life: sometimes living together, sometimes living apart.

In 1904, at the age of thirty-two, Aurobindo began to practice yoga to find the spiritual strength to carry out his political mission. Earlier in his life, he had had several spontaneous spiritual experiences. One time, in Bombay, a vast calm had descended on him. On another occasion, while walking in Kashmir, he had the realization of the vacant Infinite. A third experience occurred while he was visiting a shrine to the mother goddess Kali, whose living presence appeared before him.

In 1906, at the age of thirty-four, Aurobindo was living in Calcutta, separated once again from Mrinalini, who was living in Deoghar, a town some 300 miles to the northwest. Nevertheless, the warmth of their relationship can be seen in their written correspondence, such as the following letter written from Aurobindo to his young wife on December 6, 1907:

> Dear Mrinalini,
> I received your letter the day before yesterday. The shawl was sent the very same day. I do not understand why you did not get it....
> Here [in Calcutta] I do not have a minute to spare. I am in charge of the writing; I am in charge of the Congress work; I have to settle the *Bande Mataram* affair.* I am finding it difficult to cope with it all. Besides, I have my own work to do; that too cannot be neglected.
> Will you listen to one request of mine? This is a time of great anxiety for me. There are pulls from every side that are enough to drive one mad. If at this time you get restless, it can only increase my worry and anxiety. But if you could write encouraging and comforting letters, that would give me great strength. I should then be able to

overcome all fears and dangers with a cheerful heart. I know it is hard for you to live alone at Deoghar. But if you keep your mind firm and have faith, your sorrows will not be able to overcome you to such an extent. As you have married me, this kind of sorrow is inevitable for you. Occasional separations cannot be avoided, for unlike the ordinary Bengali, I cannot make the happiness of family and relatives my primary aim in life. Under these circumstances there is no way out for you except to consider my ideal as your ideal and find your happiness in the success of my appointed work....

Yours,[2]

In a letter that Aurobindo wrote to his father-in-law around this time, he again explained why family life took a back seat for him to his political and literary activities:

I am afraid I shall never be good for much in the way of domestic virtues. I have tried, very ineffectively, to do some part of my duty as a son, a brother, and a husband, but there is something too strong in me which forces me to subordinate everything else to it.[3]

On February 17, 1908, Aurobindo wrote to Mrinalini again, trying to console her for the "wrongs" he has done her:

Dear Mrinalini,
    I have not written to you for a long time. This is my eternal failing; if you do not pardon me out of your own goodness, what shall I do? What is ingrained in one does not go out in a day. Perhaps it will take me the whole of this life to

correct this fault.

I was to come on the 8th January, but I could not. This did not happen of my own accord. I had to go where God took me. This time I did not go for my own work; it was for His work that I went. The state of my mind has undergone a change. But of this I shall not speak in this letter. Come here, and I shall tell you what is to be told. But there is only one thing which must be said now, and that is that from now on I no longer am the master of my own will. Like a puppet I must go wherever God takes me; like a puppet I must do whatever He makes me do. It will be difficult for you to grasp the meaning of these words just now, but it is necessary to inform you, otherwise my movements may cause you regret and sorrow. You may think that in my work I am neglecting you, but do not do so. Already I have done you many wrongs, and it is natural that this should have displeased you. But I am no longer free. From now on you will have to understand that all I do depends not on my will but is done at the command [adesh] of God. When you come here, you will understand the meaning of my words. I hope that God will show you the Light He has shown me in His infinite Grace. But that depends on His Will. If you wish to share my life and ideal, you must strive to your utmost so that, on the strength of your ardent desire, He may in His Grace reveal the path to you also. Do not let anyone see this letter, for what I have said is extremely secret. I have not spoken about this to anyone but you; I am forbidden to do so. This much for today.

Your husband[4]

About December-January 1908, Aurobindo met a yogi named Lele. Within three days, he had achieved a vacant mind, and knowledge poured into him without any effort. He later described this kind of experience as follows:

> The Yogi…sees that thoughts come from outside, from the universal Mind or universal Nature, sometimes formed and distinct, sometimes unformed, and then they are given shape somewhere in us. The principal business of our mind is either a response of acceptance or a refusal to these thought-waves (as also vital waves, subtle physical energy waves) or this giving a personal-mental form to thought-stuff (or vital movements) from the environing Nature-Force. It was my great debt to Lele that he showed me this. "Sit in meditation," he said, "but do not think, look only at your mind; you will see thoughts *coming into it*; before they can enter throw these away from your mind till your mind is capable of entire silence." I had never heard before of thoughts coming visibly into the mind from outside, but I did not think either of questioning the truth or the possibility, I simply sat down and did it. In a moment my mind became silent as a windless air on a high mountain summit, and then I saw one thought and then another coming in a concrete way from outside; I flung them away before they could enter and take hold of the brain, and in three days I was free. From that moment, in principle, the mental being in me became a free Intelligence, a universal Mind, not limited to the narrow circle of personal thought as a laborer in a thought factory, but a receiver of knowledge from all the hundred realms of being and free to choose what it willed in this vast sight-empire and thought-empire.[5]

This universal state of mind became permanent in Aurobindo and ultimately enabled him to write prodigiously on a vast array of subjects. During his student days, he had read constantly, mostly Western authors, and had the capacity to remember everything he read.

On the political front, as the editor of the *Bande Mataram*, Aurobindo continued to promote his views for the independence of India. He also worked politically behind the scenes. He was one of the leaders of the Nationalist Party and the organizer of its policy and strategy in Bengal. In one of his newspaper articles, he wrote:

> All political ideals must have relation to the temperament and past history of the race. The genius of India is separate from that of any other race in the world, and perhaps there is no race in the world whose temperament, culture, and ideals are so foreign to her own as those of the practical, hard-headed, Pharisaic, shopkeeping Anglo-Saxon. The culture of the Anglo-Saxon is the very antipodes of Indian culture. The temper of the Anglo-Saxon is the very reverse of the Indian temper. His ideals are of the earth, earthy. His institutions are without warmth, sympathy, human feeling, rigid and accurate like his machinery, meant for immediate and practical gains. The reading of democracy which he has adopted and is trying to introduce first in the colonies because the mother country is still too much shackled by the past, is the most sordid possible, centered on material aims and void of generous idealism. In such a civilization, as part of such an Empire, India can have no future. If she is to model herself on the Anglo-Saxon type, she must first kill everything in her which is her own. If she is to be a province of the British Empire, part of its life, sharing its institutions,

governed by its policy, the fate of Greece under
Roman dominion will surely be hers.[6]

By April 1908, Aurobindo and Mrinalini were again living
together, this time in Calcutta. On Friday, May 1, 1908, at 5:30
A.M., they were abruptly awakened and their home invaded by
the police. Although he proclaimed his innocence, Aurobindo
was the prime suspect in a bombing that had been planned and
executed by his brother Barin, who had intended to commit a
political assassination but instead had accidentally killed two
European women. The police found a letter that Aurobindo had
written to Mrinalini, in which he had expressed his nonviolent
approach to liberating India:

> Whereas others regard the country as an inert
> object, and know it as consisting of some plains,
> fields, forests, mountains, and rivers, I look upon
> my country as my Mother, I worship and adore
> her as mother. What would a son do when a
> demon is sitting on the breast of his mother and
> drinking her blood? Would he sit down content
> to take his meals and go on enjoying himself in
> the company of his wife and children, or would
> he, rather, run to the rescue of his mother? I know
> I have the strength to uplift this fallen race; it is
> not physical strength; I am not going to fight with
> sword or with gun, but with the power of
> knowledge. The strength of the warriors is not
> the only kind of strength; there is also the power
> of the Brahman, which is founded on knowledge.[7]

For the next year after his arrest, Aurobindo was held in
Alipore Jail outside Calcutta, much of the time in solitary
confinement in a tiny cell, five feet by nine, exposed to the
elements of intensive heat and rain. The jail is still operational
today, but Aurobindo's cell, at the end of a row of six, has become

a national landmark.

Aurobindo later wrote an account of his imprisonment, called *Tales of Prison Life*.[8] His confinement turned out to be a significant transition for his life from politics to spirituality. Prior to his arrest, he had had no idea that he was the prime suspect in the case. After a year's imprisonment, he emerged as a new being embarking on a new course of action. In spite of the hardships, he spoke of the jail as an ashram or hermitage:

> For long I had made great efforts for a direct vision of the Lord of my Heart; I had entertained the immense hope of knowing the Preserver of the World, the Supreme Person, as Friend and Master. But due to the pull of a thousand worldly desires, the attachment towards numerous activities, and the deep darkness of ignorance, I did not succeed in that effort. At long last the most merciful all-good Lord destroyed all enemies at one stroke and helped me in my path, pointed to the *yogashram*, Himself staying as guru and companion in my little abode of retirement and spiritual discipline. The British prison was that ashram. I have watched this strange contradiction in my life that however much good my well-intentioned friends might do for me, it is those who have harmed me—whom shall I call an enemy, since enemy I have none?—my opponents have helped me even more.[9]

In essence, Aurobindo learned in solitary confinement to conquer the weakness of his mind. Furthermore, he learned to love all creatures from within, seeing God in every form—in his fellow revolutionaries, in the lowest of criminals, in the judge, and even in inanimate objects. The lesson of his yoga practice, he discovered, was not to come from his personal efforts but from faith and complete self-surrender. He also learned at this time the efficacy of prayer.

While in prison, Aurobindo also observed the thirty revolutionary Bengali youths who had been arrested with him, and was mightily impressed with their fearlessness and cheerfulness. In the face of great danger, even death, these young men, most of them well-educated, displayed no sign of despair or grief. Even in the courtroom, they paid no attention to the proceedings, but spent the time reading the *Bhagavad Gita* or books about yoga, or European philosophy.

Aurobindo's knowledge during this period was enriched, however, not so much from the reading of books as from direct contact with great spiritual teachers of the past. More than once, he was visited in his cell by Sri Krishna. For fifteen days, Aurobindo was taught the workings of the higher consciousness and the Truth-Consciousness, which leads towards the Supermind, by Swami Vivekananda, who had died six years earlier, in 1902.

All of these experiences and observations were preparing Aurobindo not only for the independence of India but the next stage in the evolution of the human race. For such a prodigious undertaking, a sublime humility was needed, which he found in the simplest of prisoners—an illiterate cowherd who was wrongly imprisoned but remained cheerful and kind to everyone, even the jailers, and whose thoughts were only for the welfare of the other prisoners. Aurobindo later wrote:

> He had a heart a thousand times nobler than mine,
> I would feel ashamed at his humility, to have to
> accept the old man's services embarrassed me,
> but he would not be held back so easily. He was
> all the time anxious about my comfort. As with
> me, so with the others, his kindly attention and
> humble service and respect seemed to be much
> greater especially for the innocent and miserable
> ones. Yet on his face and in his conduct there
> glowed a natural serene gravity and majesty. He
> had a great love for the country too. I shall always

remember the white-whiskered serene visage of this old convict full of kindness and generosity. Even in these days of decline among the Indian peasantry—whom we describe as uneducated, "small people," *chhotolok*—may be found such representatives of the Indian race. India's future is hopeful only because of this. The educated youth and the unlettered peasantry, the future of India lies with these two classes.[10]

To Pondicherry

In May 1909, a full year after his arrest, Aurobindo was acquitted of the bombing charge and released. Shortly after that, with the British still spying on him, he had an inner command to go to Pondicherry, a port city in French India to the south of Madras, on the Bay of Bengal. When he arrived, he left the political field and activism behind and began to develop his system of Integral Yoga. Where he had earlier focused his energies on awakening the Indian people to demand their freedom, he now devoted himself to awakening humanity at large to the possibility of a new freedom, that of the Spirit in the body giving meaning to this material earthly existence.

A few friends and political followers went with him to Pondicherry, all of them, like Aurobindo himself, virtually penniless. Until they got established, they were supported by political sympathizers, as well as by whatever money family and friends could send to them.

The period from 1910 to 1914 was one of transition and preparation for Aurobindo, during which he spent most of his time reading, writing, and meditating. He also taught his companions Greek, Latin, and French, introducing them to great works of literature.

During his first year in Pondicherry, Aurobindo met a Frenchman named Paul Richard, a former minister in the Reformed Church of France, who was interested in politics and had come to India to campaign for colleagues in an election for the French legislature. Richard later said about this meeting:

> The Hour is coming of great things, of great events, and also of great men, the divine men of Asia. All my life I have sought for them across the world, for all my life I have felt they must exist somewhere in the world, that this world would die if they did not live. For they are its light, its heat, its life. It is in Asia that I have found the greatest among them—the leader, the hero of tomorrow. His name is Aurobindo Ghose.[11]

The Meeting

In 1914, Paul Richard returned with his wife, Mirra, to introduce her to Aurobindo. That meeting was a turning point in the lives of all three. Aurobindo later said about this meeting with the woman who would come to be known as the Mother:

> When I came to Pondicherry, a program was dictated to me from within for my Sadhana. I followed it and progressed for myself, but could not do much by way of helping others. Then came the Mother, and with her help I found the necessary method.[12]

Aurobindo and the Richards soon began publishing a monthly journal called *Arya* ("Holy Man"). * After a few months, however, Paul and Mirra returned to Paris when Paul was called up for military service in World War I, which had just broken out.

During the war, in 1915, Aurobindo felt the troubled conditions in the world, but he was not discouraged. In a letter to Mirra, he wrote:

> All is always for the best, but it is sometimes, from the external point of view, an awkward best....

The whole earth is now under one law and answers to the same vibrations, and I am sceptical of finding any place where the clash of the struggle will not pursue us. In any case, an effective retirement does not seem to be my destiny. I must remain in touch with the world until I have either mastered adverse circumstances or succumbed or carried on the struggle between the spiritual and physical so far as I am destined to carry it on. This is how I have always seen things and still see them. As for failure, difficulty, and apparent impossibility, I am too much habituated to them to be much impressed by their constant self-presentation, except for passing moments....

One needs to have a calm heart, a settled will, entire self-abnegation, and the eyes constantly fixed on the beyond to live undiscouraged in times like these, which are truly a period of universal decomposition. For myself, I follow the Voice and look neither to right nor to left of me. The result is not mine and hardly at all now even the labor.[13]

By 1918, Aurobindo was already anticipating India's independence, as is clear in this exchange with his disciple A. B. Purani:

PURANI: I must do something for the freedom of India. I have been unable to sleep soundly for the last two years and a half....

AUROBINDO: Suppose an assurance is given to you that India will be free?

PURANI: Who can give such an assurance?

AUROBINDO: Suppose I give you the assurance?

PURANI: If you give the assurance, I can accept it.

AUROBINDO: Then I give you the assurance that India will be free.[14]

It was around this same time, after a ten-year separation, that Aurobindo finally felt established enough in Pondicherry to send for his wife, Mrinalini, who was back in Calcutta, staying with family. The last time they had lived together was in 1908, when the British had stormed their house and arrested him. For the past ten years, their relationship—which was more one of guru and disciple than husband and wife—had been carried on entirely in letters. Tragically, while preparing to leave Calcutta to join Aurobindo in December 1918, Mrinalini died in an influenza epidemic. Afterward, Aurobindo wrote to his father-in-law:

> With regard to this fatal event in both our lives: words are useless in face of the feelings it has caused, if even they can ever express our deepest emotions. God has seen good to lay upon me the one sorrow that could still touch me to the center. He knows better than ourselves what is best for each of us, and now that the first sense of the irreparable has passed, I can bow with submission to his divine purpose. The physical tie between us is, as you say, severed; but the tie of affection subsists for me. Where I have once loved, I do not cease from loving. Besides, she who was the cause of it still is near, though not visible to our physical vision.
>
> It is needless to say much about the matters of which you write in your letter. I approve of everything that you propose. Whatever Mrinalini

would have desired, should be done, and I have
no doubt this is what she would have approved
of. I consent to the *chudis* [gold bangles worn by
a Hindu wife] being kept by her mother; but I
should be glad if you would send me two or three
of her books, especially if there are any in which
her name is written. I have only of her, her letters
and a photograph.[15]

During the period between 1914 and 1921, Aurobindo wrote
his major philosophical, social, and spiritual works, all of them
published in *Arya*. Also during this time, he began composing
his epic poem *Savitri*, which he revised throughout his life. The
poem depicts the Mother as Savitri, a legendary Indian heroine,
conquering death. Aurobindo later described the evolution of
his own spiritual enlightenment as follows:

My philosophy was formed first by the study of
the Upanishads and the Gita; the Veda came later.
They were the basis of my first practice of Yoga; I
tried to realize what I read in my spiritual
experience and succeeded; in fact, I was never
satisfied till experience came, and it was on this
experience that later on I founded my philosophy,
not on ideas by themselves. I owed nothing in
my philosophy to intellectual abstractions,
ratiocination, or dialectics—when I have used
these means, it was simply to explain my
philosophy and justify it to the intellect of others;
the other source of my philosophy was the
knowledge that flowed from above when I sat in
meditation, especially from the plane of the
Higher Mind when I reached that level; they came
down in a mighty flood, which swelled into a sea
of direct knowledge always translating itself into
experience, or they were in intuitions starting
from an experience and leading to other intuitions
and a corresponding experience. This source was

exceedingly catholic and many-sided, and descents of ideas came in which might have belonged to conflicting philosophies, but they were here reconciled in a large synthetic whole.[16]

By 1926, Aurobindo needed to isolate himself, not out of asceticism, but for his own focus to carry on his work and to bring about the next stage of consciousness for the Earth. Around this time, people began to refer to him as Sri Aurobindo, (Sri—pronounced "shree")—which is a title of reverence.

Aside from his daily contact with the Mother, Sri Aurobindo maintained connection with the outside world primarily through writing letters to disciples and others for up to twelve hours a day. When he wasn't doing that, he was usually walking in his room, which he did for up to eight hours a day. The walking was a form of meditation, a means of maintaining physical fitness, and a way to ground the spiritual force that was coursing through his body.

The period from 1926 to 1938 produced a great deal of correspondence between Sri Aurobindo and his disciples. Here are some extracts that indicate the variety of subjects covered during those thirteen years:

[1928:]

SRI AUROBINDO: It is not everyone who has the *adhikara* ["capacity"] to help in the work of the Ashram.*

Those only can do so who have faith in it, or sympathy, or at least confidence in Sri Aurobindo....

Sri Aurobindo is not anxious to increase the number of his disciples, and only those are accepted usually who have the call and capacity for Yoga and are ready to satisfy the conditions.[17]

[1931:]

SRI AUROBINDO: The Mother has had a very severe attack, and she must absolutely husband her forces in view of the strain the 24th [of] November [Darshan Day] will mean to her. It is quite out of the question for her to begin seeing everybody and receiving them meanwhile—a single morning of that kind of thing would exhaust her altogether. You must remember that for her a physical contact of this kind with others is not a mere social or domestic meeting with a few superficial movements which make no great difference one way or the other. It means for her an interchange, a pouring out of her forces, and a receiving of things good, bad, and mixed from them, which often involves a great labor of adjustment and elimination, and in many cases, though not in all, a severe strain on the body. If it had been only a question of two or three people, it would have been a different matter; but there is the whole Ashram here ready to enforce each one his claim the moment she opens her doors. You surely do not want to put all that upon her before she has recovered her health and strength!

In the interests of the work itself—the Mother has never cared in the least for her body or her health for its own sake, and that indifference has been one reason, though only an outward one, for the damage done—I must insist on her going slowly in the resumption of the work and doing only so much at first as her health can bear. It seems to me that all who care for her ought to feel in the way I do.[18]

[1933:]

DISCIPLE: I tried to read Aristotle but found him very dry and abstract.

SRI AUROBINDO: I always found him exceedingly dry. It is a purely mental philosophy, not like Plato's.[19]

[1935:]

DISCIPLE: The Overmind seems so distant from us, and your Himalayan austerity and grandeur takes my breath away, making my heart palpitate!

SRI AUROBINDO: O rubbish! I am austere and grand, grim and stern! every blasted thing I never was! I groan in an un-Aurobindian despair when I hear such things. What has happened to the common sense of all of you people? In order to reach the Overmind, it is not at all necessary to take leave of this simple but useful quality. Common sense, by the way, is not logic (which is the least commonsense-like thing in the world); it is simply looking at things as they are without inflation or deflation—not imagining wild imaginations—or, for that matter, despairing "I know not why" despairs.[20]

[1936:]

DISCIPLE: We have been wondering why you should have to write and rewrite your poetry— for instance, *Savitri* ten or twelve times—when you have all the inspiration at your command and do not have to receive it with the difficulty that faces budding Yogis like us.

SRI AUROBINDO: That is very simple. I used *Savitri* as a means of ascension. I began with it on a certain mental level; each time I could reach a higher level, I rewrote from that level. Moreover, I was particular—if part seemed to me to come from any lower levels, I was not satisfied to leave it because it was good poetry. All had to be, as far as possible, of the same mint. In fact, *Savitri* has not been regarded by me as a poem to be written and finished, but as a field of experimentation to see how far poetry could be written from one's own yogic consciousness and how that could be made creative.[21]

[1936:]

SRI AUROBINDO: Hitler and his chief lieutenants Goering and Goebbels are certainly vital beings or possessed by vital beings, so you can't expect common sense from them. The Kaiser, though all-satanical, was a much more human person; these people are hardly human at all. The nineteenth century in Europe was a pre-eminently human era—now the vital world seems to be descending there.[22]

[1937:]

SRI AUROBINDO: The Divine may be difficult, but His difficulties can be overcome if one keeps at Him. Even my smilelessness was overcome, which Nevinson [a British journalist] had remarked with horrors more than twenty years before—"the most dangerous man in India," Aurobindo Ghose who "never smiles." He ought to have added: "but who always jokes"— but he did not know that, as I was very solemn with him, or perhaps I had not developed sufficiently on that side then. Anyhow, if you could overcome *that*—my smilelessness—you are bound to overcome all the other difficulties also.[23]

Sri Aurobindo felt that the Supermind was about to manifest in 1938. There was an interruption at this point, both in that manifestation and in Sri Aurobindo's life, when he fell in his room and broke his leg. That was an attack by the hostile forces, who were behind the impending catastrophe in Europe. Nirodbaran, a close disciple of Sri Aurobindo, made these comments about the master's fall and broken leg:

In the crucial year 1938, dark war-clouds were gathering, and rumblings were heard all over Europe. There was a strong possibility that fighting would break out in December, just a week or two after the night of November 23, when Sri Aurobindo had his accident. But, as he indicated in our talks, his Force pushed it back to a later date, for war at that time would have been a great hindrance to his work. It is possible to surmise that the irresistible forces, which no human power could check, turned their fury on one who had checked them. Long before Hitler's actual invasion of Poland, long before anyone else, Sri Aurobindo had seen this dark Asuric Power rising in Germany and striding over Europe, making Hitler its demoniac instrument, a pseudo-colossus, a self-acclaimed Napoleon.[24]

Sri Aurobindo's broken leg brought him out of seclusion, and he began to have dialogues with a group of disciples about the world situation and more personal issues, such as the following:

DR. MANILAL: At one time I felt as if my

head were lying at the Mother's feet. What does that mean, sir?

SRI AUROBINDO: It is the experience of the psychic being. So you had the psychic experience.

DR. MANILAL: But unfortunately I couldn't recognise it. *[laughter]*

SRI AUROBINDO: It is this "I" that comes in the way. One must forget it, as if the experiences were happening to somebody else. If one could do this, it would be a great conquest. When I had the experience of nirvana [in 1908], I forgot myself completely. I was a sort of nobody. What's the use of Dr. Manilal So-and-so living with this "I"? If in discovering your inner being, you even had died, it would have been a glorious death.

DR. MANILAL: What happens when the human consciousness is replaced by the divine consciousness?

SRI AUROBINDO: One feels a perpetual calm, perpetual strength, one is aware of infinity and lives not only in infinity but also in eternity. One feels immortality and does not care about the death of the body. And then one has the consciousness of the One in all. Everything becomes the manifestation of the Brahman. For instance, as I look round this room, I see everything as the Brahman. No, it is not mere thinking. It is a concrete experience. Even the wall, the books are Brahman. I see you no more as Dr. Manilal but as the Divine living in the Divine. It is a wonderful experience.[25]

When World War II broke out in Europe in September 1939, Sri Aurobindo perceived it as a direct assault by the dark occult forces that were behind Hitler. These forces, he believed, were resisting his and the Mother's attempt to transform the Earth. In 1940, he publicly supported France and England, which shocked many in India because of their anti-British attitude.

By 1945, Sri Aurobindo was widely known throughout India and abroad. Several distinguished people, including Aldous Huxley, praised his magnum opus, *The Life Divine*. In 1949, two Nobel laureates, Gabriela Mistral and Pearl Buck, nominated him for a Nobel Prize in Literature.

When India got its independence, Sri Aurobindo was asked by All India Radio to address the nation for the occasion. His speech, read on the air by an announcer, began as follows:

> August 15th, 1947, is the birthday of free India. It marks for her the end of an old era, the beginning of a new age. But we can also make it by our life and acts as a free nation an important date in a new age opening for the whole world, for the political, social, cultural, and spiritual future of humanity.
>
> August 15th is my own birthday, and it is naturally gratifying to me that it should have assumed this vast significance. I take this coincidence, not as a fortuitous accident, but as the sanction and seal of the Divine Force that guides my steps on the work with which I began life, the beginning of its full fruition. Indeed, on this day I can watch almost all the world-movements which I hoped to see fulfilled in my lifetime, though then they looked like impracticable dreams, arriving at fruition or on their way to achievement. In all these movements, free India may well play a large part and take a leading position.
>
> The first of these dreams was a revolutionary movement which would create a free and united India. India today is free, but she has not achieved unity....
>
> Another dream was for the resurgence and

liberation of the peoples of Asia and her return to her great role in the progress of human civilization….

The third dream was a world-union forming the outer basis of a fairer, brighter, and nobler life for all mankind. That unification of the human world is under way….

Another dream, the spiritual gift of India to the world, has already begun. India's spirituality is entering Europe and America in an ever increasing measure. That movement will grow….

The final dream was a step in evolution which would raise man to a higher and larger consciousness and begin the solution of the problems which have perplexed and vexed him since he first began to think and to dream of individual perfection and a perfect society.[26]

Sri Aurobindo's Departure

Extreme opposition to the descent of the Supermind required drastic measures. Sri Aurobindo told the Mother that one of them would have to leave the body and reside in the subtle physical plane to carry on the work of transformation on Earth. He insisted that he would be the one to do this. The Mother's body, he said, was much stronger than his and more suitable for the work of transformation on the physical plane.

In early December 1950 Sri Aurobindo fell into a coma. What happened next has been poignantly described by Peter Heehs:

A dedicated team of physicians was in attendance, but Sri Aurobindo declined to receive any major treatment, or even to use his therapeutic power on himself. Asked why, he said simply, "Can't explain; you won't understand." He fell into what the doctors assumed to be a terminal uraemic coma; but it was a strange sort of coma, from which the patient seemed able to emerge at will.

During his periods of full outward awareness, Sri Aurobindo spoke to his attendants, and even, when the end drew near, kissed those faithful companions of his last years. Some time after midnight on 5 December 1950, he plunged within for the last time, and at 1:26 A.M. his vital functions ceased.[27]

Notes

*On August 16, 1907, Aurobindo was arrested on a charge of sedition for writings that had appeared in the *Bande Mataram*. He was released on bail the same day. Five weeks later, on September 23, he was acquitted of the charges. What he was still doing about the case in December is unclear.

*The full meaning of *Arya* is "a holy man; a man of the highest aspiration, noblest religious dispositions along with an undaunted courage in the upward march of the human race, and one with self surrendered to the Divine Will. From the verb-root *ri*, 'to rise upward.'" (Judith M. Tyberg, *The Language of the Gods: Sanskrit Keys to India's Wisdom* [Los Angeles: East-West Cultural Centre, 1970], p. 1.)

Adhikara, briefly defined as "capacity," was more specifically defined by Sri Aurobindo as "something in the immediate power of a man's nature that determines by its characteristics his right to this or that way of Yoga, of union, which, whatever its merits or its limitations, is his right way because it is most helpful to him personally"

(Sri Aurobindo, *Birth Centenary Library*, vol. 9: *The Future Poetry* [Pondicherry, India: Sri Aurobindo Ashram Press, 1972], p. 40).

[1]Sri Aurobindo, "Some Personal Notes by Sri Aurobindo," *Mother India: Monthly Review of Culture*, 23, no. 2 (March 1971), 101.

[2]Sri Aurobindo, *Sri Aurobindo in Baroda*, compiled and edited by Roshan and Apurva (Pondicherry, India: Sri Aurobindo Ashram, 1993), pp. 69–70.

[3]Peter Heehs, *Sri Aurobindo: A Brief Biography* (New Delhi: Oxford University Press, 1989), p. 27.

[4]Sri Aurobindo, *Sri Aurobindo in Baroda*, pp. 70–71.

[5]Sri Aurobindo, *Birth Centenary Library*, vol. 26: *On Himself* (Pondicherry, India: Sri Aurobindo Ashram Press, 1972), pp. 83–84.

[6]Sri Aurobindo, *Birth Centenary Library*, vol. 1: *Bande Mataram* (Pondicherry, India: Sri Aurobindo Ashram Press, 1972), p. 903.

[7]Quoted here from A. B. Purani, *Sri Aurobindo: Some Aspects of His Vision*, 2nd ed. (Bombay, India: Bharatiya Vidya Bhavan, 1977), p. 31.

[8]Sri Aurobindo, *Tales of Prison Life*, translated by Sisirkumar Ghose (Calcutta, India: Sri Aurobindo Pathamandir, 1979).

[9]Sri Aurobindo, *Tales of Prison Life*, pp. 8–9.

[10]Sri Aurobindo, *Tales of Prison Life*, pp. 117–118.

[11]The Mother, *Glimpses of the Mother's Life*, vol. 1, compiled by Nilima Das, edited by K. D. Sethna (Pondicherry, India: Sri Aurobindo Ashram, 1978), p. 144.

[12]Quoted here from the Mother, *Glimpses*, vol. 1, p. 132.

[13]Quoted here from the Mother, *Glimpses*, vol. 1, pp. 166–167.

[14]Quoted here from K. R. Srinivasa Iyengar, *On the Mother: The Chronicle of a Manifestation and Ministry*, vol. 1 (Pondicherry, India: Sri Aurobindo International Centre of Education, 1978), p. 130.

[15]Sri Aurobindo, *Birth Centenary Library*, vol. 27: *Supplement* (Pondicherry, India: Sri Aurobindo Ashram Press, 1972), p. 422.

[16]Sri Aurobindo, "Some Personal Notes," pp. 101–102.

[17]Sri Aurobindo, *On Himself*, p. 177.

[18]Quoted here from the Mother, *Glimpses of the Mother's Life*, vol. 2, compiled by Nilima Das, edited by K. D. Sethna (Pondicherry, India: Sri Aurobindo Ashram, 1980), pp. 61–62.

[19]Sri Aurobindo, *On Himself*, p. 383.

[20]Sri Aurobindo, *On Himself*, pp. 354–355.

[21]Sri Aurobindo, *Birth Centenary Library*, vol. 29: *Savitri* (Pondicherry, India: Sri Aurobindo Ashram Press, 1972), pp. 727–728.

[22]Sri Aurobindo, *On Himself*, p. 388.

[23]Sri Aurobindo, *On Himself*, p. 354.

[24]Quoted here from the Mother, *Glimpses*, vol. 2, p. 145.

[25]Heehs, *Sri Aurobindo*, p. 142.

[26]Sri Aurobindo, *On Himself*, pp. 404–406.

[27]Heehs, *Sri Aurobindo*, pp. 146–147.

5

The Mother

The physical is CAPABLE *of receiving the higher Light, the Truth, the true Consciousness, and of man-i-fest-ing it.*

—*The Mother*[1]

Like Sri Aurobindo, the Mother was educated and grounded in the culture and values of the West. She was born Mirra Alfassa in Paris in 1878. Her father, a Turkish banker, and her Egyptian mother, had emigrated to Paris from the Middle East just before her birth. Mirra later appreciated her early upbringing because it made her see things as they were without any fanciful notions of reality. She later carried this no-nonsense approach to the farthest reaches of her exploration of reality, never taking anything for granted. This approach would be absolutely essential when she dove into the depths of matter and her own body.

In her early childhood, Mirra was a devout atheist herself, for she could not comprehend how a Supreme Being who was supposed to be loving could allow the cruelties and injustices that were everywhere in the world. In her adolescence, how-

ever, she totally changed course, as she later explained to a
disciple:

> Between 11 and 13, a series of psychic and spiri-
> tual experiences revealed to me not only the ex-
> istence of God but man's possibility of uniting
> with Him, of realizing Him integrally in con-
> sciousness and action, of manifesting Him upon
> earth in a life divine. This, along with a practical
> discipline for its fulfillment, was given to me dur-
> ing my body's sleep by several teachers, some of
> whom I met afterwards on the physical plane.
>
> Later on, as the interior and exterior develop-
> ment proceeded, the spiritual and psychic rela-
> tion with one of these beings became more and
> more clear and frequent; and although I knew
> little of the Indian philosophies and religions at
> that time, I was led to call him Krishna, and hence-
> forth I was aware that it was with him (whom I
> knew I should meet on earth one day) that the
> divine work was to be done.[2]

Mirra studied at the prestigious Acadèmie Julian in Paris,
where she became an accomplished musician, mathematician,
and artist of the Neo-Impressionist school that was flourishing
in Paris at the time. In 1897, at the age of nineteen, she married
an artist, Henri Morisset, with whom she had one child, André,
born on August 23, 1898.

Mirra was now a housewife, mother, and artist. After André's
birth, she developed a floating kidney, from which she was bedridden for several months. During this period, she read some
950 books and also educated her inner senses. For example, she
learned how to exteriorize her consciousness to other rooms in
the house. She also attained, without anyone else's help, a conscious and constant union with the divine Presence.

Although Mirra lived among and worked with the great turn-
of-the-century artists in Paris, she was much younger than they
and considered her own artistic talent quite ordinary; however,
art helped her to be a keen observer of life.

In 1905 an occultist, Max Theon, invited Mirra to Tlemcen in Algeria to study with him and his wife, Alma. Mirra learned through Max's *Revue cosmique* how to find the Divine in her heart. As a student of Max and Alma, she became a master of the invisible realm. For example, Mirra learned from Alma how to go from one subtle body to another, twelve times in succession.

In 1908, Mirra divorced Morisset and met Paul Richard, who would become her second husband in 1911.

In 1912, Mirra was meeting weekly with a small group she had started, of other spiritual seekers, each of whom would prepare a short paper on an agreed-upon topic. What Mirra wrote in her first paper was remarkably similar to Sri Aurobindo's ideal for humanity. Here is her original statement with her later comments:

> The subject for the first meeting was: What is the aim to be achieved, the work to be done, the means of achievement? And here is my answer:
> *"The general aim to be achieved is the advent of a progressive universal harmony."*
> This is the Supermind.
> I did not know Sri Aurobindo at that time, and he had not written anything yet....
> *In regard to the earth, the means of achieving this aim is the realization of human unity by the awakening in all and the manifestation by all of the inner Divinity who is one.*
> *In other words: to create unity by establishing the kingdom of God, which is in all.*
> *Hence, the most useful work to be done is:*
> *1) For everyone individually the becoming aware in oneself of the divine Presence and one's identification with it.*
> *2) The individualization of*

states of being which have so far never been conscious in man and, conse-quently, the putting the earth into touch with one or several sources of universal force, which are yet sealed to it.

...That is to say, there are superposed states of consciousness, and there are new regions which have never yet been manifested on earth, and which Sri Aurobindo called supramental. It is that, this was the same idea. That is, one must go into the depths or the heights of creation which have never been manifested upon earth and become conscious of that, and manifest it on earth. Sri Aurobindo called it the Supermind. I simply say these are states of being which were never yet conscious in man (that is, that man has so far never been aware of them). One must get identified with them, then bring them into the outer consciousness, and manifest them in action. And then, I add (exactly what I foresaw, I did not know that Sri Aurobindo would do it, but still I foresaw that this had to be done):

3) To speak to the world, under a new form adapted to the present state of its mentality, the eternal word.

That is, the supreme Truth, Harmony. It was the whole program of what Sri Aurobindo had done, and the method of doing the work on earth, and I had foreseen this in 1912. I met Sri Aurobindo for the first time in 1914, that is, two years later, and I had already made the whole program.[3]

As is clear from this passage and her comments, Mirra had already conceived the process of transformation that was later called the Triple Transformation: individual, universal, and transcendental.

Also around 1912, Mirra started a diary, in which she wrote

about her daily meditation. Twenty years later, in 1932, she published extracts from that diary, under the title *Prières et Méditations de la Mère* (Prayers and Meditations of The Mother), to which she wrote the following introduction (translated here from the French):

> This book comprises extracts from a diary written during years of intensive yogic discipline. It may serve as a spiritual guide to three principal categories of seekers: those who have undertaken self-mastery, those who want to find the road leading to the Divine, those who aspire to consecrate themselves more and more to the Divine Work.[4]

In the 1940s, Mirra wrote the following introduction for the English edition of *Prayers and Meditations*:

> Some give their soul to the Divine, some their life, some offer their work, some their money. A few consecrate all of themselves and all they have— soul, life, work, wealth; these are the true children of God. Others give nothing. These, whatever their position, power, and riches, are for the Divine purpose valueless ciphers.
>
> This book is meant for those who aspire for an utter consecration to the Divine.[5]

Most of us struggle to attain wealth, power, knowledge, and status. If we are fortunate enough to attain any of these, we tend to hold on to them for dear life, because they give us comfort, control, security, and pride. Rare is the person who can relinquish these for the good of humanity. One who does relinquish them will feel a sense of freedom, joy, and peace. In 1913, Mirra prayed:

> O sweet harmony that dwellest in all things, sweet harmony that fillest my heart, manifest thyself in

the most external forms of life, in every feeling, every thought, every action.

All is to me beautiful, harmonious, silent, despite the outer turmoil. And in this silence it is Thou, O Lord, whom I see; and I see Thee in so unique a way that I can express this perception only as that of an unvarying smile. In truth, the real nature of the feeling experienced in the presence of the sweetest, most calm, most compassionate smile has a poor resemblance to what I feel when I see Thee in this way.

May Thy Peace be with all.[6]

Sri Aurobindo wrote of *Prayers and Meditations*:

The prayers are mostly written in identification with the earth-consciousness. It is the Mother in the lower nature addressing the Mother in the higher nature, the Mother herself carrying on the *sadhana* of the earth-consciousness for the transformation, praying to herself above from whom the forces of transformation come. This continues till the identification of the earth-consciousness and the higher consciousness is effected.... There is the Mother who is carrying on the *sadhana* and the Divine Mother, both being one but in different poises, and both turn to the Seigneur or Divine Master. This kind of prayer from the Divine to the Divine you will find also in the Ramayana and the Mahabharata.[7]

When Mirra met Aurobindo for the first time, in 1914, she immediately recognized him as the teacher in her visions whom she had called Krishna. At the time, she wrote of that meeting:

It matters little that there are thousands of beings plunged in the densest ignorance. He whom we

saw yesterday is on earth; his presence is enough
to prove that a day will come when darkness shall
be transformed into light, and Thy reign shall be
indeed established upon earth.[8]

Mirra and Aurobindo were destined to collaborate on their
journey of transformation, and at their first meeting Mirra exhibited a remarkable capacity to surrender. The longtime disciple Nolini Kanta Gupta commented:

> The first time Sri Aurobindo happened to describe
> [the Mother's] qualities, he said he had never seen
> anywhere a self-surrender so absolute and unre-
> served. He had added a comment that perhaps it
> was only women who were capable of giving
> themselves so entirely and with such sovereign
> ease. This implies a complete obliteration of the
> past, erasing with it its virtues and faults. The
> Mother has referred to this in one of her Prayers
> and Meditations. When she came here, she gave
> herself up to the Lord, Sri Aurobindo, with the
> candid simplicity of a child, after erasing from
> herself all her past, all her spiritual attainments,
> all the riches of her consciousness. Like a new-
> born babe, she felt she possessed nothing, she was
> to learn everything right from the start, as if she
> had known or heard about nothing.[9]

Many decades after this first meeting with Sri Aurobindo,
the Mother said of that occasion:

> When I first met Sri Aurobindo in Pondicherry, I
> was in deep concentration, seeing things in the
> Supermind, things that were to be but which were
> somehow not manifesting. I told Sri Aurobindo
> what I had seen and asked him if they would
> manifest. He simply said, "Yes." And immediately

> I saw that the Supramental had touched the earth
> and was beginning to be realized! This was the
> first time I had witnessed the power to make real
> what is true.[10]

Years later, when Sri Aurobindo's brother Barin asked him, "what was your feeling when you saw the Mother?" Aurobindo thought for a moment and replied: "That was the first time I knew that perfect surrender to the last physical cell was humanly possible; it was when the Mother came and bowed down that I saw that perfect complete surrender in action."[11]

Nolini, who had been arrested with Aurobindo for the bombing in 1908, and acquitted with him in 1909, followed Aurobindo to Pondicherry and remained there for the rest of his life. He recorded his own first impressions of Mirra and her early relationship with Aurobindo:

> The first thing I heard and came to know about the
> Mother was that she was a great spiritual person. I
> did not know then that she might have other gifts;
> these were revealed to me gradually. First I came
> to know that she was a very fine painter; and after-
> wards that she was an equally gifted musician. But
> there were other surprises in store. For instance, she
> had an intellectual side no less richly endowed, that
> is to say, she had read and studied enormously, and
> had engaged in intellectual pursuits even as the
> learned do. I was still more surprised to find that
> while in France she had already studied and trans-
> lated a good number of Indian texts, like the Gita,
> the Upanishads, the Yoga-sutras, [and] the Bhakti-
> sutras of Narada.... In the early days, when she had
> just taken charge of our spiritual life, she told me
> one day in private, perhaps seeing that I might have
> a pride in being an intellectual, "At one time I used
> to take an interest in philosophy and other intellec-
> tual pursuits. All that is now gone below the sur-
> face, but I can bring it up again at will."

This capacity for an entire rejection of the past has been one of the powers of her spiritual consciousness and realization. It is not an easy thing for a human being to wash himself clean of all past acquisitions, be it intellectual knowledge or the habits of the vital, not to speak of the body's needs, and step forth in his nude purity. And yet this is the first and most important step in the spiritual discipline. The Mother has given us a living example of this. That is why she decided to shed all her past, forget all about it, and begin anew the a-b-c of her training and initiation with Sri Aurobindo. And it was in fact at the hands of Sri Aurobindo that she received as a token and outward symbol her first lessons in Bengali and Sanskrit, beginning with the alphabet.[12]

World War I kept Mirra and Aurobindo apart when she left in February 1915 although they corresponded frequently. On November 26, 1915, Mirra wrote to Aurobindo describing an experience she had had in which her physical body, exceeding its limits, grew into a global consciousness, then into a universal consciousness, and on toward the Divine, where it saw a "radiant Being standing on a many-headed serpent whose body coiled infinitely around the universe."[13] The Being mastered the serpent and the universe that issued from it, giving the universe eternal birth. Aurobindo replied to Mirra's letter a month later, on December 31, 1915:

> The experience you have described is Vedic in the real sense, though not one which would be easily recognized by the modern systems of Yoga.... It is the union of the "earth" of the Veda and Purana with the divine Principle, an earth which is said to be above our earth, that is to say, the physical being and consciousness of which the world and the body are only images. But the modern Yogas hardly recognize the possibility of a material union with the Divine.[14]

Mirra's experience flies in the face of what virtually all religions have thought impossible: the attainment of Heaven on Earth. However, Mirra and Aurobindo were not to be deterred from their mission. They spent the rest of their lives to bring about a new consciousness on Earth.

Mirra was profoundly touched by the suffering she saw all around her during World War I, but she realized that such suffering can open one to Spirit:

> I have visited trains, each one bringing between five and six hundred wounded from the front. It is a moving sight, not so much because of all that these unfortunate men are suffering, but above all because of the noble manner in which most of them bear their sufferings. Their soul shines through their eyes, the slightest contact with the deeper forces awakens it. And from the intensity, the fullness of the powers of true love which could, in their presence, be manifested in perfect silence, it was easy to realize the value of their receptivity.[15]

On December 8, 1916, Mirra recorded a remarkable conversation with the Supreme Lord, who told her:

> I have appointed Thee from all eternity to be my exceptional representative upon earth, not only invisibly, in a hidden way, but also openly before the eyes of all men. And what thou was created to be, thou wilt be.[16]

Our thoughts and prayers have more power than we think. On December 20, 1916, twelve days after Mirra had the above communication from the Lord, she received the following message from a great spiritual being from centuries ago:

> As thou art contemplating me, I shall speak to thee this evening. I see in thy heart a diamond surrounded by a golden light. It is at once pure and warm, something which can manifest imper-

sonal love; but why dost thou keep this treasure enclosed in that dark casket lined with deep purple? The outermost covering is of a deep lusterless blue, a real mantle of darkness. It would seem that thou art afraid of showing thy splendor. Learn to radiate and do not fear the storm: the wind carries us far from the shore, but also shows us the world. Wouldst thou be thrifty of thy tenderness? But the source of love is infinite. Dost thou fear to be misunderstood? But where hast thou seen man capable of understanding the Divine? And if the eternal truth finds in thee a means of manifesting itself, what dost thou care for all the rest? Thou art like a pilgrim coming out of the sanctuary; standing on the threshold in front of the crowd, he hesitates before revealing his precious secret, that of his supreme discovery. Listen, I too hesitated for days, for I could foresee both my preaching and its results: the imperfection of expression and the still greater imperfection of understanding. And yet I turned to the earth and men and brought them my message. Turn to the earth and men—isn't this the command thou always hearest in thy heart?—in thy heart, for it is that which carries a blessed message for those who are athirst for compassion. Henceforth nothing can attack the diamond. It is unassailable in its perfect constitution, and the soft radiance that flashes from it can change many things in the hearts of men. Thou doubtest thy power and fearest thy ignorance? It is precisely this that wraps up thy strength in that dark mantle of starless night. Thou hesitatest and tremblest as on the threshold of a mystery, for now the mystery of the manifestation seems to thee more terrible and unfashionable than that of the Eternal Cause. But thou must take courage again and obey the injunction from the depths. It is I who am telling thee this, for I know thee and love thee as thou didst know and love me once. I have appeared clearly before thy sight so that thou mayst in no way doubt my word. And also to thy eyes I showed thy heart so that thou couldst thus see what the supreme Truth has willed for it, so that thou mayest discover in it the law of thy being. The thing still seems to thee quite difficult: a day will come when thou wilt wonder how for so long it could have been otherwise.

—Sakyamuni [Buddha][17]

When Mirra was in Japan, where she lived from 1916 to 1920, she voiced humanity's refusal to receive her spiritual gift:
"I prepared the Feast."

It was a banquet I prepared for men. Instead of a life of misery and suffering, of obscurity and ignorance, I brought to them a life of light and joy and freedom. I took all the pains the task demanded, and when it was ready I offered it to a mankind to partake of it. But man in his foolishness and pigheadedness rejected it, did not want it. He preferred to remain in his dark miserable hole. Now, what I am to do with my feast? I cannot let it go to waste, throw it to the winds. So I offered it to my Lord and laid it at his feet. He accepted it. He alone can enjoy it and honor it.

The feast is that of Transformation, the Divine Life on earth. Man is not capable of it naturally, cannot attain it by his own effort or personal worth. It is the Divine who is to bring it down Himself. He is to manifest Himself and thus establish His own life here below. Then only will it be possible for the human creature to open to the urgency of the new beauty and offer his surrender.

It is not easy to prepare the Feast. I had to bear the full load of the cross and ascend the Calvary. Jesus as he mounted to his destiny with the

Cross on his back stumbled often and fell and rose again with bruised limbs to begin again the arduous journey. Even so, this being too had to go through many disillusions and deceptions, many painful and brutal experiences. It was not a smooth and straight going, but a tortuous and dangerous ascent. But at the end of the tunnel there is always the light. The calvary and the crucifixion culminated in the Resurrection: the divine Passion of Christ flowered into this supreme Recompense. Here too after all the dark and adverse vicissitudes lies the fulfillment of transformation. One must pass through the entire valley of death and rise to the topmost summit to receive and achieve the fullness of the glory. One must leave behind all the lower ranges of ignorance, the entire domain of human consciousness, come out of the imperfection man is made of; then only will he put on the divine nature as his own body and substance.[18]

In April 1920, as Mirra was returning to Pondicherry from Japan, she felt something shortly before the ship docked. She later described the experience as follows:

When I came from Japan, I was on the boat, at sea, not expecting anything (I was of course busy with the inner life, but I was living physically on the boat), when all of a sudden, abruptly, about two nautical miles from Pondicherry, the quality, I may even say the physical quality of the atmosphere, of the air, changed so much that I knew we were entering the aura of Sri Aurobindo. It was a physical experience, and I guarantee that whoever has a sufficiently awakened consciousness can feel the same thing.[19]

(I had an experience like this myself in December 1992. Shortly after I arrived in Pondicherry for one of my many stays, I was invited to see someone in the city of Madurai, two hundred miles to the south. A few days later, when I returned to Pondicherry in the evening, I saw a golden haze over the entire ashram area that had a mesmerizing stillness to it that I could almost touch. To notice this stillness, I had had to leave Pondicherry and return.)

After Mirra returned to India in 1920, she remained in Pondicherry for the rest of her life, serving as Aurobindo's collaborator in their adventure in consciousness. "Without him," she said later, "I exist not; without me he would be unmanifest."[20]

When Mirra returned to Pondicherry, she put the household in order. The following year, Aurobindo asked her to take full charge of the household. She soon found a cat dwelling there, for whom she developed a special fondness:

> I had a very sweet little cat, absolutely civilized, a marvelous cat. It was born in the house, and it had the habit all cats have, that is to say, if something moved, it played with that. Just then there was in the house a huge scorpion; as was its habit, the cat started playing with the scorpion. And the scorpion stung it. But it was an exceptional cat; it came to me, it was almost dying, but it showed me its paw where it was bitten—it was already swollen and in a terrible state. I took my little cat— it was really sweet—and put it on a table and called Sri Aurobindo. I told him, "Kiki has been stung by a scorpion, it must be cured." The cat stretched its neck and looked at Sri Aurobindo, its eyes already a little glassy. Sri Aurobindo sat before it and looked at it also. Then we saw this little cat gradually beginning to recover, to come round, and an hour later it jumped to its feet and went away completely healed…. In those days I had the habit of holding a meditation in the room where Sri Aurobindo slept…and it was regularly the same people who came; everything was ar-

ranged. But there was an armchair in which this very cat always settled beforehand—it did not wait for anyone to get into the chair, it got in first itself! And regularly it went into a trance! It was not sleeping, it was not in the pose cats take when sleeping: it was in a trance, it used to start up, it certainly had visions. And it let out little sounds. It was in a profound trance. It remained thus for hours together. And when it came out of that state, it refused to eat. It was awakened and given food, but it refused: it went back to the chair and fell again into a trance! This was becoming very dangerous for a little cat.... But this was not an ordinary cat.[21]

In 1922, there were only a dozen members of this small spiritual group, but occasional visitors also came to visit Aurobindo. One of these, Philippe Barbier St.-Hilaire, a bright young Frenchman, arrived from Japan in 1925 on a spiritual quest and stayed on for the rest of his life, given the name Pavitra. When he developed difficulties with his meditation, Aurobindo asked Mirra to help him. After she sat with him for thirty minutes, she said:

At the beginning you had a very strong aspiration. Then something must have disturbed you...you have a power of aspiration, but it has been almost completely strangled by the mind.

The force which descended at first is a force of wisdom, of pure knowledge, which descended to the level of the solar plexus.... A force of calm, a silence, descended afterwards...in that, in this calm, there was Ananda.

There was some response in the lower center, but the response was feeble and mostly recorded by the subconscient.[22]

Two weeks later, Mirra told Pavitra:

> Do not seek the truth with your mind!... All that
> you have done so far, all you have learnt, ought
> to be put aside. What holds you back is your edu-
> cation and your mental habits.
> ...Your inner being opened, put itself in a re-
> ceptive attitude, which allowed the descent. In-
> stead of trying to reason, plunge into the experi-
> ence itself.[23]

Months later, Mirra gave Pavitra some additional advice:

> As soon as you are seated, the force descends and
> you receive it. What is missing is something in
> the consciousness. You do not get sufficiently ab-
> sorbed in the inner experience. If that were so,
> you would return with the full knowledge of what
> happened.
> Between your head and chest, a line of light
> is set up...this white light comes from
> Maheshwari, it is a light of knowledge and pu-
> rity. It is she who is the great preparer of the Yoga.
> When that is ready, generally an aspect of power
> (Mahakali) descends.... At the same time, a third
> ring separated you.... This force comes from
> Mahalakshmi.
> The force of purification is always there now,
> preparing, regulating. I am always following you,
> though I do not see you physically.[24]

Descent of the Overmind

In addition to preparing and guiding the disciples,
Aurobindo and Mirra had a larger goal, which was to manifest
the next evolutionary stage of consciousness. When the
Overmind descended to Earth in 1926, there were twenty-four
disciples in the ashram, including six women. Sri Aurobindo later

wrote about this event:

> The 24th November 1926 was the descent of Krishna into the physical. Krishna is not the supramental Light. The descent of Krishna would mean the descent of the Overmind Godhead preparing, though not itself actually, the descent of Supermind and Ananda. Krishna is the Anandamaya: he supports the evolution through the Overmind, leading it towards his Ananda.[25]

The following months were magical and even miraculous. K. D. Sethna, editor of *Mother India*, wrote about this event from accounts by eyewitnesses:

> The nine or ten months after the Overmind descent were a history of spectacular events. All who were present have testified that miracles were the order of the day. What can be called miracles happen every day even now in the Ashram—whenever a great spiritual Force is at work, the miraculous is inevitable—but many such events occur without any éclat and often wear even the appearance of natural phenomena. Those which were common occurrences in those ten months were most strikingly miraculous and, if they had continued, a new religion could have been established with the whole world's eyes focused in wonder on Pondicherry. But the spectacular period terminated with an incident of profound significance. The Mother received one day what she has called the Word of Creation; just as the God Brahma is said to have brought forth the world with the Word of Creation, the fiat of a new world that could be marvelously built, lay ready. A superhuman world was on the verge of being materialized.
>
> With this power the Mother went to Sri Aurobindo's room and told him: "I have got the

Word of Creation." Sri Aurobindo sat silent for a while and then said: "This Creation is from the Overmind. And we do not want that. We have to build the Supermind's world." The Mother went back to her own room. She concentrated intensely for two hours, and at the end of them she had completely dissolved the whole new Creation that had been on the brink of precipitation on the earth. The greatest power in any hands during human history was set aside as if it were a trifle— and all because Sri Aurobindo had said that nothing short of the highest divine truth was the ideal of manifestation for him and her. Miraculously grand though the manifestation would have been of the Overmind deities, it would not have been an utter transformation of life and would have stood in the way of a still greater glory. The very grandeur of it would have filled the aspiring gaze of mankind and checked it from straining for anything beyond it—at least for millennia.[26]

After the descent of the Overmind on November 24, 1926, Aurobindo, who from this point on was called Sri Aurobindo, went into seclusion to prepare for the descent of the Supermind. Mirra became known from this time on as the Mother. With Sri Aurobindo in seclusion, the Mother became the visible head of the ashram and actively supervised its operation and development.

The period from 1926 to 1938 was one of development of the ashram and of preparation for the descent of the Supermind. Generally, everything went smoothly on both fronts. These New Year messages from 1933 to 1938 indicate the Mother's march toward victory:

1933: Let the birth of the New Year be the new birth of our consciousness.
Leaving the past far behind us, let us run towards a luminous future.

1934: Lord, the year is dying and our gratitude

bows down to Thee.
Lord, the year is reborn, our prayer rises
up to Thee. Let it
be for us also the dawn of a new life.

1935: We surrender to Thee this evening all that
is artificial and false, all that pretends and
imitates.
Let it disappear with the year that is at an
end.
May only what is perfectly true, sincere,
straight, and
pure subsist in the year that is beginning.

1936: O Lord! grant that this year may be the year
of Thy victory. We aspire for a perfect faith-
fulness, which would make us worthy of
it.

1937: Glory to Thee, O Lord, who triumphest
over every obstacle! Grant that nothing in
us may be an impediment to Thy work.

1938: Lord, grant that everything in us may be
ready for Thy realization. On the threshold of the New Year, we bow down to Thee,
O Lord, Supreme Realizer.[27]

The Mother had daily reports sent to her from each department of the ashram. She would review these and then return
handwritten notes indicating the work to be done the next day.

The physical structure of the ashram changed around 1933.
Given the constant arrival of new residents, the small dining
room, which could accommodate thirty people, became inadequate, so a large French colonial building was utilized, which
was across the street from the nearby city park.

The quality of the rice that the ashram was purchasing was inadequate, so the Mother purchased land on which the ashramites could grow their own rice, as well as other vegetables, including cauliflower and cucumbers. In 1934, the Mother bought cows, and some ashramites learned cattle breeding at a dairy farm in Bangalore. Overseeing every detail of the ashram's operation, the Mother gave some of the cows names and visited them on Sunday.

Sri Aurobindo's Accident

On November 24, 1938, about 1:30 a.m. a catastrophic event occurred at the ashram just as rumblings about an impending war were being heard all over Europe: Sri Aurobindo fell in his room and broke his right leg, which totally incapacitated him. The Asuric forces were about to cause World War II. Not surprisingly, Sri Aurobindo's and the Mother's work of transformation was the target of these dark forces, which wanted to dominate the world by any means. Sri Aurobindo and the Mother, who were intent upon liberating humanity, making their work central to the earth's evolution.

The Mother was aware of the severity of the fracture in Sri Aurobindo's leg, which could be life-threatening because of the proximity of the broken bone fragments to major arteries and nerves. Medical specialists from Madras arrived, took x-rays, and advised the Mother to have Dr. Manilal, who was visiting the ashram from Gujarat, put the limb in plaster and exert a steady traction by means of splints, but avoiding any forceful traction or other drastic measures. Nirodbaran, a sadhak–doctor, who was an eyewitness to all these events, commented on the Mother's surprising reaction when Dr. Manilal made his prognosis:

> Dr. Manilal had to face from the Mother such an unexpected thundering assault that we felt our hearts would stop with fear and consternation. It was Mahakali's wrath. I have never since seen her in such a fiery mood. Sri Aurobindo was lying quietly; the Mother came into the room and,

standing by his bed, asked Dr. Manilal what he thought of the fracture. The doctor either purposely gave an evasive reply with some hesitation or did not consider the case serious. The Mother exploded, "Don't hide it! We know the truth." Then I saw something rare that I shall never forget. The Mother prostrated herself on the floor before Sri Aurobindo and, I believe, began to pray to him. From this supplication I could realize the gravity of the situation. Yet, she had shown no trace of it until then. Calm and solemn, Sri Aurobindo heard the silent prayer.[28]

The Mother's grave demeanor and her prayer suggest imminent danger for Sri Aurobindo. With the personal care and assistance of the Mother, who even prepared his meals, Sri Aurobindo gradually recovered over the next several months. By April 24, 1939, he was well enough to give darshan.

The eruption of World War II caused an influx of families to the ashram, creating a shift in emphasis. Before, the ashramites had been a tightly knit group that was focused on yoga under the watchful eye of the Mother. Now, the Mother had another charge: to provide for the needs of the newcomers. She became very accessible to the children and nurtured them. She started a school in 1943. An educational institution was developed, which also had a strong emphasis on physical education. Although the intensity of the Integral Yoga became more diffuse, the ashram became more inclusive of humanity-at-large. Eventually, all of humanity had to be represented by the various personality types for the coming transformation.

For example, if a man who had a problem with greed came to live in the ashram, his greediness could soon become magnified to the point that he would have to choose whether to transform himself or remain in darkness. If he chose to transform himself, he would ultimately transcend his greediness and thereby benefit others in the ashram who had the same defect. As more and more people transform their character, the impetus for transformation becomes stronger and easier.

Battle of the Sexes

Perhaps a more universal problem is the perpetual conflict between the sexes. The Mother had lived in the West for forty-two years before settling in Pondicherry and was well aware of the plight of women in all societies. She talked extensively about the relations between men and women and the supposed differences between them. The problem of gender inequality has existed since time immemorial. "Man feels himself superior," said the Mother, "and wants to dominate, the woman feels oppressed and revolts, openly or secretly; and the eternal quarrel between the sexes continues from age to age, identical in essence, innumerable in its forms and shades."[29] As long as each sex blames the other, each remains a slave:

> Thus woman is the slave of man because of the attraction she feels for the male and his strength, because of the desire for a "home" and for the security it brings, lastly because of the attachment to maternity; man too on his side is a slave of woman because of his spirit of possession, his thirst for power and domination, because of his desire for sexual relation, and because of his attachment to the little comforts and conveniences of a married life.
>
> That is why no law can liberate women unless they free themselves: men too likewise cannot, in spite of all their habits of domination, cease to be slaves unless they are freed from all their inner slavery.
>
> This state of secret conflict, often not admitted, but always present in the subconscious, even in the best cases, seems inevitable, unless human beings rise above their ordinary consciousness to identify themselves with the perfect consciousness, to be unified with the supreme Reality. For when you attain this higher consciousness, you perceive that the difference between man and woman reduces itself to a difference purely physical.[30]

We are well aware of the physical differences between the sexes. In fact, we are bombarded with sexuality in movies, books, magazines, television, advertising, and a million other places, so that the physical differences are accentuated over and over again. We have become obsessed with this male-female game.

In her own personal life, especially before she settled in Pondicherry in 1920, the Mother defied convention and was always an independent thinker. Nevertheless, she was able to successfully embody the most traditional feminine qualities, such as surrender, which is all-important in yoga. In this respect, she remarked, women have an innate advantage over men:

> Women are not more bound to the vital and material consciousness than men are. On the contrary, as they have not, in general, the arrogant mental pretensions of men, it is easier for them to discover their psychic being and to allow it to guide them.
> In general, they are not conscious in a mental way which can be expressed in words, but they are conscious in their feelings and the best of them are so even in their actions.[31]

After Sri Aurobindo's passing in 1950, the Mother was left to continue ministering to the needs of around 750 people who were living at the ashram, maintaining the finances and also carrying on the personal transformation of her body.

Under the Mother's guidance, the ashram continued to flourish. On May 1, 1951, a new sports ground was opened, complete with a swimming pool in 1957 and a 400-meter cinder track. In 1951, the Mother opened the library, and then the music and dance rooms the following year.

In March 1952, the Mother made the following declaration:

> Sri Aurobindo is still alive, as living as ever, and will continue to live…. We are determined—he and I—to complete the work he lived for…. In-

dia must maintain the spiritual leadership of the world. If she does not, she will collapse, and with her will go the whole world.[32]

Parts of India, including Pondicherry, were still under French rule long after India got its independence from Britain. However, on November 1, 1954, French India was merged with India proper. In the previous August, the Mother had expressed her desire to become an Indian citizen:

> I want to mark this day by the expression of a long cherished wish; that of becoming an Indian citizen. From the first time I came to India—in 1914—I felt that India was my true country, the country of my soul and spirit.... Now the time has come when I can declare myself.
>
> But, in accordance with Sri Aurobindo's ideal, my purpose is to show that truth lies in union rather than in division. To reject one nationality in order to obtain another is not an ideal solution. So I hope I shall be allowed to adopt a double nationality, that is to say, to remain French while I become an Indian.
>
> I am French by birth and early education, I am Indian by choice and predilection. In my consciousness there is no antagonism between the two; on the contrary, they combine very well and complete one another. I know also that I can be of service to both equally, for my only aim in life is to give concrete form to Sri Aurobindo's great teaching, and in his teaching he reveals that all the nations are essentially one and meant to express the Divine Unity upon earth through an organized and harmonious diversity.[33]

Jawaharlal Nehru, the Prime Minister of India, visited the ashram twice in 1955. His daughter Indira, who accompanied him once and she made two subsequent visits when she became

Prime Minister.

The Mother's New Year's message for 1956 gave a hint of a long-awaited event:

> The greatest victories are the least noisy. The manifestation of a New World is not proclaimed by the beat of drum.[34]

Supramental Descent

The following month, on February 29, 1956, the Supramental Consciousness descended into the Earth's atmosphere:

> Lord, Thou hast willed, and I execute,
> A new light breaks upon the earth,
> A new world is born,
> The things that were promised are fulfilled.[35]

This was a revision of a prayer she had made forty-two years earlier, on September 25, 1914:

> The Lord has willed and Thou dost execute:
> A new Light shall break upon the earth.
> A new world shall be born,
> And the things that were promised shall be fulfilled.[36]

The Supramental Force was acting globally, not just in the ashram, wherever there was any receptivity. On February 29, 1960, the first leap year anniversary of the Supramental descent, the Mother explained what had happened on February 29, 1956. The Divine presence was there, she said, and she faced a giant door barring the world from it. She struck the massive door with a mighty blow that shattered it, and the supramental Light, Force, and Consciousness rushed down upon earth in an uninterrupted flow.

Alongside the development of the inner life, there were activities of a more mundane nature at the ashram. The ashram school was started on December 2, 1943. The Sri Aurobindo International Centre of Education was opened an April 24, 1952.

On August 15, 1960, the Mother agreed to inaugurate the New Horizon Sugar Mills, located just outside Pondicherry. On December 9, 1960, she opened the New Horizon Stainless Steel Factory. Neither are Ashram departments but about her interest in business, she stated:

> First of all, from the financial point of view, the principle on which our action is built is that money is not meant to bring more money—this idea…is a falsehood and a perversion—money is meant to increase the wealth, the prosperity, and the productiveness of a group, a country, or, preferably, the whole earth…. It is by activity and circulation that it grows and intensifies, not by accumulation and stagnation.
>
> What we are attempting here, is to prove to the world, through a concrete example, that by some inner psychological realization and some outer organization a world can be created where most of the causes of human misery will cease to exist.[37]

In 1962, the Mother's heavy workload took its toll, and she had to mostly confine herself to her rooms. Nevertheless, she continued to see visitors and to reply to letters.

On March 5, 1963, she was asked, "Can you *now* say that the Divine has decided to preserve the present human civilization?" She replied, "It will be *settled* in 1967."[38] This was during the proliferation of atomic weapons.

On August 15, 1964, Sri Aurobindo's ninety-second birthday, the Indian government released a commemorative stamp. The Mother made the first cancellation, announcing at the time that Sri Aurobindo "has come to bid the Earth to prepare for its luminous future."[39]

Auroville

The Mother began plans in 1965 for a city of the future, to be called Auroville. It was to be, in her words:

A place that no nation could claim as its sole property…a place where the needs of the spirit and the care for progress would get precedence over the satisfaction of desires and passions, the seeking for material pleasures and enjoyment.[40]

On September 8, 1965, she declared:

Auroville wants to be a universal town where men and women of all countries are able to live in peace and progressive harmony, above all creeds, all politics, and all nationalities.
　　　The purpose of Auroville is to realize human unity.[41]

On February 21, 1967, Huta, another one of the Mother's disciples, exhibited 460 paintings that had been directly inspired by the Mother's teachings and sketches. In fact, those sketches were placed alongside Huta's paintings at the exhibition. Presently, a building is under construction at Savitri Bhavan in Auroville to display this art.

The official groundbreaking for Auroville occurred on February 28, 1968. The participants in the ceremony included one boy and one girl from each of 124 nations and 23 Indian states, each bringing soil from their native countries to be placed in an urn. UNESCO became a sponsor of Auroville.

Auroville is an attempt at collective realization of Supramental Consciousness. The only requirement for participating in it is a "simple good will to make a collective experiment for the progress of humanity."[42]

Superman Consciousness

On January 1, 1969, the Supramental Consciousness descended further into matter itself, into the body. It was described by the Mother as the Superman or the intermediary consciousness. This superhuman effort by the Mother, which almost defies our imagination, required an indomitable will to reach this point in evolution, where the Supramental Consciousness first manifests as power and penetrates matter. The Mother described this Consciousness as acting externally as a personality but she also said that there is a simultaneous action in the environment *and* in the body (cells).

In November 1971, with her health still precarious and her body wearing out in the race against time, the Mother said:

> We are at a moment of transition in the history of the earth.... But this moment is long compared to human life. Matter is changing to prepare itself for a new manifestation; but the human body is not plastic enough and offers resistance; this is the reason why illnesses and even incomprehensible illnesses are increasing in number....
>   The remedy is in union with the Divine Forces that are at work and a receptivity full of truth and peace that will make the labor easy.[43]

On April 2, 1972, the Mother made an announcement about her physical situation:

> If you believe that I am here because I am bound, it is not true. I am not bound. I am here because my body has been given for the first attempt at transformation.... It is not very pleasant, but I do it willingly because...everybody will be able to profit from it.[44]

On May 20, 1973, at the age of ninety-five, the Mother's condition remained unstable. She continued to eat very little, and her state did not improve for the next six months.

During this period, the Mother lived in seclusion. For the past twenty-three years, since 1951, she had been having a series of conversations with her disciple Satprem, which now came to an end. For the first seven years, Satprem had only taken notes on their dialogues. In 1958, he had begun tape-recording the sessions, selections of which had been published in the ashram's quarterly *Bulletin of the Sri Aurobindo International Centre of Education* under the heading "Notes on the Way." Satprem later published the entire series of conversations from 1951 to 1973, including his notes for the first seven years, under the title *Mother's Agenda*[45] but without approval from the Ashram.

On August 15, 1973, Sri Aurobindo's one hundred and first birthday, the Mother walked to her balcony and gave darshan to 8,000 people who had assembled below.

The Mother was still totally focused on bodily transformation when she passed away on November 17, 1973, at the age of 95.

India's Prime Minister, Indira Gandhi, declared to the world:

> The Mother was a dynamic, radiant personality with tremendous force of character and extraordinary spiritual attainments. Yet she never lost her sound practical wisdom, which concerned itself with the running of the Ashram, the welfare of society, the founding and development of Auroville, and any scheme which would promote the ideals expressed by Sri Aurobindo.
> She was young in spirit, modern in mind, but most expressive with her abiding faith in the spiritual greatness of India and the role which India could play in giving new light to mankind.[46]

Notes

[1]The Mother, *Mother's Agenda*, vol. 11: *1970*, ed. by Satprem (New York: Institute for Evolutionary Research, 2000), p. 102.

[2]The Mother, *Collected Works of The Mother*, vol. 13: *Words of The Mother* (Pondicherry, India: Sri Aurobindo Ashram Press, 1980), p. 39.

[3]The Mother, *Glimpses of The Mother's Life*, vol. 1, compiled by Nilima Das, edited by K. D. Sethna (Pondicherry, India: Sri Aurobindo Ashram, 1978), pp. 111–112.

[4]The Mother, *Collected Works of The Mother*, vol. 1: *Prayers and Meditations* (Pondicherry, India: Sri Aurobindo Ashram Press, 1979), p. viii.

[5]The Mother, *Prayers and Meditations*, p. vii.

[6]The Mother, *Prayers and Meditations*, p. 27.

[7]Quoted here from The Mother, *Glimpses*, vol. 1, pp. 114–115.

[8]The Mother, *Prayers and Meditations*, p. 113.

[9]Quoted here from The Mother, *Glimpses*, vol. 1, p. 136.

[10]The Mother, *Glimpses*, vol. 1, p. 132.

[11]The Mother, *Glimpses*, vol. 1, p. 252.

[12]Quoted here from The Mother, *Glimpses*, vol. 1, pp. 136–137.

[13]The Mother, *Glimpses*, vol. 1, p. 168.

[14]Quoted here from The Mother, *Glimpses*, vol. 1, p. 169.

[15]The Mother, *Glimpses*, vol. 1, p. 163.

[16]The Mother, *Glimpses*, vol. 1, p. 176.

[17]Quoted here from The Mother, *Glimpses*, vol. 1, pp. 176–177.

[18]The Mother, *Glimpses*, vol. 1, pp. 206–208.

[19]The Mother, *Glimpses*, vol. 1, p. 208.

[20]The Mother, *Glimpses*, vol. 1, p. 132.

[21]The Mother, *Glimpses*, vol. 1, pp. 223–224.

[22]Quoted here from K. R. Srinivasa Iyengar, *On The Mother: The Chronicle of a Manifestation and Ministry*, 2nd ed. (Pondicherry: Sri Aurobindo International Centre of Education, 1978), vol. 1, p. 228.

[23]Quoted here from Iyengar, *On The Mother*, vol. 1, p. 228.

[24]Quoted here from Iyengar, *On The Mother*, vol. 1, p. 228.

[25]The Mother, *Glimpses*, vol. 1, p. 233.

[26]Quoted here from The Mother, *Glimpses*, vol. 1, pp. 234–235.

[27]The Mother, *Glimpses*, vol. 2, p. 74.

[28]Quoted here from The Mother, *Glimpses*, vol. 2, p. 149.

[29]The Mother, "The Problem of Women," in *On Women*, compiled by Vijay from the writings of Sri Aurobindo and The Mother (Pondicherry, India: Sri Aurobindo Society, 1978), p. 3.

[30]The Mother, "The Problem of Women," pp. 4–5.

³¹The Mother, "Man and Woman—An Unnecessary Conflict," in *On Women*, compiled by Vijay from the writings of Sri Aurobindo and The Mother (Pondicherry, India: Sri Aurobindo Society, 1978), p. 47.

³²Quoted here from Iyengar, *On The Mother*, vol. 2, p. 531.

³³Quoted here from Iyengar, *On The Mother*, vol. 2, pp. 565–566.

³⁴Quoted here from Iyengar, *On The Mother*, vol. 2, p. 599.

³⁵The Mother, *Glimpses*, vol. 2, p. 277.

³⁶The Mother, *Glimpses*, vol. 2, p. 277.

³⁷Quoted here from Iyengar, *On The Mother*, vol. 2, p. 674.

³⁸Quoted here from Iyengar, *On The Mother*, vol. 2, p. 696.

³⁹Quoted here from Iyengar, *On The Mother*, vol. 2, p. 704.

⁴⁰Quoted here from Iyengar, *On The Mother*, vol. 2, p. 713.

⁴¹Quoted here from Iyengar, *On The Mother*, vol. 2, p. 713.

⁴²Quoted here from Iyengar, *On The Mother*, vol. 2, p. 753.

⁴³Quoted here from Iyengar, *On The Mother*, vol. 2, p. 783.

⁴⁴Quoted here from Iyengar, *On The Mother*, vol. 2, p. 788.

⁴⁵The Mother, *Mother's Agenda*, 13 vols., edited by Satprem (New York: Institute for Evolutionary Research, 1979–2000).

⁴⁶Quoted here from Iyengar, *On The Mother*, vol. 2, p. 804.

6

Action in the World

*None can reach heaven who
has not passed through hell.*

—Sri Aurobindo[1]

*During the First World War,
every part of my body
represented a battlefield.*

—The Mother[2]

Sri Aurobindo said to never distrust one's own experiences—
assuming, of course, that one is mentally balanced. Because of
the accumulation of the many letters that he wrote to his
disciples, who had many questions about their *sadhana* (spiritual
practice), we have a wealth of information from him to help us
understand our own experiences and processes.

For example, in April 1969, after I had been practicing
meditation on a daily basis for four months, I had my first out-
of-body experience. After sitting quietly for longer than my usual

twenty minutes, I noticed a pressure building up in my head. It became stronger and stronger, much like a squeezing sphygmomanometer, that medical apparatus used to take blood pressure—except that this was a tightening around my skull rather than my arm. Suddenly, my consciousness shot out through the top of my head, and I felt myself soaring in space like a rocket. I had the impression of going very fast, with the wind rushing by me. It was dark, but I could see the stars. I soared and soared until I suddenly came back to consciousness in my body.

I didn't know what to make of this experience until years later, when I read in Sri Aurobindo's *Letters on Yoga* an answer he gave to a disciple who had a similar experience. Sri Aurobindo said that it was called "Splitting of the Skull," which involves the consciousness going back to its source. Since that time, I have been able to find most of my spiritual experiences described in the *Letters on Yoga, Mother's Agenda*, or *Savitri*. However, it is not always a good idea to look for a rational explanation of such experiences, at least right away. I have found that explanations appear spontaneously at the appropriate time. Mentalizing can nullify or partially impede the benefits of such experiences.

Although the Mother describes many spiritual experiences in *Mother's Agenda*, these represent only a small fraction of the ones she had during the twenty-three years covered in the book. Some she forgot. Some she never got around to mentioning. And some were beyond words.

We often explain things by comparisons. For example, we may say that something smells like a rose. But what happens when there is *nothing* to which one can compare an experience? Time and again, the Mother complained that her descriptions sounded too flat or too ordinary, failing to capture the essence of the experience. Only when we have the experience ourselves can we truly understand it.

Aside from Sri Aurobindo and the Mother, very few practitioners of Integral Yoga have published books or articles about their spiritual experiences, especially transformation of their bodies. Even simple words, such as *peace, light, love, joy, bliss,* and *power,* have a general connotation, but when one experiences them in the inner life, devoid of any subject-object relationship, the experience has a totally unique feeling. Perhaps the closest we can come to capturing such experiences is through poetry. Sri Aurobindo conveyed his journey, his experience of all the dimensions of consciousness, through his epic poem *Savitri,* the story of a woman who represents the Mother on her quest for immortality.

According to Georges Van Vrekhem, in his illuminating book *Beyond the Human Species,* the Mother completed her mission on Earth with the descent of the Supermind in 1956.[3] She continued on with the transformation of her own body until November 17, 1973, the day she died. Both Sri Aurobindo and the Mother are still extremely active on the subtle physical plane and may be contacted there. When the Mother was alive, she was asked how one can contact this subtle physical plane. She said that she didn't know any method; she simply was *there.* A region of the subtle physical plane is supramentalized, so that one can see the supramental gold everywhere. There is a wondrous atmosphere of a divine Presence, and one feels infused in Spirit with all its luminosity. The physical and subtle physical are superimposed, and one can move from one to the other in the blink of an eye.

Many, many people throughout the world have had contact with Sri Aurobindo and the Mother in one form or another, either through inner vision or being with them in another dimension. It is also possible to see them in the waking state with eyes wide open. When this happens, one is in an altered state of consciousness. We can also see other disciples who have died but are actively working for the transformation. There are, of course, numerous instances of visions by persons who share other beliefs—for example, Catholics who have seen the Virgin Mary.

Although Sri Aurobindo and the Mother are active on the subtle physical plane, during their lives they were also intimately involved, unlike most yogis, in worldly matters. For example, they were deeply interested in the outcome of World War II, believing that the dark and evil occult forces behind Hitler were in direct opposition to their own mission of transforming the Earth. Sri Aurobindo said that if Hitler had been victorious, his own work of transformation with the Mother would have been delayed for centuries, or worse:

> The victory of one side (the Allies) would keep the path open for the evolutionary forces: the victory of the other side would drag back humanity, degrade it horribly, and might lead even, at the worst, to its eventual failure as a race, as others in the past evolution failed and perished. That is the whole question, and all other considerations are either irrelevant or of a minor importance. The Allies at least have stood for human values, though they may often act against their own best ideals (human beings always do that); Hitler stands for diabolical values or for human values exaggerated in the wrong way until they become diabolical (e.g., the virtues of the Herrenvolk, the master race). That does not make the English or Americans nations of spotless angels nor the Germans a wicked and sinful race, but as an indicator it has a primary importance.[4]

Sri Aurobindo's view of Hitler is revealed in a story told by Maggi Lidchi-Grassi, an ashramite in Pondicherry. One day, Sri Aurobindo came across a copy of *Mein Kampf*, which was the Bible of the Nazis. He said that it was a tissue of lies that he would not touch. When a French magazine, *L'Illustration*, published a photograph of Hitler, Goebbels, and Goering, Sri Aurobindo commented on it:

> Hitler gives the impression of the face of a street-criminal. In his case, it is successful ruffianism with a diabolical cunning and behind it the

psychic of a London cabman—crude and undeveloped. That is to say, the psychic character in the man consists of some futile and silly sentimentalism. He is possessed by some supernatural Power, and it is from this Power that the voice, as he calls it, comes. Have you noted that people who at one time were inimical to him come into contact with him and leave as his admirers? It is a sign of that Power. It is from this Power that he has constantly received suggestions, and the constant repetition of the suggestions has taken hold of the German people. You will also mark that in his speeches he goes on stressing the same ideas—that is evidently a sign of that vital possession.[5]

Saga of an American Soldier in WWII

Although Sri Aurobindo and the Mother often operated on the highest international levels, they could also operate on an individual one—for example, with an infantryman in the trenches. One fascinating divine intervention by Sri Aurobindo has been described by an American soldier named John Kelly.

In an interview in 1984 with the editor of *Collaboration*, a journal for the Sri Aurobindo community in the United States, Kelly related his experience in World War II as follows:

I had no knowledge of yoga. I quit high school in my second year after the football season to earn money…the family was in poor circumstances. When I became 18, I was drafted into the army. In a very short period of time, I was in France in the infantry, and we went into the attack, surprisingly, I found out later, on Mother's birthday in February of 1945, the closing months of World War Two. France was still occupied by the Germans, and this was the time of the Battle of the Bulge, and Bastogne. We were replacements for a lot of people who had fallen in those battles. So we were in this town, I don't know if it was one or two days into the battle, day and night, hit by rockets from 15 to 20 miles called "screaming meemies"...all sorts of terrible noise.... Anyway, because of one of those rockets that could flip you up in the air and toss you like a flapjack, I must have opened up. The head must have opened to these frequencies.... That might be one possible explanation.

We were in a zigzag trench down this mountain, which was a graveyard from the first World War. I had heard that from the Napoleonic wars there were people buried there.... There were crosses. We were near a wood road up in the forest. The original company had been wiped out almost to a man...as far as I know. There were German and American bodies laying on the field amid the pine trees. It was a big jungle of torn-up trees and earth.

I had the first vision there. You know, they say there's no atheist in a foxhole, well, I wanted to see...I thought I was going to be on the other side any minute. So I said, "Let's get there first!" It was about the only thing worth trying for. I had heard from my childhood brought up in a Catholic school of people who had some kind of transformation vision and experience. God or the angels could descend and enlighten you, you see. So here's the situation: a cemetery, all these dead from past wars, I in another "plot" alive.... They haven't thrown the dirt in on top of me—that's the only difference between me and these fellows. I said, "What the hell is this all about?" I'm a person a little thick. To bring something home to me you practically have to hit me on the head, and this was that type of situation..., and I found out in India that experiences happen in graveyards. So I was in a psychological state. Believe me. Desperation.

After some time, one day, two days, god knows, it was freezing up there, in the middle of winter. Time stood still. Finally one night late..., there was nobody near me…. I saw a wisp of white smoke in front of me, and a little whiff of smoke like cigarette smoke. Little sparks of light started to emanate out of that little wisp. It was moving to my right from "no-man's-land…." My eyes were fastened on it like a rabbit's. The smoke kept growing and turned into a haze, and the sparks coming out of it were enormous. My mind was working feverishly, very rapid…so…out of that came a bubbling laughter, gentle laughter of a wise old man. It came out like champagne, and actually I heard the "ppp" of a bottle and the fizz. That effervescent sound with the light in front of me became a delightful fascination. And frightening. The laughter kept getting louder, in my head perhaps. I don't know. But it was very gentle and very wise, and suddenly I see a mouth and a beard start to form, then the eyes, and the eyes sent out this light that hit me, and I fell back in the hole. I said, "Oh god, I think I struck pay dirt here."

The laughter continued. I felt a bubbling in my stomach, a buoying of my spirits, you see. Suddenly the voice says (low) "What is it you wish, my child?" It had the accent of a high Englishman. Here I am from Brooklyn. I said, "Oh my god (my father was a rebel)…. God is an Englishman." I thought, "What am I gonna say to God?" I pinched myself. I said, "Jesus, I'm making this up in my head." No, it was real. I'm awake and this is happening.

So the first thing I thought of was, "Get me the hell out of here…take me to Paris where I can sit down, drink some wine, and dance with the girls. This is a serious situation, but at the same time I was completely delirious. There was some kind of spirit here. I wasn't lonely. If I got killed now I didn't give a damn. There was a certain inner delight about the whole relationship that occurred. So I said, "I've got to think of something sensible to say," so I said, "Great Sir," that's what I called him because everyone's Sir in the army. So I said, "O great Sir, all I really wish is…to know." So he laughed, and I ducked down because I didn't want to get hit with that light in the head. I wouldn't look at his eyes because of the force that came emanating out.

The laughter was one of the most incredible things of tone value that I have ever heard. What I felt was that the laughter itself was talking to me. Now, you see, there is such a thing as mocking laughter, hilarious laughter, you can laugh every way. You can laugh, you know, for all kinds of reasons. There's a whole vocabulary of laughter that I became attuned to and the nuances of the laughter. There was a whole thing we were going through as if this wasn't the first time it had happened.

I thought, "I'd better not say anything more or I'll get in trouble." So he said, "If my help you choose, then your religion you will lose." I thought, "Aha, I've got the devil!" But then I didn't care at this point about religion or whether it was hell or heaven I was going to, as long as I went. I mean, I was brought up a Catholic, but I never really had Christ in me. I was given a label like a Democrat or Republican. It was on the surface of my being. So I said to him, "You know, I don't have a religion in that sense, the true sense of having the founding force of a religion. You have to give it to me." I was begging for spirit. And I was putting the ball in his court…. I got the ball across the net, you see. That's all it amounted to for me. Like a ping-pong game. I ducked down, waiting for his reply, and suddenly the laughter stops. "Oh, oh, " I thought, "I said the wrong thing." But then I looked up, and standing there in front of me, on the battlefield, was the full figure, a man with a white beard and white hair hanging down in a sheet like a Roman emperor. He's leaning against this tree a little bit, and he's signing to my left. I don't know if the moon was out that night, but the light on his face was golden.

You could see a certain kind of refinement in this being that was extraordinary, an aesthetic face that really doesn't show up in his photographs at all. There was suffering and the conquering of suffering. All of that was there.

So as I look to the left, out of the forest I see a waffling motion and something moving down like a big platform zipping in, like a UFO long before I ever heard of these things. It moved and set itself. It was a Greek temple like those small Parthenon-type things with four columns. People sit on them in wicker chairs and have tea. That kind of set-up. And there was a lady lying down! I said, "Oh, this is a fairy tale. This is ridiculous, delightful." She's on a big divan with a black housecoat of velvet. The columns of this thing are like luminescent light, like a very high-quality neon light…. It reminded me of alabaster, radiant soft light…, indirect lighting…, the supreme in indirect lighting.

I look, and there she is sitting in a pose exactly as we see her in those old photographs of 1914. I came to learn over the years that this pose was like the mudra of the Greek goddess of wisdom. So I'm in this trench, and it seemed like I was on the steps of the temple looking up at her. Her face changed…. It was a long nose…, very much Mother. And then that same face said, "I am Mother, Mother, Mother, Mother. I am all Mothers." The face kept changing like a strobe light effect. That face changed and changed constantly and then would come back and rest at that face again.

I was absolutely enchanted. It was extraordinary. With that it's getting very heavy on my head. My head is really singing. I said, "Listen, sweetheart, you'd better remove that thing, that temple, from the field of battle because we're having a hell of a time here." She didn't want to go. I said, "If you don't go soon, I won't have anything in my head. I'll be insane…with delight." So, reluctantly, it faded away into the gloom. Then I was so happy I did a somersault, or maybe I fainted, I don't know. I collapsed. The next thing I recall is a solder saying, "Hey, Kelly, get up. Wake up. We're going off of this hill. We've been relieved." This was dawn, I think. The place was always so overhung with clouds you didn't know what it was.

As we go down, I start to recall what happened, and I hear two guys talking behind me. One says to the other, "Did you see the light on the hill last night?" "Yeah, wasn't that something?" They saw it, too! That thing was like a 3-D manifestation. It kept growing from those wisps of smoke. I thought, "I've got to forget this." But every time there was a bombardment, all I did was think about her, sitting in that temple. And I said, "Gee, I wonder who she is."

Another day goes by, and suddenly I hear the old man in the sky. You see, I used to walk behind my men—they made me a sergeant for a few days because all of the others were sick or wounded or whatever. Anyway, the old man says to me, "That underpass is going to be hit." There was a train overpass that we had to go under, and he almost gives me the picture of the bombardment occurring. So I ran down to the Lieutenant and said, "Where are we going?" I was stalling. He showed me the map and a German headquarters building on the other side of the underpass. That's where we were going. I tried to convince him to go another way, but he wouldn't listen.

So I went back to my men, and then the old man in the sky says, "Take your men and go first." I said, "What? Now you want me to go first?" There I was, cringing and cowardly, trying to find another way out. Anyway, he convinced me to go first and quickly. So I went and told the Lieutenant that we would go first. He says, "You will?"

We ran down the hill like a track team through the underpass, and the idea was not to stop until we got to the building. And we did. They shot at us. We shot back. As soon as we closed the door, the whole goddamn place exploded. But they didn't hit that building. It was their own building. There was nobody in it, thank god. When the smoke cleared, we looked, and there was nobody back there. The whole platoon was gone. Well, they had gone around just like I thought *we* should.

Anyway, the contact was constant. He was giving directions, and I was always refusing to accept them. And he was like a periscope. He could look around. He could see in the distance, where it was safe and where we should go. That was very beneficial to me. But still, you can have your father take you by the hand and lead you into the candy store, and still you're gonna be disgruntled. I was disgruntled. Though I was in a very advantageous position with having such a guide. Still, the gloom. At least I had somebody to complain to!

Well, the war ended. We got through the Ziegfried line and through the concentration camps. Eventually we got up along the border with the Russians. We were now the occupation army. Anyway, I was trying to figure all this out. I didn't know about bi- location, you see, that masters do exist and have existed through the ages, and that he and she were of that class, that order of beings. I had put them in the class of god, the devil, and the holy ghost, beings of another world, when, in fact, they were living beings on our own Earth. That's the real significance of this story.

I asked Mother these things specifically later on when I got to India. She said that it was as if the day the World War started the telephone exchange slowly and invisibly—like an enormous box—came down slowly and settled on her. And with that box, it made all kinds of sounds like "tu-tu-tu-tu", was like a telephone exchange, that's the words she used. She was, in a sense, plugged in to all these distress calls from all over the battlefields of the world. Anybody that was in jeopardy or peril...would be calling, and sometimes she would faint, in the schoolyard, the playground, or she would go into a trance and there was no stopping it or controlling it. And there was no remembering it because it was constant. She was part of that hookup. Higher emanations were going out of her in all directions—that was what was given to her as a work, and she said the happiest day of her life was the day the war ended and the box went back up again.

So, after a while, I came back from the line, and I was in this building. Now the tension from all this had built up in my body, all the confusion and craziness and these visions. I was like a taut wire, but it was occult—I had no control over it. That wire was so high-strung—I thought that I was insane, you know. I was out in no-man's land and no-mind's land. That's a strange place, not knowing that there is such a place and that you can get accustomed to it.

I had other visions. I saw an old guy with a pipe who I later thought must have been Carl Jung. I saw a priest, a big tough-looking guy, big black beard, pirate eyebrows, but very sweet, and I told him I wanted to see that woman again, and he said that he would speak to her.

It just kept building up and up. Finally I dropped dead right on the bed. The heart stopped, and I go out of my head. All of this force goes right out of the top of my head, but I was still coherent and then Sri Aurobindo came. There was a flame shot around the room—it was the psychic plane, that dimension. That was a magic circle or something, and up through the magic circle we go. He tells me to stay on his heels and not to look right or left. Out we go into the night sky over Germany, headed towards Switzerland, out towards Italy, down towards Rome. At the same time, there are all sorts of besieging entities on all sides trying to come at us in this plane. Ghosts and otherworldly beings trying to make contact and send messages to this world. But I was told not to look right or left. Finally, we broke out of that world, that gloom world, into the night sky. It seemed to be the physical night sky—I can't tell you for sure. We headed out over the Mediterranean Sea and got to Egypt and saw the sands of Egypt turning to dawn. By the time we hit the coast of India, it was daylight, and I'm in the Ashram on the floor, and there are these chintzy pink clouds on the floor!

He's sitting in his chair. Mother's over there. But these clouds! I was hitting the floor. What are they doing there? He was smiling and laughing. "Do you know what an ashram is?" he says. I didn't know, but I bluffed. So we're in the Ashram and talking, and I found out I could go over…to past lives, and I found out I'd been in ashrams before, in past lives. Then he told me certain things, and we had a whole series of visionary experiences in other planes, as he mentions in *Savitri*. Finally, I came back to the bed, the heart started up, and the cataleptic trance left—that's actually what I was in, a cataleptic trance.

I'm so deliriously happy when I wake up. I remember looking out the window—there was a drunken soldier coming up the road with a bottle of wine in his hand, singing a dirty song, and that was spiritual! It was under the haze of dawn light, and this debauched guy was some part of this spiritual atmosphere in some mysterious manner. I wake up. I get dressed, and a hush falls on the room. I knew the old man was back, and there, coming through the wall, there he is sitting in the chair, and the Mother is with him but less visible. So I stand straight like a soldier. He's very benevolent. There's wonderful force, emanations, and circles radiating out, seas of bliss and light and joy all coming out. And this enormous benevolence.

I had said, I wonder who he is, this wonderful being who had helped me through the war all this time to get me through these states and give me these experiences, and he moves his head— he picked it right up—and he says to me (barely audible), "Sri Aurobindo," I said, "Auro?" he says, "Au...ro...bin...do." He's smiling, almost ready to burst out laughing. He can hardly contain himself. He's breaking up.

I said, "O.K., Aurobindo, What is that? Is that a password? You and me got a password?" Basically he says yes. I never heard a word like that. Then Mother said to me, "Come to Pondicherry," I thought, "I'm supposed to go to a place very far away?" It was much farther than today—everybody still went by ship then—I wasn't that clear. Bringing it over to the physical mind, when there wasn't that much there, wasn't an easy choice. My associations and relationships took half a lifetime...truly.

It wasn't meant to be, either. I told them I had to stay and help my mother. She was sick, and the old man's a bum, and he's drinking, and I've got to stay to take care of the family. He understood and said he understood. "You will come in twenty years," he said.

That's basically the story. There are many

others. I went back to America, became a fireman in New York City, retired from that after my mother passed away. She died in 1965. A year later, I went off to India and saw Mother. She was very happy. We had a lovely relationship. I met other people who had seen Sri Aurobindo like I had, in the war or someplace in the world. That was a big boost. As long as someone else had seen them, then I knew I was in the right group. I got there too late to see Sri Aurobindo in the body, but his *darshan* is always there.[6]

Reprinted with permission by Gordon Korstange,
editor and interviewer for Collaboration

I have heard numerous stories from other individuals about the strange set of circumstances that led them to Sri Aurobindo and the Mother. In Auroville, a young woman told me that she had seen a photo in a newspaper held by another passenger on a bus in Brazil, and through a strange set of circumstances later discovered that the man in the picture was Sri Aurobindo.

A homeopath in southern California was in a library when a copy of *The Life Divine* by Sri Aurobindo fell off a shelf and hit him on the head. That was his introduction to Sri Aurobindo.

The late Reverend Joseph Martinez related to me how he became acquainted with the teachings of Sri Aurobindo. He had left a Jesuit monastery in Napa County, worked for a while in medical sales, and finally stopped doing anything. One day, he was walking down Market Street in San Francisco and went into a bookstore. While randomly looking at books, he took a small volume off the shelf, *The Mind of Light* by Sri Aurobindo, and opened it. "Then," he said, "it started talking to me, just as I am talking to you now."

An ashramite in Pondicherry, Shyam Kumari, has compiled a number of stories in multiple volumes about how people came to Sri Aurobindo and the Mother, as well as reminiscences and inspiring stories of grace.

It is no accident that we have these two spiritual figures, one male and one female, one from the East and one from the West. Both were active in the material life before they focused exclusively on their mission. They were well grounded in the ways of the world and had no illusions about the difficulty or the enormity of the task before them. By the time each had arrived in Pondicherry, they were fully self-realized beings ready to begin their work of transformation and all that that entailed.

Notes

[1]Sri Aurobindo, *Birth Centenary Library*, vol. 28: *Savitri* (Pondicherry, India: Sri Aurobindo Ashram Press, 1972), p. 227.

[2]The Mother, *Mother's Agenda*, vol. 4: *1963*, edited by Satprem (New York: Institute for Evolutionary Research, 1987), p. 468.

[3]Georges Van Vrekhem, *Beyond the Human Species: The Life and Work of Sri Aurobindo and The Mother* (St. Paul, MN: Paragon House, 1997), pp. 319–320.

[4]Sri Aurobindo, *Birth Centenary Library*, vol. 26: *On Himself* (Pondicherry, India: Sri Aurobindo Ashram Press, 1972), p. 396.

[5]Maggi Lidchi-Grassi, *The Light that Shone into the Dark Abyss* (Pondicherry: Sri Aurobindo Ashram Press, 1994), p. 48.

[6]Interview with John Kelly, *Collaboration*, 10(2), Spring–Summer 1984, 16–18.

Part Two

7

Good and Evil

Be not repelled by the world's crookedness; the world is a wounded and venomous snake wriggling towards a destined off-sloughing and perfection. Wait, for it is a divine wager; and out of this baseness, God will emerge brilliant and triumphant.

—Sri Aurobindo[1]

And there is a moment when one would be unable to say, "This is divine and that is not divine," for a time comes when one sees the whole universe in so total and comprehensive a way that, to tell the truth, it is impossible to take away anything from it without disturbing everything.

—The Mother[2]

Our evolution is incomplete. There is indeed a huge gap between our present state and what we are evolving into. This gap will continue to exist until we understand and integrate the complexities of good and evil, one of the most perplexing issues of life. Good and evil symbolize the duality of our lower nature. How they came into existence must be brought to light. We must understand that the adverse or hostile forces known to us as evil have a very important role to play in human evolution. They test us every step of the way, and all events of our lives are cause for examination. The surprising thing is that we ourselves may serve sometimes as examiner and sometimes as examined in this remarkable universe. At the very core of the dark and hostile Asuric forces is a sense of separation from the Supreme, which is the formation of the ego.

We are all immersed in a duality of nature. I am using good and evil here as a metaphor for that duality. Good versus evil is the play of opposites that we tend to ignore. The dark side becomes evident when we want to progress. Presently, we are all involved in the transformation of matter, willing or not. At some point, we will realize that good and evil are always together. The best and the worst of us are side by side, but we tend to deny the dark or shadow side. We are here to experience our opposites, but all the possibilities will not manifest so long as there is separation. Ironically, the "dark forces" can be very beautiful and dazzling in their appearance.

The play of opposing forces creates a tension within us, or a resistance, that we must overcome to achieve integration. Many people see this resistance, or at least a part of it, as evil. This so-called evil has an important part to play in our transformation. In a letter to a disciple, Sri Aurobindo talked about the evil persona:

> What you say about the "Evil Persona" interests me greatly, as it answers to my consistent experience that a person greatly endowed for the work has, always or almost always—perhaps one ought not to make a too rigid universal rule about these things—a being attached to him, sometimes

appearing like a part of him, which is just the contradiction of the thing he centrally represents in the work to be done. Or, if it is not there at first, not bound to his personality, a force of this kind enters into his environment as soon as he begins his movement to realize. Its business seems to be to oppose, to create stumblings and wrong conditions, in a word, to set before him the whole problem of the work he has started to do. It would seem as if the problem could not, in the occult economy of things, be solved otherwise than by the predestined instrument making the difficulty his own. That would explain many things that seem very disconcerting on the surface.[3]

Religious fundamentalists are obsessed with the devil. In their eyes, we are always under attack, and it is our duty to win the battle or be doomed. But this is not so. If it were, we would be in a hopeless situation. In our culture, we are tormented with guilt and sin and the devil. However, I don't discount the influence of these teachings on our psyche. In fact, they are ingrained in us. Some years ago, I was surprised by a powerful dream that I had about how guilty and sinful I was. I did not have a strong religious background, but still the dream indicated its deep roots in my psyche.

We cannot understand the role of good and evil unless we view the historical evidence for creation as well as our make-up from the way we are biologically conceived. We also have to look at morality and its implications. We cannot understand the true meaning of a single religious scripture unless we know the entire book and its message. All of the parts have to fit into the whole.

God as Creator or as a Projection?

When we speak of our universe as the creation, we are immediately drawn into a misleading premise—namely, that God created the world and us. As long as we believe this, there will always be a separation from our creator, God. A better way to view our creation is as a God-made manifestation or projection of himself or herself. An artist creates. The artist becomes inspired, perhaps has an idea or a vision, and attempts to recreate this on the canvas. Certainly, something of the artist's consciousness is in the painting and can move us emotionally years or even centuries after its creation. But the painting is still confined to one locale. We can know something of an artist—but only a part—through his or her work. We can know God through his or her manifestation and in matter itself. In the very early stages of evolution, life awakened from matter. In the next stage of evolution, mind awakened. In 1956, the Supermind manifested itself in the Earth's atmosphere. In 1969, it manifested itself in matter itself.

On the material level, electricity was discovered after being hidden for centuries. The same thing happened with the atomic energy that was inherent in the atom. The Supreme Consciousness is contained within each atom. If we can identify with the conscious-force within one atom, we can know God, for there is the same consciousness within every atom in the universe. In our quest for this knowledge of unity, we have to deal with the polarities in our world, the duality of opposites and especially of good and evil. The contradictions that are inherent in evil hold the key to our understanding.

If God is truth and goodness and love, why is the planet in such a mess, and why is there so much misery? We in America continually hear that this is the greatest country in the world. If so, why is there so much unhappiness here? The first thing we have to understand is the condition imposed on us, which is one of freedom and free choice.

Four Principal Beings

The Mother said that originally there were four beings who ruled the Earth: Truth, Life, Light, and Love. These beings had tremendous power. They also had subordinates or emanations, who in turn had emanations, and so on. Since absolute power corrupts, the four beings became more and more distanced from their source, which was the beginning of the ego—that is, the ego is a separate entity cut off from or unaware of its source.

By their separation and autonomy, these four beings turned into their opposites: truth into falsehood, life into death, light into darkness, and love into suffering.

Inconscience

The Divine Mother saw what happened and established the divine consciousness in matter itself, in what Sri Aurobindo called the Inconscience:

> The Inconscience is in an inverse reproduction of the supreme superconscience: it has the same absoluteness of being and automatic action, but in a vast involved trance; it is being lost in itself, plunged in its own abyss of infinity.[4]

Evolution is the progressive unfolding or revealing of that Inconscience. Mind cannot be the last phase of evolution, because it is ignorance trying to know itself. On the one hand, we have the possibility of the Divine emerging from matter; on the other hand, each of us already has the divine presence within us, waiting for us to recognize it. This latter possibility has always been available to us. The revelation of the Divine, or Truth Consciousness, in matter is the new condition we are now in. The Divine *transforms* matter; it does not *replace* it.

We cannot participate in this new work of manifesting the Divine in matter by withdrawing from the world or becoming ascetics. We must use every circumstance from life in our quest for self-knowledge. No incident is insignificant. The small things in life can be the most important, for they are often the ones we tend to overlook. We need interaction with others to expose our own shortcomings and to see what we need to work on.

What exactly do we do with matter? For now, let us just say that nothing is to be done but to fix the Supramental force in our body. This change in consciousness will do the work for us.

If the forces of evil seem abstract, nothing could be further from the truth. They are at work everywhere, creating disruptions and chaos. According to the Mother, they were behind World Wars I and II. They are not, however, our constant adversaries in ordinary life. They have no need to intercede, because our lower nature will cause enough conflict for us. But they will be especially active when we get onto the spiritual path. They can affect us mentally, emotionally, and physically, all of which affects our relationships. They are extremely clever. We are never alone, because the forces of evil are always with us, and they know all of our weaknesses. One of their functions is to test us.

In 1938, Sri Aurobindo was walking in his room when he fell and broke his leg. He said later that he had let his consciousness slip while thinking about the safety of the Mother. This is the only time this kind of thing happened to him on a physical level. When I first heard this story, I could understand how unseen forces could affect one psychologically, but I could not comprehend how they could throw one to the ground.

Hostile Attacks

In June 1989, Surama and I, who had become the managers of the Sri Aurobindo Association, received fifty boxes of books from New York, mostly the writings of Sri Aurobindo and the Mother, to sell throughout the United States, Canada, and Europe. The first week in July, we drove up to the state of Washington with as many books as we could pack in the car, to sell at the annual Integral Yoga meeting. When I went down to the room assigned to us, I discovered that it was not set up for book sales, so I started to move the furniture around. As I was pushing a sofa across the carpeted floor, both of my legs suddenly went up in the air behind me, and I was thrust forward over the armrest with my face pushed down into the cushions. I was shocked as well as amused by this, knowing that I could never duplicate this physical movement on my own. At the time, I didn't know what to make of this.

A few months later, as I was taking my usual evening walk in Berkeley, I stumbled slightly. A pressure then pushed on my back, forcing me to lurch forward to the sidewalk, where I broke my fall with my hands. The pressure continued to push me to the side until I was lying in the middle of the walk on my back with my arms and legs sticking up in the air. This time I was not amused, as I could easily have broken my wrists if I had not landed squarely on my palms.

After these incidents and others of a similar nature, I no longer underestimated the power of these forces. They don't only have physical impact, but can also play on our mind and emotions, and can be very clever at creating misunderstandings and causing arguments with others. Nothing escapes them. These adverse forces are intent on keeping the status quo of chaos, disorder, and ill will because they know they will be finished if the divine light and presence become dominant on Earth. It is not good to give too much attention to them, but we need to be aware of their presence and power. If we do give too much attention to them, we can easily become obsessed with them and even draw them to us.

There is strong peer pressure in Integral Yoga and in other spiritual paths to keep quiet about our experiences. In December 1999, when I had decided to write this book, I was considering how to present it. Nothing seemed right until, one day in January, I told Surama that I had decided to make it personal and not academic—that is, I had decided *not* to keep quiet about my experiences. I told her that I did not see how the book could be effective any other way. The remainder of that day I felt miserable. That night I had chaotic dreams. In short, I felt that I had entered Hell. Surama said she was having similar feelings. In fact, we exchanged sharp words with each other throughout that day. The next day, I realized that I had been attacked by the hostile forces. With that awareness, my whole mood suddenly changed, and I recognized that the attack had been an affirmation that my approach to this book was correct.

Morality changes from one society to another and from one era to another. Basically, in every society today, might is right. Those people with wealth and position have not necessarily earned that right. There are countless injustices in our society.

Hypocrisy is rampant everywhere. It is not necessarily getting worse, only more obvious.

The Mother said that our world is absurd because it is so superficial. This world is false because its material appearance does not express the deeper truth of things. There is a disconnection. In the Supramental world, which will manifest in the future, the Consciousness-Force will act directly on matter, which will be obedient to this Force. For example, if someone is naked and wants to be clothed, a garment will immediately materialize. In our present situation on Earth, anyone can have power if he or she has the material means, with or without earning it. In the Supramental world, all power will be in the hands of Supramental beings.

One check and balance that we have here on Earth if we want to go beyond conventional morality is the presence of the so-called adverse forces. When we go beyond the conventional means of enforcement and conformity, there is a pressure that pushes us to sincerity. There is no place to hide. This is more evident today than ever before because of the pressure of the Truth-Consciousness, or Supermind. Thus, the adverse forces, in effect, serve to bring our negative aspects up to the surface, where we can cleanse ourselves of them.

Once I gave a presentation to a group of young people between the ages of seventeen and thirty. When I finished talking, they commented how much they disliked rules and regulations and how much they wanted more freedom. I told them that Integral Yoga was just the thing for them, because there are virtually no rules other than to know yourself and be true to yourself. However, this can be infinitely more difficult when we do not have some guru or organization to guide us and map out our program for us. Nevertheless, the guidance is always there within us and around us if we recognize it.

The adverse or hostile forces around us can actually be our teachers. They can lead us to sincerity by their very opposition to it. As the Mother stated:

Each person carries with himself in his atmosphere what Sri Aurobindo calls the "Censors"; they are in a way permanent delegates of the adverse forces. Their role is to criticize mercilessly every act, every thought, the slightest movement of the consciousness, and to bring you face to face with the most hidden springs of your actions, to bring to light the slightest vibration of a lower kind accompanying what seem to be your purest and highest thoughts and acts….

Every time I meet these gentlemen I welcome them, for they compel you to be absolutely sincere, they track down the most subtle hypocrisy and make you at every moment face your most secret vibrations…. Nothing escapes them. But what gives a hostile tinge to these beings is the fact that they are first and foremost defeatists. They always paint the picture for you in the darkest colors; if need be they distort your own intentions. They are truly instruments of sincerity. But they always forget one thing, deliberately, something that they cast far behind as if it did not exist: the divine Grace. They forget prayer, that spontaneous prayer which suddenly springs up from the depths of the being like an intense call, and brings down the Grace and changes the course of things.[5]

Because these agents of the adverse forces are themselves incomplete, they cannot lead us toward perfection, but they can provoke us to examine ourselves. If we look carefully, we will see that the lines between good and evil are blurred—there is no exact demarcation. If we give great emphasis to either aspect, good or evil, it can revert to its opposite. One needs the other for the play. We cannot have saints without the presence of sinners. Judas was necessary to fulfill the mission of Jesus. When everything in the universe has found its proper place, that is when absolute perfection will be achieved. All hostile forces help us to overcome the obstacles in our path to achieve this integration.

Humility

It takes a good deal of humility to know the Truth, because we are so judgmental. Our preoccupation with our judgments of good and evil prevents the Truth of our being from manifesting. The emergence of our soul is not a rational act; it is an act of love and grace. We offer ourselves, our being, our dark as well as our light sides, to the Divine. Nothing is left behind. Only when we become empty can we be filled with the divine light.

The Mother said about this:

> Our ideas of good and evil are so ridiculous! So ridiculous is our notion of what is close to the Divine or far from the Divine. The experience I had the other day…was for me revelatory, I came out of it completely changed….
>
> And all the time the experience lasted, one hour—one hour of that time is long—I was in a state of extraordinary joyfulness, almost in an intoxicated state…. The difference between the two states of consciousness is so great that when you are in one, the other seems unreal, like a dream. When I came back, what struck me first of all was the futility of life here; our little conceptions down here seem so laughable, so comical…. We say that some people are mad, but their madness is perhaps a great wisdom, from the supramental point of view, and their behavior is perhaps nearer to the truth of things—I am not speaking of the obscure madmen whose brains have been damaged, but of many other incomprehensible madmen, the luminous mad: they have wanted to cross the border too quickly, and the rest have not followed.[6]

Ambition

It is dangerous to be ambitious on our spiritual path, because we often bite off more than we can chew. I know a man who wanted fervently to embody the Supramental Consciousness.

He once told me that the Divine had promised him that he would receive it. But he had an enormous ego and neglected his own imperfections. Thus, when the Supramental Consciousness came, his body could not handle the Force, and he became bedridden for days at a time.

Examinations

If we are observant and patiently do our homework, we will be presented with innumerable opportunities in everyday life to achieve an integrated being, one without shadows, so that we can absorb and assimilate these forces in our body. The Mother explained this process:

> The integral yoga consists of an uninterrupted series of examinations that one has to undergo without any previous warning, thus obliging you to be constantly on the alert and attentive.
>
> Three groups of examiners set up these tests. They appear to have nothing to do with one another, and their methods are so different, sometimes even so apparently contradictory, that it seems as if they could not possibly be leading towards their same goal. Nevertheless, they complement one another, work towards the same end, and are all indispensable to the completeness of the result.
>
> The three types of examination are: those set by the forces of Nature, those set by spiritual and divine forces, and those set by hostile forces. These last are the most deceptive in their appearance, and to avoid being caught unawares and unprepared requires a state of constant watchfulness, sincerity, and humility.
>
> The most commonplace circumstances, the events of everyday life, the most apparently insignificant people and things all belong to one or other of these three kinds of examiners. In this vast and complex organization of tests, those events that are generally considered the most

important in life are the easiest examinations to undergo, because they find you ready and on your guard. It is easier to stumble over the little stones in your path, because they attract no attention.

Endurance and plasticity, cheerfulness and fearlessness are the qualities specially needed for the examinations of physical nature.

Aspiration, trust, idealism, enthusiasm, and generous self-giving, for spiritual examinations.

Vigilance, sincerity, and humility for the examinations from hostile forces.

And do not imagine that there are, on the one hand, people who undergo the examinations and, on the other, people who set them. Depending on the circumstances and the moment, we are all both examiners and examinees, and it may even happen that one is at the same time both examiner and examinee....

To conclude, a final piece of advice: never set yourself up as an examiner. For while it is good to remember constantly that one may be undergoing a very important examination, it is extremely dangerous to imagine that one is responsible for setting examinations for others. That is the open door to the most ridiculous and harmful kinds of vanity. It is the Supreme Wisdom which decides these things, and not the ignorant human will.[7]

All of these negative aspects are important in our evolution because they must be transformed if we are to move into the stage where no shadows exist. When our defects are brought to light, we can meet them face to face and transform them. We cannot see them so long as they are in the shadows. Their exposure is occurring now on a global scale to everyone, and not just to a select few. People living in an urbanized, industrialized society build up an invisible barrier for protection because there are too many forces impinging on their being. This is most evident in large cities, where residents take on a gruff exterior because of the tension in the atmosphere. But this tension is there for all of us, to some extent. Each time I return to Pondicherry, I have to go through a "cleansing" period, although it becomes shorter and shorter with each visit. I have to shed that protective coating so that I can receive the divine forces so prevalent there. This process continues until the Supramental force is fixed in the body. Then the body itself contains the joy.

Final Test

It is not just the negative aspects of our being, or those aspects that we perceive as negative, that have to be addressed. The final test is success. We usually take up the spiritual path because of dissatisfaction with our life and the world around us. What happens if, in the meantime, we become successful—whether by position, wealth, or recognition? Do we continue on our spiritual journey? I have known devotees who initially appeared to be very dedicated, but once they became successful in their field of endeavor, their spiritual aspirations faded.

People who thrive on tension, deadlines, and work will never get an intimation of this other life. There is no way the divine grace can reach them, except through illness, mental breakdown, or catastrophe—in short, some sudden reversal of fortune. This can become a life-or-death situation, depending on how the affected party responds. Unfortunately, in our materialistic society, the alternatives are very limited.

In all of our inner endeavors and spiritual quests, we have to establish peace within ourselves. This is the foundation we can build upon: a quiet mind and calm emotional being. True progress stems from this peace. We cannot sustain this peace until we have established an equilibrium or equality in our being. Later, as the energies increase within us, as happened to me when I first started reading *Savitri*, we cannot contain them. We get excited, or nervous, and let the energy escape—like steam pouring out of a teakettle. Sri Aurobindo walked in his room for hours a day so that his body could assimilate these forces. We do need movement, but without agitation.

Refuge in the Divine is always the surest remedy when hostile forces attack us. As the Mother said:

> What I have told you is the Truth, it is the *only* remedy:
> To exist only for the Divine.
> To exist only through the Divine.
> To exist only in the service of the Divine.
> To exist only...by becoming the Divine.
> There you are.[8]

This is indeed a tall order, but we have to start somewhere if we really want to attain peace in ourselves and in the world. We may find that the process is easier than we think. Often, a small movement or adjustment is all we need, while our mind is continually raising insuperable roadblocks, often in the name of good and evil. The Mother gave us hope, in a simple prayer she wrote in 1931:

> Oh my Lord, my sweet Master, for the accomplishment of Thy work I have sunk down into the unfathomable depths of Matter, I have touched with my finger the horror of the falsehood and the inconscience, I have reached the seat of oblivion and a supreme obscurity. But in my heart was the Remembrance, from my heart there leaped the call, which could arrive to Thee: "Lord, Lord, everywhere Thy enemies appear triumphant; falsehood is the monarch of the world; life without Thee is a death, a perpetual hell; doubt has usurped the place of Hope, and revolt has pushed out Submission; Faith is spent, Gratitude is not born; blind passions and murderous instincts and a guilty weakness have covered and stifled Thy sweet law of love. Lord, wilt Thou permit Thy enemies to prevail, falsehood and ugliness and suffering to triumph?

Lord, give the command to conquer, and victory will be there. I know we are unworthy, I know the world is not yet ready. But I cry to Thee with an absolute faith in Thy Grace, and I know that Thy Grace will save.

Thus, my prayer rushed up towards Thee; and, from the depths of the abyss, I beheld Thee in Thy radiant splendor; Thou didst appear and Thou saidst to me: "Lose not courage, be firm, be confident—I COME."[9]

Notes

[1]Sri Aurobindo, *Birth Centenary Library*, vol. 17: *The Hour of God* (Pondicherry, India: Sri Aurobindo Ashram Press, 1972), p. 114.

[2]The Mother, *Collected Works of The Mother*, vol. 8: *Questions and Answers, 1956* (Pondicherry, India: Sri Aurobindo Ashram Press, 1976), p. 2.

[3]Sri Aurobindo, *Birth Centenary Library*, vol. 24: *Letters on Yoga* (Pondicherry, India: Sri Aurobindo Ashram Press, 1972), p. 1660.

[4]Sri Aurobindo, *Birth Centenary Library*, vols. 18–19: *The Life Divine* (Pondicherry, India: Sri Aurobindo Ashram Press, 1972), p. 550.

[5]The Mother, *Collected Works of The Mother*, vol. 9: *Questions and Answers, 1957–58* (Pondicherry, India: Sri Aurobindo Ashram Press, 1976), pp. 279–280.

[6]The Mother, *Questions and Answers, 1957–58*, pp. 280–281.

[7]The Mother, *Collected Works of The Mother*, vol. 14: *Words of the Mother* (Pondicherry, India: Sri Aurobindo Ashram Press, 1976), pp. 42–43.

[8]The Mother, *Collected Works of The Mother*, vol. 11: *Notes on the Way* (Pondicherry, India: Sri Aurobindo Ashram Press, 1976), p. 259.

[9]The Mother, *Collected Works of The Mother*, vol. 1: *Prayers and Meditations* (Pondicherry, India: Sri Aurobindo Ashram Press, 1976), p. 376.

Oneness

To love God, excluding the world, is to give Him an intense but imperfect adoration.

—Sri Aurobindo[1]

All of our troubles stem from a separation from others and from the Supreme Being. We are one in consciousness and existence. While many have rhetorically professed Oneness in consciousness, we want now to make it real in practice. Paradoxically, we can demonstrate the possibility of Oneness by showing separateness—that is, by separating our consciousness from our body. An unfettered consciousness functioning independently of the body can indicate the potential for unity in people, animals, and plants.

This may be a difficult concept for us to accept because we have spent all our lives becoming separate and individualized human beings. We take pride in our individuality. The process started in our infancy and continued into our childhood as we learned to distinguish ourselves from others. That is the essence of maturation. The process was extended into our adulthood as we began to think that our thoughts, feelings, and bodies were unique.

Becoming an individual is a common goal for all of us, and it is essential for us to form a strong ego for a healthy existence. But this is only a stage in our maturation and not an end result. Once we have established our own identity, we can explore the greater dimensions of being.

Imagination

On the mental level, there are a number of ways that we attempt to move out of our bodily confines. The most common one is the use of imagination. The images we conjure up are an attempt to expand our mind to new possibilities. The Mother made the following remarks about imagination in the early 1930s:

> The imagination is really the power of mental formation. When this power is put at the service of the Divine, it is not only formative but also creative. There is, however, no such thing as an unreal formation, because every image is a reality on the mental plane. The plot of a novel, for instance, is all there on the mental plane existing independently of the physical. Each of us is a novelist to a certain extent and possesses the capacity to make forms on that plane; and, in fact, a good deal of our life embodies the products of our imagination. Every time you indulge your imagination in an unhealthy way, giving a form to your fears and anticipating accidents and misfortunes, you are undermining your own future. On the other hand, the more optimistic your imagination, the greater the chance of your realizing your aim. Monsieur Coué got hold of this potent truth and cured hundreds of people by simply teaching them to imagine themselves out of misery. He once related the case of a lady

whose hair was falling off. She began to suggest to herself that she was improving every day and that her hair was surely growing. By constantly imagining it, her hair really began to grow and even reached an enviable length, owing to still further auto-suggestion. The power of mental formation is most useful in Yoga also; when the mind is put in communication with the Divine Will, the supramental Truth begins to descend through the layers intervening between the mind and the highest Light, and if, on reaching the mind, it finds there the power of making forms, it easily becomes embodied and stays as a creative force in you. Therefore, I say to you, never be dejected and disappointed, but let your imagination be always hopeful and joyously plastic to the stress of the higher Truth, so that the latter may find you full of the necessary formations to hold its creative light.

The imagination is like a knife which may be used for good or evil purposes. If you always dwell in the idea and feeling that you are going to be transformed, then you will help the process of the Yoga. If, on the contrary, you give in to dejection and bewail that you are not fit or that you are incapable of realization, you poison your own being. It is just on account of this very important truth that I am so tirelessly insistent in telling you to let anything happen but, for heaven's sake, not to get depressed. Live rather in the constant hope and conviction that what we are doing will prove a success. In other words, let your imagination be molded by your faith in Sri Aurobindo; for, is not such faith the very hope and conviction that the will of Sri Aurobindo is bound to be done, that his work on transformation cannot but end in a supreme victory, and that what he calls the supramental world will be brought down on earth and realized by us here and now?[2]

Oneness in Nature

My paranormal experiences with animals have shown me that there is a universal intelligence that transcends our ordinary mental state. This universal consciousness also permeates nature. Therefore, if we identify with a natural object, such as a tree, it will reveal its innermost essence. Regarding the Oneness of nature, the Mother related the following experience:

> A deep concentration seized on me, and I perceived that I was identifying myself with a single cherry-blossom, then through it with all cherry-blossoms; and as I descended deeper in the consciousness, following a stream of bluish force, I became suddenly the cherry-tree itself, stretching towards the sky like so many arms, its innumerable branches laden with their sacrifice of flowers. Then I heard distinctly this sentence:
>
>> "Thus hast thou made thyself one with the soul of the cherry-trees, and so thou canst take note that it is the Divine who makes the offering of this flower-prayer to heaven."
>
> When I had written it, all was effaced; but now the blood of the cherry-tree flows in my veins, and with it flows an incomparable peace and force. What difference is there between the human body and the body of a tree? In truth, there is none: the consciousness which animates them is identically the same.
> Then the cherry-tree whispered in my ear:
>
>> "It is in the cherry-blossom that there lies the remedy for the disorders of the spring."[3]

Love is the attraction to all that is. There is an irresistible pull to merge or unite with everything that appears to be outside us. In fact, everything is pulled to merge with everything else. A tree, for example, yearns for the light—the light of love that brings joy, beauty, and life itself. These are all qualities latent in matter. Love is inherent in all of nature, as the Mother noted:

> The movement of love is not limited to human beings, and it is perhaps less distorted in worlds other than the human world. Look at the flowers and trees. When the sun sets and all becomes silent, sit down for a moment and put yourself into communion with Nature. You will feel, rising from the earth, from below the roots of the trees and mounting upward and coursing through their fibres, up to the highest outstretching branches, the aspiration of an intense love and longing—a longing for something that brings light and gives happiness for the light that is gone and they wish to have back again. There is a yearning so pure and intense that if you can feel the movement in the trees, your own being, too, will go up in an ardent prayer for the peace and light and love that are unmanifested here.[4]

Animals can embody more consciousness than one might think, as can be seen in the Mother's description of one of her cats:

> I had a cat—in those days I used to sleep on the floor—which always came and slipped under the mosquito-net and slept beside me. Well, this cat slept quite straight, it did not sleep as cats do, it put its head here and then lay down like this (*gesture*), alongside my legs with its two forepaws like this, and its two little hind legs quite straight. And there was something very, very curious about it which I saw one night, like that. I used to ask myself why it was like this, and one night I

saw a little Russian woman of the people with a fur bonnet and three little children, and this woman had a kind of adoration for her children and always wanted to look for a shelter for them; I don't know, I don't know the story, but I saw that she had her three little children, very small ones, with her…one like this, one like that, one like that (*Mother shows the difference in height*), and she was dragging them along with her and looking for a corner to put them in safety. Something must have happened to her, she must have died suddenly with a kind of very animal maternal instinct of a certain kind, but all full of fear—fear, anguish, and worry—and this something must have come from there and in some way or other had reincarnated. It was a movement—it was not a person, you know, it was a movement which belonged to this person and must have come up in the cat. It was there for some reason or other, you see, I don't know how it happened, I know nothing about it, but this cat was completely human in its ways. And very soon afterwards it had three kittens, like that; and it was extraordinary, it didn't want to leave them, it refused to leave them…. It did not eat, did not go to satisfy its needs, it was always with its young. When one day it had an idea—nobody had said anything, of course—it took one kitten, as they take them, by the skin of the neck, and came and put it between my feet; I did not stir; it returned, took the second, put it there; it took the third, it put it there, and when all three were there, it looked at me, mewed, and was gone. And this was the first time it went out after having had them; it went to the garden, went to satisfy its needs and to eat, because it was at peace, they were there between my feet. And when it had its young, it wanted to carry them on its back like a woman. And when it slept beside me, it slept on the back. It was never like a cat.

Well, these things are habits of the species, movements of the species. There are many others of the kind, you see, but this is an example.[5]

At this point, a disciple asked the Mother if extraordinary animals like this one come back after death in a human body. The Mother replied:

Ah!

There was a cat...what its name was I don't know; and I had many cats, you know, so I don't remember now, there was one called Kiki, it was the first son of this cat, and then there was another, its second son (that is to say, born another time) which was called Brownie.

This one was admirable, and it died of the cat disease—as there is a disease of the dogs, there is a disease of the kittens—I don't know how it caught the thing, but it was wonderful during its illness, and I was taking care of it as of a child. And it always expressed a kind of aspiration. There was a time before it fell ill...we used to have in those days meditation in a room of the Library House, in the room there—Sri Aurobindo's own room—and we used to sit on the floor. And there was an armchair in a corner, and when we gathered for the meditation, this cat came every time and settled in the armchair and literally it entered into a trance, it had movements of trance; it did not sleep, it was not asleep, it was truly in a trance; it gave signs of that and had astonishing movements, as when animals dream; and it didn't want to come out from it, it refused to come out, it remained in it for hours. But it never came in until we were beginning the meditation. It settled there and remained there throughout the meditation. We indeed had finished, but it remained, and it was only when I went to take it, called it in a particular way, brought it back into its body, that it consented to go away; otherwise, no matter who came and called it, it did not move. Well, this cat always had a great aspiration, a kind of aspiration to become a human being, and in fact, when it left its body it entered a human body. Only it was a very tiny part of the consciousness, you see, of the human being, it was like the opposite movement from that of the woman with the other cat. But this one was a cat which leaped over many births, so to say, many psychic stages to enter into contact with a human body.[6]

I have also had experiences with animals that indicate that a higher or universal intelligence is manifesting through them. I take an extended walk every day, and on occasion I go up a canyon above the University of California campus and past the football stadium to a fire trail in the hills. The walk takes me about seventy-five minutes from my house. Many students and faculty use the trail for hiking or jogging.

One day, I saw three snakes on the trail and thought it was an omen because I had never seen even one snake before out in the wild. After I had seen the first two, I thought there must be another one out there somewhere to make a trinity. Sure enough, ten minutes later, I passed another one on the side of the trail. As I arrived back at my house, half an hour later, I heard my cat, Lefty, meowing. When I went out the front door, I saw him holding a snake in his mouth. The snake, which was not moving, was coiled into a perfect figure eight, as in the symbol for infinity, which Lefty was holding horizontally.

When Lefty headed for the house, I rushed inside and closed the door. A minute later, I went outside again and found Lefty on the brick pathway along the side of the house. I picked him up and shook him until he dropped the snake. It lay on the walk, still in a figure eight, and still not moving. I looked to see if it was a real snake, and saw that Lefty's teeth had made a superficial wound on its flesh. I took Lefty inside, and when I looked out the window a minute or two later, the snake was gone.

In less than two hours, I had seen four snakes in an urban environment. Snakes have various connotations, including evil and sexuality, but they can also symbolize energy, transformation, and evolution. The number 4 is symbolic of completion.

Sexual Energy

In July 1984, some three or four months after this incident with the snakes, I was on a business trip to southern California. I was staying at a motel in Laguna Beach, and one evening, about 6:00 P.M., as I was reclining on a chaise lounge on the balcony overlooking the ocean, I noticed a pulsation in my groin. I thought at first that my legs might be crossed, restricting the blood flow. But they were not crossed. I observed my body for a couple of minutes as the pulsation continued; it seemed to be coming from outside of me. After this experience, my sexual energy was purified, and all my sexual desire was gone. In fact, since that day, it has never returned. What I was unable to do in months of trying was done for me in minutes. Was the prior incident with the snakes a precursor, indicating a universal consciousness at play?

Although I have never been attracted to reptiles, they seem to have some significance for me. Recently, I was walking at Point Reyes National Shoreline on the coast above San Francisco. I was on the main trail that leads up the hill from the Visitor's Center to a meadow. At the top of the hill, I walked off the trail onto a narrow path and sat for fifteen minutes to look down at the valley. When I started to head back to the main trail, I suddenly let out a shriek. One more step and I would have landed right on a five-foot snake stretched out in a straight line across the path. The snake was not startled at all, and was perfectly still. I thought of leaping over it, but decided to walk around instead. When I looked back, the snake was still motionless, even after I tossed a small pine cone at it that bounced off its back. As I reflected on this incident later, I decided that it was time to take a leap of faith and let others see my book. Shortly after that, I contacted a book editor.

On another walk, this time through a commercial district in Berkeley, I passed a street person, who made derogatory remarks to me. Then, a block away, a bag lady cursed me for not giving her any change. Another block down the street, a husky dog appeared out of nowhere. I talked to it, but it wasn't interested. It began walking a few feet in front of me, as if leading me home. This went on for more than twenty minutes. As I approached the last corner, intending to turn left to go up the hill to my house, I watched to see what the dog would do. Sure enough, it turned left and led me up the hill. However, he went past my driveway. I turned in quickly and went inside. The dog kept walking, and I've never seen it since. I have taken that walk more than four thousand times (at four times a week for twenty years), and, with the exception of that day, have never seen a stray dog or been insulted by street people. Sometimes I have wondered if that dog appeared on the scene to protect me from hostile forces.

A third animal incident occurred at Wilbur Hot Springs, a spa north of San Francisco. One day, as I was walking deep in thought along the one-lane gravel entrance road, a huge jackrabbit sprang out of the bushes right in front of me, some ten to twelve feet away, and just stood there staring at me, but without any sign of fear. After two or three minutes, I decided to talk to it, but it remained frozen, not even blinking. After another minute or two, it hopped slowly to the other side of the road, and then stopped and resumed staring at me. Finally, it walked casually past me along the other side of the road. I started walking again, and after fifty feet or so I turned around, and there, a hundred feet away, the rabbit was staring back at me. I was definitely under observation. When I got back home from the retreat the next day, Surama told me that she had seen me the day before lying in bed, looking ill, and she had been concerned about me.

For me, all of these experiences were paranormal in nature, although occurring in the material world, and indicated a greater mind or spirit at work. The experience with the snake was even precognitive.

Three other paranormal experiences also come to mind, although they have nothing to do with animals. The first occurred in 1972 as I was walking in the Richmond District of San Francisco. It suddenly occurred to me how good I was feeling. But when I observed my body, I noticed that it was just feeling so-so. Clearly, it was my consciousness that was giving me the pleasant sensation. Obviously, there was a separation here between my consciousness and my body.

The second experience occurred in 1975 in Berkeley as I was meditating in my home. Suddenly, I had a vision of myself walking blissfully on a crowded street that reminded me of Old Delhi, which I had visited in October 1973. Then I realized that the reason I felt so good was that I was meditating in Berkeley.

The third experience occurred on a Friday in 1989, when I developed red spots on my chest. They were more unusual than bothersome, since I had never had anything of this sort before. Over the weekend, the rash spread and began to itch. I intended to see a doctor on Monday about this, but by Monday the rash had nearly disappeared. That evening, my sister Pat called from her home in St. Louis to tell me that our mother had had a mild stroke. Then she related to me how she had learned about this, since our mother lived by herself an hour away. An old friend, Jim, who now lived in California, was visiting the area after many years and stopped by my mother's house. Because of her stroke, my mother could not speak, although she could still walk. Jim called my sister, who came over and took my mother to the hospital. Apparently, her stroke had begun the same day my rash had appeared, and my rash had ended on the day she was found. Was there some cellular connection between my mother's body and mine?

Synchronicity

Synchronicity is the occurrence of two seemingly unrelated events that have meaning somehow in their connection. In 1984, I was on the search committee for a new school building in San

Francisco for the California Institute of Integral Studies. I found a couple of buildings through a real estate broker, but they were not quite right. Then I went up to spend a few days at a bed-and-breakfast in the Russian River area, some sixty miles north of San Francisco. At the end of my stay, I took a walk along a gravel road. The gravel was gray, and sprinkled in it were small items like bottle caps and cigarette butts. As I walked along, I came across three coins—first a penny, then a quarter, and finally a dime. I started to look for more coins, but not only did I not find any, but I got dizzy trying. I decided that finding the three coins was an omen of some kind.

When I got back to San Francisco, I went to see another building that the realtor wanted to show me. It was a former Catholic boys' school, known as St. Agnes, which turned out to be ideal for CIIS. Soon after this happened, my stepson, Richard, traveled to London on vacation. He knew nothing of my activity in the school search. However, when he returned a couple of weeks later, he showed me a tarnished silver school ring that he had found in a crack in the sidewalk in London. It was a cheap little ring, so he wasn't even sure, he said, why he had kept it. When I inspected it, I saw the name Agnes engraved on the top of it.

When synchronicity occurs, the implication is that a universal or cosmic intelligence is behind it all. There is almost an element of humor, as if someone were piquing our interest.

Recently, I received a call from a middle-aged woman in the Midwest, who was having some unusual incapacitating sensations in her body. She had been given my name, she said, by someone in the Sri Aurobindo Association in Sacramento, and had been told that I might be able to help her. During our conversation, she mentioned that she was from Mansfield, Ohio, a town I had never heard of before. A few days later, I received a letter from her, and decided to send her some blessing packets of dried flowers from the ashram in Pondicherry. The flowers carry a vibration that gives protection. Usually, I am very prompt in responding to people, but for some reason, in this case, I let the packets sit on my desk all week.

That Saturday, I was watching a football game on TV, and during the halftime, I started surfing the channels, as men are wont to do. At one point, I came across a program in which a reporting team goes from one city to another, with the location chosen by having the last person interviewed blindly throw a dart at a map of the United States. I was stunned when the woman on the program had her dart land on Mansfield, Ohio. Needless to say, I mailed the flower packets right away.

This occurrence poses many questions. There was a time window of about three seconds for me to recognize the program and decide to watch it. Was the program merely for my benefit— or rather, for the woman in Ohio? Not likely, considering the size of the national audience. On the other hand, it is too much of a coincidence to simply ignore. Was this evidence of a universal consciousness at work?

Learning from Experience

Our basic education comes from books. We stuff ourselves with more and more education. When we go out into the "real" world, we find that we need more than book learning to succeed. We also need what is called "street smarts," or knowledge of the ways of the world and what it really takes to succeed. In other words, we learn from experience.

In the spiritual field, which now encompasses all of life, we not only learn from books and gurus but, more importantly, from experience. This teaches us by having us identify with what we are trying to learn. This identification with something or someone else not only gets us out of our egocentric self but can ultimately lead us to identification with all of existence, including the Supreme, both in matter and the transcendent. Isn't that what a vision or inner experience is? We know something to be true for us because we have *experienced* it. Here is what Sri Aurobindo said about integral knowledge:

> The integral Yoga of knowledge has to recognize
> the double nature of this manifestation—for there
> is the higher nature of Sachchidananda in which

He [the Supreme Being] is found and the lower nature of mind, life, and body in which He is veiled—and to reconcile and unite the two in the oneness of the illumined realization. We have not to leave them separate so that we live a sort of double life, spiritual within or above, mental and material in our active and earthly living; we have to re-view and remold the lower living in the light, force, and joy of the higher reality. We have to realize Matter as a sense-created mold of Spirit, a vehicle for all manifestation of the light, force, and joy of Sachchidananda in the highest conditions of terrestrial being and activity. We have to see Life as a channel for the infinite Force divine and break the barrier of a sense-created and mind-created farness and division from it so that that divine Power may take possession of and direct and change all our life-activities until our vitality transfigured ceases in the end to be the limited life-force which now supports mind and body and becomes a figure of the all-blissful conscious-force of Sachchidananda....

Thus, by the integral knowledge we unify all things in the One. We take up all the chords of the universal music, strains sweet or discordant, luminous in their suggestion or obscure, powerful or faint, heard or suppressed, and find them all changed and reconciled in the indivisible harmony of Sachchidananda. The Knowledge brings also the Power and the Joy. "How shall he be deluded, whence shall he have sorrow who sees everywhere the Oneness?"[7]

At a weekend workshop at the Esalen Institute in Big Sur, I was part of a group that at one point was given an exercise to talk or otherwise communicate with a tree. Here was an opportunity for knowledge by identity. I chose a tree on the edge of a cliff overlooking the Pacific Ocean. I asked the tree questions about its age, how it liked being there, and if it were happy. As I listened, I received answers. Was this real? I don't know, but I do know that I have never forgotten the experience, and I still feel a kinship with that tree.

After I returned home, I struck up a friendship with a redwood tree by a creek on the university campus near my home. I walk by it all the time, and occasionally I will sit on the ground with my back against the tree and feel its energy. There is definitely a vibration in that tree, and a vibration is consciousness.

We are very big on relationships in this country; yet many people are still lonely, even in a crowd. The truth is, however, that we don't have to confine our relationships to people. We can have friendship with an animal, a flower, a tree, a rock, a garden, a painting, a sunset, or the Supreme Consciousness itself! And these relationships can be at least as fulfilling as those with other people. But we have to listen.

On one occasion, Udar Pinto, a longtime disciple at the Sri Aurobindo Ashram in Pondicherry, told a group of us a story about the Mother. We were sitting having tea in the breezeway at Golconde, an architecturally unique residence at the ashram. One day, back in the 1930s, Udar and the Mother were driving around, scouting for logs from which to get lumber to build Golconde. Just as they were about to go home, the Mother pointed to a very large log and said that she wanted that one also. When Udar said that the log was very awkward to move because of its size and that there were better ones, the Mother replied, "This log pleaded with me to take it." That may sound unbelievable, but the only way you will know the truth for yourself is to communicate with a tree, or your pet, or your car, and then listen.

Identification

The Mother often wrote and spoke about identification, giving numerous examples of how to identify with someone or something. In the following passage, she discusses how to identify with the universe, in response to a question from a disciple:

Is it not possible to know the universe in its reality as it is in itself, independently of the observer or thinker?

Yes, there is a way: it is by identification. But…in fact one can know only what one is. So if you want to know the universe, you must become the universe. You cannot become the universe physically, you know; but perhaps there is a way of becoming the universe: it is in the consciousness.

If you identify your consciousness with the universal consciousness, then you know what is happening.

But that's the only way; there are no others. It is an absolute fact that one knows only what one is, and if one wants to know something, one must become that. So you see, there are many people who say, "It is impossible," but that's because they remain on a certain plane. It is obvious that if you remain only on the material plane or even the mental plane, you cannot know the universe, because the mind is not universal; it is only a means of expression of the universe; and it is only by an essential identification that you can then know things, not from outside inwards but from inside outwards.[8]

The Mother was asked how she can know the character of a man by looking at his eyes. Her response:

Not only by looking at his eyes. I know the character of a man through self-identification. And then outwardly, if you want, the eyes are like doors or windows: there are some which are open, so one enters within, goes very deep inside, and one may see everything that happens there. There are others which are partly open, partly closed;

others still have a veil, a kind of curtain; and then there are others which are fastened, locked up, doors closed so well that they cannot be opened. Indeed, this is already an indication, it gives an indication of the strength of the inner life, the sincerity and transparency of the being. And so, through these doors that are open I enter and identify myself with the person within. And I see what he sees, understand what he understands, think what he thinks, and I could do what he does (but usually I refrain from that!) and in this way I get to know what people are like. And it doesn't need much time; it goes very fast. It can even be done through a photograph, but not so well.[9]

Identification has a practical purpose for everything we do. We can become immersed in our work if we want it to have life. As the Mother stated:

Take someone who is writing a book, for instance. If he looks at himself writing the book, you can't imagine how dull the book will become; it smells immediately of the small human personality which is there, and it loses all its value. When a painter paints a picture, if he observes himself painting the picture, the picture will never be good, it will always be a kind of projection of the painter's personality; it will be without life, without force, without beauty. But if, all of a sudden, he becomes the thing he wants to express, if he becomes the brushes, the painting, the canvas, the subject, the image, the colors, the value, the whole thing, and is entirely inside it and lives it, he will make something magnificent.

For everything, everything, it is the same. There is nothing which cannot be a yogic discipline if one does it properly.[10]

On the other hand, when one does not have yogic discipline,

one can become immersed in and attached to all kinds of petty preoccupations that can lead to ego confrontations. For example, Surama and I recently attended a wonderful exhibit of Van Gogh paintings at the Los Angeles County Museum. While we were waiting in line, the couple in front of us were impatient to get in and, apparently feeling that they should be accorded special privileges, got into an argument with the attendant. This couple had already edged themselves in front of us, but we didn't bother to protest. The attendant, however, had no patience with their arrogance and got very agitated himself. How could this couple then go into the exhibition and be open to the consciousness of Vincent Van Gogh? the Mother had such situations in mind when she made the following remarks:

> Most of you live on the surface of your being, exposed to the touch of external influences. You live almost projected, as it were, outside your own body, and when you meet some unpleasant being similarly projected, you get upset. The whole trouble arises out of your not being accustomed to stepping back. You must always step back into yourself—learn to go deep within—step back and you will be safe. Do not lend yourself to the superficial forces which move in the outside world. Even if you are in a hurry to do something, step back for a while and you will discover to your surprise how much sooner and with what greater success your work can be done. If someone is angry with you, do not be caught in his vibrations, but simply step back, and his anger, finding no support or response, will vanish. Always keep your peace, resist all temptation to lose it. Never decide anything without stepping back, never speak a word without stepping back, never throw yourself into action without stepping back. All that belongs to the ordinary world is impermanent and fugitive, so there is nothing in it worth getting upset about. What is lasting, eternal, immortal, and infinite—that indeed is

worth having, worth conquering, worth possessing. It is Divine Light, Divine Love, Divine Life—it is also Supreme Peace, Perfect Joy, and All-Mastery upon earth with the Complete Manifestation as the crowning. When you get the sense of the relativity of things, then whatever happens you can step back and look; you can remain quiet and call on the Divine Force and wait for an answer. Then you will know exactly what to do. Remember, therefore, that you cannot receive the answer before you are very peaceful. Practice that inner peace, make at least a small beginning, and go on in your practice until it becomes a habit with you.[11]

If we believe—or better yet, *know*—Oneness to be a fact of existence, then we also know that reality has many modes of existence. Our ordinary waking consciousness is only one level. All of us have awakened from a dream in which we felt we were experiencing something as real, perhaps even more real than in waking life. The colors were more vibrant, and everything seemed to be more alive. In all probability, we were not dreaming but were visiting the plane or dimension of consciousness that Sri Aurobindo called the "subtle physical," which is a region very close to our physical world. "All that can be seen with closed eyes," he wrote, "can be seen with open eyes also; it is sufficient that the inner sight should extend to the subtle physical consciousness for that to happen."[12] A vision, he noted, can be seen through the physical eyes and the subtle physical consciousness simultaneously, with one consciousness superimposed on the other.

One time when Surama was at the tax office with her accountant, she saw the deceased Nolini with her eyes open, but the accountant saw nothing. Surama was seeing Nolini in another dimension superimposed on the physical. Vincent Van Gogh was probably expressing this same alternate state of consciousness in his paintings.

We also have a subtle physical body superimposed upon our physical body. Amputees feel their subtle limb after their physical limb has been removed. The chakras or energy centers are not in our physical body but in the subtle body. Similarly, our soul has a separate existence from our body, even though it is located behind our heart area.

Oneness extends to all parts of our being, even our body. In truth, as much as we may feel isolated, we are never alone. The divine consciousness is always around us and in us. Every thought and feeling that we have and every act that we perform is known, whether it happened today or fifty years ago. People who do not know this are blessed, for they would be truly embarrassed otherwise. On the other hand, people who *do* know it are even more blessed, but they also have more responsibility for their acts.

Judgment Day happens every day. When we realize that, we change. The judgment is not for punishment; it is to learn and to progress. The other day, I heard a voice in my meditation, which said, "Remember the conversation you had in India in 1974, when you asked someone why he didn't use window screens to keep out mosquitoes? And he replied that it would keep out the fresh air." This was a very, very insignificant dialogue that happened twenty-five years ago, and yet it is recorded somewhere.

Oneness is becoming more than a concept to us. Reality as part of this Oneness is divisible only in our ignorance. We are experiencing today, worldwide, a surge toward that realization, as fast as we can stand it (and actually some can't). A new light-power-consciousness is emerging and is now coming through the body. It is Oneness, in matter itself, and it is real.

Notes

[1]Sri Aurobindo, *Birth Centenary Library*, vol. 17: *The Hour of God* (Pondicherry, India: Sri Aurobindo Ashram Press, 1972), p. 133.

[2]The Mother, *Collected Works of the Mother*, vol. 3: *Questions and Answers* (Pondicherry, India: Sri Aurobindo Ashram Press, 1976), pp. 156–157.

[3]The Mother, *Flowers and Their Messages* (Auroville, India: Auropress Trust, 1973), p. ix.

[4]The Mother, *Flowers*, pp. viii–ix.

[5]The Mother, *Collected Works of the Mother*, vol. 7: *Questions and Answers, 1955* (Pondicherry, India: Sri Aurobindo Ashram Press, 1976), pp. 98–99.

[6]The Mother, *Questions and Answers, 1955*, pp. 99–100.

[7]Quoted here from Sri Aurobindo, *Birth Centenary Library*, vol. 20: *The Synthesis of Yoga* (Pondicherry, India: Sri Aurobindo Ashram Press, 1972), pp. 403–404, 407.

[8]The Mother, *Questions and Answers, 1955*, pp. 319–320.

[9]The Mother, *Collected Works of the Mother*, vol. 5: *Questions and Answers, 1953* (Pondicherry, India: Sri Aurobindo Ashram Press, 1976), p. 219.

[10]The Mother, *Collected Works of the Mother*, vol. 4: *Questions and Answers, 1950–51* (Pondicherry, India: Sri Aurobindo Ashram Press, 1976), p. 364.

[11]The Mother, *Questions and Answers*, p. 160.

[12]Sri Aurobindo, *Birth Centenary Library*, vol. 23: *Letters on Yoga* (Pondicherry, India: Sri Aurobindo Ashram Press, 1972), p. 949.

9

Suffering

*Do not take the sorrows of life
for what they seem to be; they
are in truth a way to greater
achievements.*

—The Mother[1]

If God loves His children, why does He allow us to suffer? Most people cannot get past this question. If one is religious, one has to proceed on faith. Some people become agnostics because God seems to be cruel and uncaring.

With the advent of television and global communication, we are more in touch then ever with the suffering of others. Television bombards us with local, national, and international tragedies in the form of earthquakes, fires, hurricanes, tornadoes, tidal waves, starvation, auto accidents, murders, torture, civil wars, terrorism, and other varieties of natural and human catastrophe.

Many people are aware of their own suffering through

physical and mental pain, but few of us pause to think of our existential suffering—that is, just by being born, we are bound to suffer. And it is not only the needy and homeless who suffer. Suffering is the great leveler for everyone, rich and poor. No one is exempt, not even the avatars, those divine emanations who incarnate on Earth. Indeed, they too must suffer in order to make contact with us.

Terrorism

Recently a terrible tragedy has occurred in which two teenage boys massacred thirteen people. Not only were the multiple killings senseless, but they were no less than diabolical. The boys belonged to a gang called the "Trench Coat Mafia," which openly identified with the dark forces, including Adolf Hitler, whom they regarded as a hero. It was no accident that the shootings occurred on Hitler's birthday.

As incredible as it may seem, we are all being subjected to occult terrorism. In the past, only isolated individuals such as Hitler were possessed, as the Mother noted, by hostile forces ruled by the Lord of Falsehood. Today, these forces are invading anyone open to them to carry out their demonic intentions. We have had a number of horrible incidents over the past few years, and they will probably increase in frequency. The hostile forces are rising up in opposition to the Supramental Light that descended on Earth in 1956.

Sri Aurobindo and the Mother wrote about their battles with these forces in the 1930s and 1940s. The intent of these forces is to cause fear, isolation, alienation, stagnation, and chaos.* They use diversionary tactics to keep us from progressing in our inner being. Out of all this enormous suffering, there will be a few who will rise above it and open up to a higher consciousness and power through love and forgiveness.

Separated from the Source

For those directly affected, including families, classmates, and teachers of the victims, the suffering is acute; there is no mistaking that. However, there is another kind of suffering that is not so evident and is generally in the background, but it has always been with us. This suffering is chronic, but at certain moments in our lives can become acute.

For most of my earlier years—say, until I was about thirty-five—I could make no sense of life in the United States. People seemed to have no purpose and had little sustained joy for living. There was a great deal of hypocrisy all around me. After a life of struggles, death was the only release. But who understood death? The only solace for most people was the family, especially the hope that the children would have a better life. But there could never be any resolution to the endless cycle of pain and struggle. People—and I include myself in this—would pursue pleasure, avoid pain, and live mostly in indifference. With our present material affluence, we live more and more in the pursuit of pleasure, but that only pushes us more and more into indifference. The more we devour, the more we are consumed. And the pain becomes more unconscious. We continually strive for balance in our lives, but what Sri Aurobindo called the All-Delight eludes us, if we even know it is there.

By the time I left for India in October 1973, I had begun to lift myself out of this despair, but I was desperate to begin *living* the meaning of life, which I had already discovered intellectually in the writings of Sri Aurobindo and the Mother. Although the Mother had left her physical body one week before I arrived in Pondicherry, I knew her presence was still there. Several times a day, I stood before her tomb in the ashram courtyard and pleaded with her to fill me with divine consciousness. When I returned home, five months later, my suffering had turned to joy.

Inconscient

The divine nature is concealed, buried in the bedrock of world existence, the inconscient, and it is only the vibration of suffering that can pull matter out of its inertia. The purpose of our existence, the working out of our evolution, is not a judgment or a punishment. We are destined to become aware of our own self-concealment of the inner Divine within each of us. But how does this happen? Most of us need a jump start—something that finally makes us take a good look and say, "It can't be like this. There has to be more to life than this!" We usually don't even ask why we are here until someone close to us dies or we ourselves are in very difficult circumstances.

Crisis Mode

Many years ago, I was visiting someone at a substance abuse rehabilitation center on the Pacific coast of Oregon. As I was sitting in on a group discussion, one of the parents said that she was very pleased, even gratified, that her son was at the center. Because of his commitment there, she said, he was finally taking charge of his life after admitting his problems, and she could see the tremendous improvement he had made. Then she said something that startled me: "I wish my daughter had a drug or drinking problem, so she could get help, too. She has a terrible attitude, but there isn't any one thing that she's done to get help for. She's drifting from one mini-crisis to the next." Most of us are in such denial about our suffering that we have to virtually fall apart before we do something about it.

Today, we are continually being pushed to the edge by the manifestation of the Supramental Force to bring out the truth of our being. We need to redress our alienation from our original self. Fundamentally, all suffering results from a separation from our soul. We feel lonely and isolated, but with just a little twist in our consciousness we could experience that inner center. Suffering can be the catalyst. Unfortunately, most of us are very slow learners. We have to be turned on our head, over and over and over again, until we realize how simple the process can be. Eventually, I realized that my suffering was not all of my own doing. I simply had not known any better. Our culture in the West does not support this inner movement, this looking within. The education is not there because the teachers in our society do not know themselves.

Soul's Mission

So, again I ask: If God loves His children, why does He allow us to suffer? The question is insoluble because it is put badly. If we realized that *we* are God, then we would know that God is bringing the suffering upon *Himself*. If someone does something to us that we don't like, we might call that cruel. But if we do the same thing to ourselves, it takes on a different slant. One must remember, too, that our souls planned the events in our life before we took a body, and drew to it people and circumstances to complete the experiences necessary for our growth. Meanwhile, our surface self, our ego, is looking constantly for self-gratification and pleasure, while avoiding pain and seeking to maintain the status quo. God favors those most whom He treats most severely.

At one time or another, each society usually has a highly evolved being to show humanity the way. In most cases, that person is subjected to suffering. Sri Aurobindo said about this:

> We must realize that the existence of ignorance, error, limitation, suffering, division, and discord in the world need not by itself, as we too hastily imagine, be a denial or a disproof of the divine being, consciousness, power, knowledge, will, delight in the universe. They can be that if we have to take them by themselves separately, but need not be so taken if we get a clear vision of their place and significance in a complete view of the universal workings. A part broken off from the whole may be imperfect, ugly, incomprehensible; but when we see it in the whole, it recovers its place in the harmony, it has a meaning and a use.[2]

Division is created by our ego, our limiting and dividing surface consciousness that sees, feels, and experiences everything as separate from itself. Humanity reaches a certain global tension to break down this division. We are in a period now in which the pressure is steadily increasing to show us the division so that we will open up to embrace the New Consciousness that is now manifest. The Mother said about this:

It is only his friends whom God treats with severity…. It is only to those who are full of hope, who will pass through this purifying flame, that the conditions for attaining the maximum result are given. And the human mind is made in such a way that you may test this; when something extremely unpleasant happens to you, you may tell yourself, "Well, this proves I am worth the trouble of being given this difficulty, this proves there is something in me which can resist the difficulty," and you will notice that instead of tormenting yourself, you rejoice—you will be so happy and so strong that even the most unpleasant things will seem to you quite charming![3]

A few people serve as examples of what can be achieved under dire consequences of suffering. Christopher Reeves, the actor, is an example of a person who radiates joy within his suffering after becoming a quadriplegic as the result of a horseback riding accident.

Transcending Suffering

Years ago, I had a friend with the appropriate given name of Carma, who had a leg amputated to stem the spread of cancer. When I saw her in the hospital after the operation, she was radiant. The cancer continued to spread, and she died not long after, but she had found the perfection of spirit existing side by side with her suffering, and she chose the former.

My wife, Surama, has gone through a trying ordeal with arthritis, which began in early 1994. At first, she felt a sharp pain in her left elbow that literally took her breath away. This was the beginning of a painful struggle that lasted three years before she was able to stabilize the disease by radically altering her lifestyle in various ways. These included making changes in her diet, taking vitamins, minerals, and anti-inflammatory medications, doing simple home exercises, using magnets on her hands, having acupuncture treatments, and drinking Chinese herbal teas. Most importantly, she stopped asking, "Why me?" and began to take charge of her life. When I asked her about her battle with arthritis and the meaning it has had for her, she said:

> None of us enjoys pain or suffering, but it is necessary for us to go through this sometimes in order to grow, to see how well we handle adversity and to make needed changes in our life. Do we give up? Do we fight? How often do we seek spiritual help? Turning to the Divine, to the Mother, to whatever spiritual helper you choose, will work miracles. Don't give up, don't get discouraged. The Mother is always with us. Listen to her and listen to your body.[4]

The moment Surama stopped being the victim and became proactive in fighting her disease, her health began to improve. This shows how important consciousness can be in shaping our lives. Positive thoughts can yield positive results, and negative thoughts can yield negative results. There have been ideas, theories, and philosophies that have existed for centuries that were either false concepts to begin with or have become irrelevant to our time. One of these is the Western concept of Original Sin. It is true that we have separated from our origin in consciousness, but this was necessary for the play of opposites.

Different Concepts

Another concept, this one from Eastern philosophy, treats the universe as *lila*, or play, meaning that we are in a cosmic game for the amusement of the Divine. This seems to trivialize our suffering.

Some of us have been told that God created us as inferior creatures so that we can praise and glorify Him. In the view of Integralism, however, we were created so that eventually we can manifest perfection, with everything in order and harmony in the manifested world.

Some believe that evil is always evil, good is always good,

and we have a choice between Heaven and Hell, or between eternal bliss and eternal damnation. These are childish ideas that entrap us in our evolution, since they assume that nothing can ever change.

Some say that we are bound to world existence by desire, which creates *Samsara*, the endless wheel of birth and rebirth, until we become enlightened and dissolve into Nirvana. What, then, is the point of existence? It is not desire but delight that is our destiny. However, grief, pain, suffering, error, and weakness are necessary to our complete value. It is not enough to call existence unreal and escape the world into Pure Being. Every weakness portends power and potentiality.

We have countless distractions in the West to deny our suffering: television, computers, the Internet, cell phones, shopping, eating, work, friends—the list is endless. And these are only the legal ones! We live in a busy world, but some balance is needed for us to reflect, to meditate, to read inspiring books, and to experience beauty.

From Suffering to Beauty

The late Dr. Rollo May, a gifted writer and psychotherapist, related in his book *My Quest for Beauty* his own transformative experience as a young man. At the age of twenty, when he was a college teacher of English in Greece, he was suddenly overcome with loneliness, which ultimately led to a nervous breakdown. While he was bedridden for two weeks, he knew that something was terribly wrong with his whole way of life.

One evening at 11:00 P.M., he got out of bed and started walking up the road toward Mt. Hortiati, about ten miles away. It was raining and soon started snowing. His clothes froze to his body, but he kept going. He had a sense that at last he was coming to a certain peace, that he was finally doing something, taking some steps. But he wasn't sure where he was going. After six hours in the darkness, wolves rushed up to him, but he ignored them. Finally, at dawn, he arrived at the little village of Hortiati, where most of the people were shepherds who spoke no English.

Nevertheless, he was able to rent a room and sleep till noon. When he went downstairs, a dozen men were gathered around a stove in the cafe. May sat down at a table and began writing on slips of paper, doing a kind of primitive self-analysis, trying to make sense of his life. At some point, he became aware of the people around him. As he tells it:

> My loquacious companions soon became curious, and finally they could refrain no longer from asking me what I was doing.
>
> One spoke out, *"Ti graphité?"* which means, "What do you write?" I knew they would not understand if I talked about philosophy, and furthermore it wasn't quite true that I was writing that anyway.
>
> So I answered in my halting Greek, "I write, *what is life?"*
>
> They all leaned back with guffaws of laughter. One of them spoke out, "That's easy! If you have bread you eat, if you do not have bread you die."[5]

This may sound like a primitive response, but I suspect that most people can relate to it. However, it was not enough for Dr. May. Later, he had a transcending experience as he walked across a field of poppies that were swaying in the breeze. The beauty of the scene lifted him out of his deep depression, and he realized he had not been listening to his inner voice.

May's story has mythical proportions: deep despair, dark night of the soul, journey into the night and up the mountain, descent, return to humanity and derision, and transcendence through beauty.

Sri Aurobindo related a similar experience in which he had not listened to his inner voice, which had been telling him to leave the political field. As a result, he was imprisoned by the British and placed in solitary confinement for most of a year. That proved to be a blessing in disguise, because his inner realizations as he meditated in his cell, and even as he slept, then led him to formulate his Integral Yoga.

The universe was created *in* delight and *for* delight. But this delight can exist only in the perfect oneness of creation that already exists. When each of us reaches corresponding levels of perfection within ourselves, we will be able to see and experience that perfection within, when everything is in its place. It only requires a shift in position—perhaps an internal one. Sri Aurobindo said, "Now everything is different, yet everything has remained the same."[6]

We are not only born into the suffering of the Earth, but we compound the situation with our egoistic actions, called karma. We bring these tendencies with us from past lives, some of which manifest at a given time as part of our learning curve until we discover how to use things in their true way.

Quiver

The Mother talked about another difficulty that causes our suffering. She called this difficulty the "quiver." People tend to accept everything or to explain everything away. We seem to have a natural tendency to be cautious when life is going well for us, waiting for the other shoe to drop. The Mother said that if we were able to look inside ourselves, we would see a type of vibration, a microscopic tremor, that is a little quiver caused by ordinary consciousness. If we notice it, we wonder how people do not go insane. It is a grace that we don't.

Sri Aurobindo and the Mother talked about suffering as a "vibration"—which is more or less the same as the quiver. It is located in the base of matter and will eventually be annulled by the Supramental. Although this may take several generations, the Mother addressed this condition in her own cells to bring peace and harmony.

This tremor or quiver is magnified when we are frightened or shocked or anxious. Then it becomes perceptible to us. It is the cells vibrating in an expanded mode. Before we can transcend this vibration of suffering, we must discard the psychological garbage that we carry with us: despair, grief, alienation, and fear—especially the fear of death. Meanwhile, it is this vibration of suffering, this quiver, that keeps us in contact with the Earth. The key to our individual and collective evolution is hidden in this vibration, as it teaches us to manifest the Divine Force.

Now we know about the physical effects during pregnancy caused by such poisons as alcohol, tobacco, and drugs. But the expectant mother's emotional and mental states, both at conception and during pregnancy, are equally important. In so-called primitive cultures, peaceful areas are set aside for expectant mothers to have their children. In some societies, one or both of the parents pray before conception for a beautiful and harmonious soul to incarnate in their coming child.

The moment of birth is quite critical in the formation of the child. The emotional and mental states of the mother will have either a deleterious or a beneficial imprint. Fear and anxiety can be transferred as well as joy and happiness.

Special Twist

The Mother said that there is something that settles in us like a residue that we identify with but is not us:

> And you have to feel that it isn't you before you can come down again into it to take possession of it and change it. As long as you say, "This is me," you are tied, bound hand and foot.
>
> What's you is this (*gesture above the head*), It's there: What sparkles in the light—that's you. This [the body] isn't you, it's the sediment....
>
> Everyone is born with...(what can I call it?) *some special twist* (*laughing*)—I know my own twist, I know it quite well! (I don't talk about it because it isn't enjoyable.) But that's what remains last of all....
>
> The first thing is to detach your consciousness, that's most important. And to say: I-AM-NOT-THIS, it's something that has been ADDED, placed to

enable me to touch Matter—but it isn't me. And then if you say, "That is me" (*gesture upward*), you'll see that you will be happy, because it is lovely—lovely, luminous, sparkling....

As long as you try (instinctively you try to arrange things with your best light, your best consciousness, your best knowledge...), it's stupid because that prolongs the struggle, and ultimately it's not very effective. There is only one effective thing, that's to step back from what's still called "me" and...with or without words, it doesn't matter, but above all with the flame of aspiration, this (*gesture to the heart*), and something perfectly, perfectly sincere: "Lord, it's You; and only You can do it, You alone can do it, I can't."[7]

Actually, the resistance—or special twist, as the Mother called it—is there for each of us at every step of our attempt to progress and get free of our cage. Everything from the Transcendent filters down to us on this earthly plane. For example, we normally experience the bliss of Ananda as pleasure. It is a diluted form of bliss. The resistance that ties us down is not really part of us, but nevertheless it has the effect of enclosing us in our box. It is like going through a brick wall. We identify with that limitation until we take a leap—which is aptly depicted by the Tarot card of the Fool, who is blithely stepping off the side of a cliff.

Resistance

When I was serving in the U.S. Army in Alaska in the 1950s, I would take advantage of any free offer I saw in a magazine, just so I would get some mail. One day, an envelope arrived from the Rosicrucians. Curious about what they had to offer, I asked a fellow soldier, who was college-educated, what he thought of them. He said, "I'm surprised at you, Wayne. I thought you were more intelligent than that. What do you want to fool around with that stuff for?" At that time, this was enough to keep me in my cage. I never sent for more information. Such behavior is common for everyone at one state of progress or another.

Even the Mother had to face resistance in herself to the progress in her physical transformation, the final stage in the transformation of her cells. There were periods in the transition during which she appeared incapacitated and perhaps even a bit foolish. In short, she lost all dignity.

Resistance exists at all levels of progress. In my own case, I resumed my spiritual explorations in the late 1960s. I took another leap in 1970, when I made a commitment to Integral Yoga. And yet another leap in 1972, when I wrote to the Mother in Pondicherry. I have made a series of leaps over the past thirty years, some small and some large, but all necessary.

A common dilemma is for one to straddle the line, wanting to take the leap but not wanting to leave behind what one has. This creates anxiety, frustration, and stagnation.

Virtually all groups and organizations create a tremendous pressure to conform to the status quo and the boundaries established for acceptable behavior. This is especially true for educational, religious, and spiritual organizations, in which members tend to be hesitant to explore new territory and announce it to the group.

The suppression of progress also exists on a very ordinary level. For example, a "country club matron," who has huge material wealth, may become bored with her life and friends. She feels hollow and empty inside. Then she begins to read about a political candidate who inspires her. She is reluctant to talk about him with her friends, because he belongs to the "wrong" party, but she brings him up casually in conversation to feel them out. After some strange and curious looks, she drops the subject. She could go ahead and vote for him and not tell anyone. Instead, she simply keeps her thoughts to herself and feels sad.

The pressure to conform is stifling. For centuries, the status quo—or slow progress at best—was the only acceptable avenue for humankind. This has not been true, however, since the Supramental descent in 1956. The lid has been lifted, the veil pierced. We have been given a way out of our suffering, but it requires openness to new possibilities. We are witnessing enormous advancement in space exploration, in computer science, and in medical technology, to name only a few areas, but we cannot perceive the unlimited possibilities in our own bodies.

Karma

Our past, including our past lives, is reflected in our karma. We carry these selected tendencies forward into our present life. The Mother was convinced that karma is all those lessons that we have not yet learned. In other words, it is our unfinished business. We have a path that has shaped our present birth and existence, which dovetails into an amalgamation with our parents, heredity, cells, environment, and karma into what we call suffering. This is not a punishment but a working out, a stage in our soul's destiny for the delight of existence. "Distrust the man," said Sri Aurobindo, "who has never failed and suffered."[8]

When we learn to live in a greater harmony and peace within ourselves and in our relations with the world, with an aspiration to unite with the divine consciousness, we transcend the effects of suffering and fulfill our spirit's destiny in the world. With the manifestation of the Truth Consciousness, the entire evolving process has been accelerated and is pushing for realization on a global scale. Suffering will have fulfilled its purpose. As the Mother wrote in 1910:

> Only those who have suffered can understand the suffering of others; understand it, commune with it, and relieve it. And I understood, O divine comforter, sublime Holocaust, that in order to sustain us in all our troubles, to soothe all our pangs, thou must have known and felt all the sufferings of earth and man, all without exception.
>
> How is it that among those who claim to be thy worshippers, some regard thee as a cruel torturer, as an inexorable judge witnessing the torments that are tolerated by thee or even created

by thy own will?

No, I now perceive that these sufferings come from the very imperfection of Matter which, in its disorder and crudeness, is unfit to manifest thee; and thou art the very first to suffer from it, to bewail it, thou art the first to toil and strive in thy ardent desire to change disorder into order, suffering into happiness, discord into harmony.

Suffering is not something inevitable or even desirable, but when it comes to us, how helpful it can be!

Each time we feel that our heart is breaking, a deeper door opens within us, revealing new horizons, ever richer in hidden treasures, whose golden influx brings once more a new and intenser life to the organism on the brink of destruction.

And when, by these successive descents, we reach the veil that reveals thee as it is lifted, O Lord, who can describe the intensity of Life that penetrates the whole being, the radiance of the Light that floods it, the sublimity of the Love that transforms it for ever![9]

Notes

*It is interesting in this connection that other recent shootings were by a high school gang who called themselves the Lords of Chaos.

[1]The Mother, *Collected Works of the Mother*, vol. 14: *Words of the Mother* (Pondicherry, India: Sri Aurobindo Ashram Press, 1976), p. 266.

[2]Sri Aurobindo, *Birth Centenary Library*, vol. 18: *The Life Divine* (Pondicherry, India: Sri Aurobindo Ashram Press, 1972), p. 401.

[3]The Mother, *Collected Works of the Mother*, vol. 4: *Questions and Answers, 1950–1951* (Pondicherry, India: Sri Aurobindo Ashram Press, 1976), pp. 354–355.

[4]Rollo May, *My Quest for Beauty* (Dallas: Saybrook, 1985).

[5]May, *My Quest for Beauty*, p. 10.

[6]The Mother, *Mother's Agenda*, vol. 7: *1966*, ed. by Satprem (New York: Institute for Evolutionary Research, 1991), p. 74.

[7]The Mother, *Mother's Agenda*, vol. 4: *1963*, ed. by Satprem (New York: Institute for Evolutionary Research, 1987), pp. 384–387.

[8]Sri Aurobindo, *Birth Centenary Library*, vol. 17: *The Hour of God* (Pondicherry, India: Sri Aurobindo Ashram Press, 1972), p. 115.

[9]The Mother, *Collected Works of the Mother*, vol. 2: *Words of Long Ago* (Pondicherry, India: Sri Aurobindo Ashram Press, 1976), pp. 19–20.

10

Karma and Rebirth

> *Rebirth is an indispensable*
> *machinery for the working*
> *out of a spiritual evolution;*
> *it is the only possible effective*
> *condition, the obvious dy-*
> *namic process of such a mani-*
> *festation in the material uni-*
> *verse.*
>
> —Sri Aurobindo[1]

Karma and rebirth or reincarnation are foreign concepts to many people. Like other Westerners, I certainly did not grow up with an understanding or knowledge of them. It was only later, when I began reading books by such authors as Edgar Cayce and Jane Roberts, that I acquired an introduction to the subject. But karma and reincarnation were presented in rather simplistic and general terms. If they were valid and authentic, I wondered, why didn't Christianity embrace them?

Bible

There are some obscure or veiled references to rebirth in the

Bible, but nothing definitive. Resurrection of the body is not re-birth, nor is it clear what kind of body is to be resurrected. In the early Christian era, the Gnostics believed in reincarnation, as did several prominent traditional theologians, including St. Clement of Alexandria (ca. 150–ca. 215 A.D.) and Origen (ca. 185–ca. 254 A.D.). However, the Emperor Justinian (483–565 A.D.) condemned the teachings of Origen, including the belief in reincarnation, in 543 A.D., and it then disappeared from the orthodox stream of Christian thought. This created many difficulties in developing a reasonable explanation for our lives on Earth, because it is not possible for a person to complete his or her life process in one birth. As a result, the concept of purgatory was promulgated, which only begs more questions. St. Augustine (354–430 A.D.) introduced guilt, remorse, and punishment into the Christian concepts of Creation, Original Sin, and Heaven and Hell.

The theory and teachings of karma and reincarnation are taken for granted by Hindus and Buddhists, who see no need to prove or justify them. In *The World Within*, Dr. Gina Cerminara tells the story of a Hindu boy who wrote in a school essay on his favorite animal: "The cat has four legs, one in each corner. He also has nine lives, which he does not use in Europe because of Christianity."[2]

Dr. Ian Stevenson, a psychiatrist, investigated hundreds of cases of reported reincarnation and identified some well-known people who have embraced the belief:

> Some of the westerners who have professed a belief in rebirth are: among writers, D. H. Lawrence, T. S. Eliot, Henry Miller, Conan Doyle, Jack London, Maeterlinck, Sir Edwin Arnold, and the leaders of Ireland's literary revival, Yeats, George Russell, James Stephens, and James Joyce. Among inventors, there was Thomas Edison, and among religious philosophers were Nicolas Berdyaev, Richard Wilhelm, Christmas Humphreys, and D. T. Suzuki. Among artists,

Gauguin, Mondrian, Kandinsky, Malevich, and Paul Klee. In the present chapter, Gandhi and H. G. Wells will be added to the list, as well as two social historians, Lewis Mumford and Theodore Roszak, together with several distinguished scientists: Einstein, Gustaf Stromberg, Camille Flammarion, and Sir William Crookes.[3]

A British psychiatrist, Dr. Arthur Guirdham, had a patient in 1961 who consulted him about persistent nightmares. Since the age of twelve, she said, she had been having disturbing dreams of murder and massacre, and had kept a written record of people and names that came into her mind without her knowing them in life. Her therapist concluded that she was a sane, ordinary housewife with no neuroses.

Prior Life in 13th Century

As a schoolgirl, the woman had written verses of songs in medieval French, a language she had never studied. Nevertheless, a professor at Toulouse University, who studied her verses, concluded that they were an accurate account of the Cathars, or Cathari, a group of Puritans who lived in Toulouse in the thirteenth century. The woman gave horrid details of being burned alive at the stake. She also gave accurate descriptions of people, places, and events, and made correct drawings of old French coins, jewelry, and buildings. Here is how she described herself burning at the stake:

> The pain was maddening. You should pray to God when you're dying, if you can pray when you're in agony. In my dream, I didn't pray to God…. I didn't know when you were burnt to death you'd bleed. I thought the blood would all dry up in the terrible heat. But I was bleeding heavily. The blood was dripping and hissing in the flames. I wished I had enough blood to put the flames out. The worst part was my eyes. I hate the thought of going blind. In this dream, I was going blind. I tried to close my eyelids, but I

couldn't. They must have burnt off, and now those flames were going to pluck my eyes out with their evil fingers…. The flames weren't so cruel after all. They began to feel cold, icy cold. It occurred to me that I wasn't burning to death but freezing to death. I was numb with the cold, and suddenly I started to laugh. I had fooled those people who thought they could burn me. I am a witch. I had magicked the fire into ice.[4]

In my own spiritual search, I could find no satisfaction in the concept of a God who generated fear, guilt, sin, judgment day, and heaven and hell, yet alone a single life here on Earth. After all, two births are not more surprising than one, said Voltaire. So many things are left unanswered by the concept of a single life on Earth that I welcomed the insight afforded by karma and rebirth. But their existence merely for the sake of liberation also raised questions for me. Something was still missing. What is the purpose of life if we are merely to escape from it? The only people who have given me satisfactory answers to this question are Sri Aurobindo and the Mother.

Faces

My first personal contact with rebirth came in 1970, when I attended a lecture by Vimala Thakar, an Indian author, at the Cultural Integration Fellowship in San Francisco. Sitting in the front row, I was absorbed in her presentation, when suddenly I began to see other faces flashing in place of hers. One face replaced another. After a while, I turned away to rest my eyes. When I looked again, the faces continued, but faster this time, with each new face lasting for less than a second. I was astonished, but not at all frightened. Did all of these faces represent her past lives?

Shortly after this experience, I saw "faces" on my teenage daughter. One was of a mentally retarded girl. At the time, my daughter was doing volunteer work with the mentally retarded. Did she feel a bond with these people because of a prior life experience?

The third time I saw these superimposed "faces" was with Carma, the lady I mentioned in the previous chapter, who had her leg amputated. After a long struggle overcoming many childhood problems, Carma gave her first public lecture, at a friend's apartment. As she was speaking, I saw "faces" on her. The one that made the deepest impression on me was that of a very serene and wise Chinese woman. Carma told me later that she had always identified with the Chinese and their philosophy, so she was not surprised when I told her what I had seen.

The "face" visions stopped after this experience with Carma, but I had been given a gift to see that we carry our past with us, even in a subtle physical sense. As with many other extraordinary experiences, we tend to dismiss or deny them because they don't fit into our known reality.

Nityagopal

I have been exploring my own past lives in a casual way for the past ten years, ever since I read *The Gospel of Sri Ramakrishna* by Mahendranath Gupta.[5] In that book, there is a photograph, taken in 1886, of Ramakrishna lying in state, surrounded by thirty-two disciples and colleagues, who are identified below the picture. I felt drawn to one of those individuals, whose name was Nityagopal. The book contains numerous dialogues between Ramakrishna and Nityagopal, which gave me an insight into his character. I was struck by how profoundly I resonated with him. I saw how his tendencies may have carried forward to the person I am now, even though our countries, religions, and lifestyles are so very different.

Since then, I have had two visions of him and in one he embraced me just before I left for Calcutta. In February 1998, I paid my respects by visiting his ashram in Calcutta. Events that occurred there corroborated my belief that Nityagopal and I have an inner connection, but whether or not he is a past life of mine is uncertain. I believe it is more likely that there has been an emanation into me of a part of his consciousness, creating a fusion from his nonmaterial plane to my material plane of consciousness.

In any event, he is only one of my previous incarnations. We do not keep recreating the same character and personality. There would be no point to that, and very little personal growth. We are here to experience different lives to eventually form a new being. Nevertheless, it is still *this* life that is of primary importance, so it is a mistake for anyone to become too consumed with former lives. All things are possible here and now, for everything we need to resolve is within us in this life.

Many people in the West have difficulty believing in karma and rebirth, but these concepts are central to the theory of evolution in consciousness. Karma has taken on a meaning in the West of reward and punishment for one's deeds—a kind of judgmental cause and effect: "As you sow, so shall you reap." But one's soul is more important than divine justice. We are here on Earth to experience, to learn, to grow, and to express, until ultimately a comprehensive and integral being is formed out of these many lives. It is not possible to accomplish this with one or even a few lives. The journey is long and slow. What keeps it going is the process of karma. If this were not so, we would have no growth or evolution. Karma and rebirth are a necessary part of our process.

It makes little sense to have only one birth and one life in which we are responsible for an ancestry, upbringing, education, and moral order we did not choose. In fact, we create our own fate and destiny. Our current life here has meaning only if we know that there will be future lives to complete the process of suffering, joy, disappointment, success, and failure. Otherwise, we are here by the edict of a cruel and unjust God. What about the millions of children and displaced persons who undergo unspeakable tragedy, only to die at a premature age? Is this their only chance at life on Earth?

We have to look at the larger picture to gain some perspective. Nature has a certain line of progression. If there is a beginning with a soul in the body, there must be an end, not an escape. The psychic or soul presence evolves over countless millennia from lower forms until it progresses to an evolved mental state. But our mental state is not the last stage of evolution. Neither does the soul regress into lower forms.

If we have all of this history within us, why don't we remember it? This is a reasonable question, but an absence of memory does not disprove reincarnation. How much do we remember of our first five years of life? Very little, if any, and it gets much more difficult remembering past lives. In the cosmic wisdom, we are spared all of the travail and turmoil so that we may start afresh, although the essence of our past life episodes and memories are latent in our psychic being. Would we really want to remember all our past sufferings, injuries, pains, and deaths? Life would be impossibly burdensome for most people if they had to consciously carry all these memories with them. Sometimes fragments emerge in dreams or in meditation. When people become fully aware of their psychic being, as Sri Aurobindo and the Mother did, their past lives are revealed to them.

In 1895, Gustav Mahler, the German composer, said to his close friend and biographer, Richard Specht:

> We all return; it is this certainty that gives meaning to life, and it does not make the slightest difference whether or not in a later incarnation we remember the former life. What counts is not the individual and his comfort, but the great aspiration to the perfect and the pure which goes on in each incarnation.[6]

Children are more susceptible than adults to past-life memories, and there are many accounts of children remembering their past lives. The Mother said these memories are usually of a life that was prematurely curtailed.

Westerners have a mind-set that tends to ignore existence before birth or after death except in the most superficial terms—perhaps of heaven and hell. Most people in the West live for instant gratification of their impulses or appetites rather than being present in the here and now. They have a simplistic concept of "living happily ever after" that obscures their meaning here. Until they come to grips with life, death will be meaningless, for life and death are part of the same continuum.

New Personality

Karma and rebirth are inseparable and complex. There are no two identical destinies, and never have been. Everyone has the same ground of being or fundamental existence, but this plays out differently for each of us. It is not our personality that is reborn. Rather, we form a different personality and character with each new life episode, which gives us new experiences. There would be no point in recreating the same me over and over again. Sometimes we take on opposite traits, or a different skin color, or a different gender, or a different religion to have another perspective and experience. Would we be more tolerant of differences if we knew that?

Soul Chooses

Our soul chooses the main lines rather than the details of our next life, attracting people and events into that new life to fulfill our new purpose. If one feels that one's life is empty and futile, it should not be for lack of external accomplishment but for not completing one's purpose in this existence. One's life may be fulfilled in a single moment, such as by an heroic act, or perhaps by experiencing a beauty that transcends our senses, or by overcoming failure. On the other hand, finding fulfillment may take a lifetime, as in living a life of selfless giving, or achieving peace and harmony, or just having a happy single or married life.

The Essence Survives

When we die, what is taken from our life, preserved, and integrated is not the experiences themselves but the essence of them. Our life experiences begin to form a new being in us, called the "psychic being" by Sri Aurobindo, much as our experiences in childhood and adolescence help to form our character. Where in our being is that time that we won the race in grade school, or overcame the taunts of classmates, or rejoiced in learning something? It is not those events per se that formed our present character, but their essences, which still remain a part of us. The essences of those events have formed something in us that is more than memories.

When iron is heated and forged, it takes on a new character and strength, becoming steel. Although we would not consciously choose it, some of our most growth-related experiences emerge from misfortune, whether in the form of poverty, illness, humiliation, cowardice, or failure. Sometimes we have to go through these adverse circumstances to know their meaning. This is karma. This is what keeps the world turning round and round and has allowed our psychic being to form. It is carried over into our next life.

In truth, we change very little over a lifetime unless our soul has chosen an especially difficult life to deal with or a discipline that accelerates our growth. The latter has been the traditional view, although even this has changed because everyone on the planet is now being pushed into an accelerated movement. We can all feel this pressure. Like it or not, we are all involved. How we deal with this accelerated energy and new consciousness determines our ease of transition.

Dying Process

When we die, we go through a process of assimilation of our life experiences. After a period of time, we enter into a rest or repose in the psychic world, awaiting our next birth. The psychic being is a subtle body that transports us from our past life through the other planes. Sri Aurobindo stated:

> We have found that there is life on other planes after death and before subsequent rebirth, a life consequent on the old and preparatory of the new stage of terrestrial existence. Other planes co-exist with ours, are part of one complex system, and act constantly upon the physical.[7]

In our next life, we will form a new character and personality, and new abilities may emerge that have been latent. We may also carry forward some old tendencies, even though hundreds of years may have elapsed since our last incarnation. Plato estimated that typically a thousand years pass between incarnations.[8] On the other hand, rebirth can be almost immediate. But no matter when we are reborn, we will have a new childhood to develop, with a new education, possibly siblings to deal with, and so on. Our body will have new genes that must be integrated with our karma. During our maturation, new karma will develop. Every act has its consequences. Every desire can enslave us.

Our thoughts and beliefs shape our life's experiences. We create and are responsible for our fate and destiny. We also create our own heaven and hell, both here and in the afterlife. But these are temporary, for there is a law of karma and rebirth that will prevail regardless of our beliefs.

The life we create here with our actions, reactions, feelings, thoughts, desires, and beliefs is influenced by a number of factors beside heredity and environment. But these become secondary to the influence of karma and especially to the soul's influence on and plan for our evolution.

Silent Concentration on Your Soul

How do we become aware of the soul's intention? One way is to set a time every day to sit quietly and comfortably. Concentrate on your soul with the intent of making contact with it. Keep trying. The attention alone will have an influence. The soul, like a child, is unable to blossom without love and attention.

Mind in the Cells

The mind is everywhere, even in the cells of our heart, which can become overloaded with thoughts, drives, desires, and frustrations. In this age of medical miracles, including heart transplants, this can create karmic confusion. For example, I read recently in the newspaper about a woman who began to experience cravings for beer and Chicken McNuggets after having a heart transplant. This puzzled her, because she did not like beer and had never had Chicken McNuggets. Eventually, she located the donor's family and asked them about the deceased. It turned out that the donor had been a teenage boy who had been killed in a motorcycle accident. "Oh, yes," his mother said. "He loved beer and Chicken McNuggets and had been eating some shortly before the accident."

As I have indicated in a prior chapter, my own experiences have shown me that I can "think" outside my body just as well as I can inside it. My mind or consciousness can function with or without the use of the brain. People on the other side—that is, who have died recently—can communicate without a body.

My Brother's Transition

For example, my younger brother, Don, passed away in 1990 from a terminal illness. He had a degree in music, and played the piano, organ, and harpsichord. When he moved to San Francisco, however, he got away from his music. Although it had been his main interest in life, he never developed it fully. When he died, he was confused and unhappy. Eight years later, with no intervening contact from him, I saw Don vividly in a dream. His entire body was vibrant, and his face was glowing. I had never seen him like this when he was alive.

For some reason, I forgot to mention this dream-experience to Surama until six or seven days later. When I did, she said: "I also had a dream of him that night. He looked incredible, and he was composing music with my pen, the one you gave me and bought from a street vendor last Christmas. Don said he had borrowed my pen from my purse. Usually, I'm angry if anyone goes into my purse without asking, but this didn't bother me at all." Interestingly, the pen never worked again after that dream-experience.

Cellular Injury

A number of times, I have had a bodily or cellular response that was inexplicable in terms of my present life. For example, on one of my visits to India, I developed a shoulder pain so severe that I could not sleep for nearly two weeks. I finally found some medication that eliminated the pain. The mystery was that I had never injured that shoulder, nor did that pain ever return. Somehow, my being in India triggered the response to a latent cellular memory. Our karma is not only mental but psychological and emotional. By the grace of God, it does not surface all at one time or in one incarnation.

Although we like to think that everything happens for the best, observation reveals otherwise. To overcome obstacles, we have to be at the summit of our consciousness, which is not easy. If we have established some peace in our being and faith in a divine presence, all that happens to us will be for the best. Otherwise, if we touch fire, it will burn. Evil begets evil—not as a punishment, but because this is the consequence of action. Similarly, good begets good.

Fate and Free Will

Fate and free will are not contradictory notions but two movements of one indivisible energy. Sri Aurobindo said, "My will is the first instrument of my Fate."[9] When Napoleon was asked why, if there is fate, he was always planning, he responded, "Because it is still Fate who wills that I should plan."[10]

Sri Aurobindo believed that fate is only one factor of existence. Being, consciousness, and will are even more important factors. Ethics and morality cannot be the whole preoccupation of cosmic law and karma. If one tries to seek reward and avoid punishment, that debases virtue into selfishness, manipulating karma into commercial bargaining.

If we are to have a reasonable explanation for our life that gives it meaning, we must have a continuity of experience, before birth and after death. One incarnation evolves into another, ultimately merging with our fundamental existence in a new expression in time and space. Sri Aurobindo said about this:

> If it is once admitted that the Spirit has involved itself in the Inconscience and is manifesting itself

in the individual being by an evolutionary gradation, then the whole process assumes meaning and consistence; the progressive ascent of the individual becomes a key-note of this cosmic significance, and the rebirth of the soul in the body becomes a natural and unavoidable consequence of the truth of the Becoming and its inherent law.[11]

Meaning of Incarnations

An isolated incarnation is meaningless, but so also is a round of incarnations in which the only objective is to escape to Nirvana or to the heavens and leave the Earth as it is. As Sri Aurobindo said:

> The soul is not bound by the formula of mental humanity: it did not begin with that and will not end with it; it had a pre-human past, it has a superhuman future.[12]

Escape the Wheel

How do we get out of the cycle of karma when it seems to go on forever? The traditional view is to achieve liberation and leave this planet for good. We do indeed have that option, but if we choose it, we do not contribute to the Earth's evolution. Religious and spiritual literature is replete with individuals who have achieved enlightenment, or liberation from their body, and presumably do not have to reincarnate unless they choose to. However, in terms of the total human population—the billions of souls who are alive today, and the billions more who lived in the past—the percentage of those who have been liberated is infinitesimal.

Surely, there must be some other more viable option for humankind. Since 1956, we have been at a juncture in Earth's history that is unprecedented. The manifestation of the Supermind is accelerating everyone's consciousness toward unprecedented heights or depths. In the transitional period, unfortunately, there will be chaos, destruction, and violence. Every living human being has an option to participate willingly in this remarkable journey. Anyone who wishes to jump ship and avoid the suffering by achieving personal liberation can do so, but he or she will also miss the joys awaiting. Sri Aurobindo expressed the point eloquently:

> A play of self-concealing and self-finding is one of the most strenuous joys that conscious being can give to itself, a play of extreme attractiveness. There is no greater pleasure for man himself than a victory which is in its very principle a conquest over difficulties, a victory in knowledge, a victory in power, a victory in creation over the impossibilities of creation, a delight in the conquest over an anguished toil and a hard ordeal of suffering. At the end of separation is the intense joy of union, the joy of meeting with a self from which we were divided. There is an attraction in ignorance itself because it provides us with the joy of discovery, the surprise of new and unforeseen creation, a great adventure of the soul; there is a joy of the journey and the search and the finding, a joy of the battle and the crown, the labor and the reward of labor. If delight of existence be the secret of creation, this too is one delight of existence; it can be regarded as the reason or at least one reason of this apparently paradoxical and contrary Lila [play].[13]

Grace

Grace can sweep away everything. Since the advent of the Supramental Consciousness in 1956, we can, according to the Mother, dissolve our karma without going through all the steps of liberation. With a sincere call and opening to the divine consciousness, we can ultimately transcend all limitations here on Earth. While this cannot come in one fell swoop, since our bodies have to go through a formidable transition, the opportunity is here to participate consciously in the journey. It is a gift available to all. Karma and rebirth are here for a reason, but they bind us hand and foot. Ultimately, even they must be superseded. On this theme, Sri Aurobindo said:

If Supermind also is a power of consciousness concealed here in the evolution, the line of rebirth cannot stop even there; it cannot cease in its ascent before the mental has been replaced by the supramental nature, and an embodied supramental being becomes the leader of terrestrial existence.[14]

The Mother and Sri Aurobindo—and a few disciples—nurtured this new consciousness until it could manifest on a global scale. It appears to me that the incubation was completed with the Mother's passing on November 17, 1973. The initial manifestation of the new consciousness was a descent into the Earth's atmosphere on February 29, 1956, but that was only the beginning. The Mother stated in 1933:

All the ages and millennia of human life that have elapsed so far have prepared the advent of the *new state*, and now the time has come for its concrete and tangible realization. That is the very essence of Sri Aurobindo's teaching, the aim of the group he has allowed to form around him, the purpose of his Ashram.[15]

Notes

[1]Sri Aurobindo, *Birth Centenary Library*, vol. 19: *The Life Divine* (Pondicherry, India: Sri Aurobindo Ashram Press, 1972), pp. 754–755.

[2]Quoted here from Joseph Head and Sylvia Cranston, *Reincarnation: The Phoenix Fire Mystery* (Pasadena, CA: Theosophical University Press, 1998), p. 456.

[3]Ian, Stevenson, *Twenty Cases Suggestive of Reincarnation* (New York: American Society for Psychical Research, 1966), p. 485.

[4]Head and Cranston, *Reincarnation*, p. 400.

[5]Mahendranath Gupta, *The Gospel of Sri Ramakrishna*, trans. Swami Nikhilananda (Madras: Sri Aurobindo Math, 1974).

[6]Quoted here from Head and Cranston, *Reincarnation*, p. 353.

[7]Sri Aurobindo, *The Life Divine*, p. 793.

[8]Plato, *The Republic*, trans. H. D. P. Lee (Baltimore: Penguin Books, 1953), p. 401.

[9]Sri Aurobindo, *Birth Centenary Library*, vol. 16: *The Supramental Manifestation* (Pondicherry, India: Sri Aurobindo Ashram Press, 1972), p. 282.

[10]Sri Aurobindo, *The Supramental Manifestation*, p. 284.

[11]Sri Aurobindo, *The Life Divine*, p. 754.

[12]Sri Aurobindo, *The Life Divine*, pp. 760–761.

[13]Sri Aurobindo, *The Life Divine*, pp. 410–411.

[14]Sri Aurobindo, *The Life Divine*, pp. 763–764.

[15]The Mother, *Collected Works of the Mother*, vol. 15: *Words of the Mother* (Pondicherry, India: Sri Aurobindo Ashram Press, 1976), p. 264.

11

Death

*What is this then thou callest
death? Can God die? O thou
who fearest death, it is Life
that has come to thee sport-
ing with a death-head and
wearing a mask of terror.*

—Sri Aurobindo[1]

One would be hard-pressed to find a more unpopular topic than death. In our materialistic culture, death is a denial of everything we live for and enjoy. Recently, I interrupted my writing and research to attend classes in continuing education for my business. At the end of the course, three of us—two students and the instructor—met at a restaurant to socialize. When the conversation turned to metaphysics, I mentioned that I was writing a book on evolution and life, and was currently working on a chapter on death. One of my companions said nothing, but scrunched up her shoulders and shivered. For me, that said it all. In this society, we are taught nothing about death and its true significance, nor are we prepared in the least for its eventuality.

As I was growing up in the Midwest in the 1930s and 1940s, I often tried to fathom this thing called death—this nothingness, this utter and eternal blackness. For that is what I understood death to be. "When you're dead," I thought, "you're dead. Dead as a doornail." Side by side with this concept in my mind was the idea of being with our creator, living eternally in Heaven or Hell after Judgment Day. It is no wonder that we are confused, and that when confusion reigns, denial is the result. We simply do not want to talk about death. No one seems to have any answers, but virtually everyone becomes superstitious at even the mention of the subject. As a result, we are totally unprepared for the most significant event of our life. For life means death, and death means life.

We cannot begin to live full lives till we come to terms with the fear of death. Many years ago, I attended a series of classes on public speaking to overcome my shyness. Some of those in the class were salespersons or in people-related professions. But the one common denominator we all had was our discomfort with public speaking. We were told that the two greatest fears that most people have are of death and public speaking. I could certainly identify with the latter, but I had difficulty relating to the fear of death. Why? Because we are seldom confronted with it directly except when relatives or friends die—and even then, the memories fade away. The sting of death is the separation from what we have known and experienced. The Mother said that the greatest obstacle to our progress is fear, and that the fear of death is the most subtle and most tenacious of fears.

We cannot conquer our fear of death until we understand what life is. Our divine essence is one and immortal; only its forms are countless and changing. This knowledge must be firmly established in our mind, and we must identify as far as possible with the eternal life that is independent of every living form. This gives us a psychological basis to begin our understanding of death.

Four Methods to Deal with Death

The Mother gave four methods for overcoming the fear of death. The first appeals to our reason, which can conclude that, since death is inevitable and unavoidable, it is absurd to fear it. In almost every case, death comes when it must; we can neither hasten nor delay its hour, even when we think or act otherwise. Death is never an accident, even though we may die "by accident." Except for a few individuals who have extraordinary powers, the hour of death seems to be inexorably fixed. Reason teaches us that it is absurd to fear something we cannot avoid. Therefore, we accept it and do the best we can day by day without worry. This method of avoiding the fear of death may be very good for intellectuals, but not so good for emotional people.

The second method is one of inner seeking. The Mother says that, beyond all our emotions, there is a silent and tranquil depth of our being where the light of our soul is shining constantly. If one searches for this light within and concentrates on it, one is sure to find it. As soon as one enters into it, one awakes to the sense of immortality, knowing that we have always lived and that our consciousness is wholly independent of our body, which is only one of the transient forms we have manifested. Thus, death is not an extinction but only a transition. However, this method of avoiding the fear of death will not work for individuals who are incapable of introspection and inner seeking.

The third method involves total faith in one's God. People who have such faith know that whatever happens to them is for their own good. They surrender their will absolutely, feeling God's love and protection as if they were lying at the feet of their beloved, enjoying perfect security. This method will only work for those who have the capacity to enter into this type of supreme trust.

The fourth method is to believe that death is a bad habit that can be conquered. This method is for born warriors who cannot accept life as it is and feel a right to immortality. Only those with an indomitable spirit should attempt it. Few have the fortitude to overcome the obstacles. The Mother described four battles that such a warrior would have to survive.

Four Battles

The first battle is mental. It has to be waged against the over-whelming, collective suggestion, based on thousands of years of experience, that there is a law of nature that has no exception: namely, that everything that lives must die. Most religions turn death into either a reward or a punishment—a deliverance to Heaven or to Hell. For one resolved to conquer death (not merely the *fear* of death), all these suggestions must have no effect.

The second battle is emotional. One must relinquish attach-ment to everyone and everything that one has loved: spouse, children, friends, home, career, and so on. It is not a question of giving up all of this, but of giving up *attachment* to it. Thus, one must feel capable of living without these persons and things, or that one could rebuild a new life, free of desire and attachment.

The third battle is with the sensations—for example, need-ing gratification from food, sex, or money. These needs are re-lentless, rising up again and again, sensing the slightest weak-ness in us.

The final battle is physical. It is fought in the body, begin-ning at birth. The two combatants in this battle are the forces of transformation and disintegration. Every indisposition, illness, or accident is the result of the force of disintegration. All growth, harmonious development, resistance to attack, and recovery from illness are due to the force of transformation. This battle must be waged without a quiver of fear. When the Mother waged this battle, she increased the receptivity of her very cells.[2] After she died in 1973, the battles she won and the inroads she made were not lost. Rather, they were passed on to all those who are open and receptive to the force of transformation, regardless of race, nationality, gender, creed, or age.

We are preparing for death from the moment we are born. As Charles Dickens once said, "We are all on the way to the grave together." The preparation is subtle, not overt. We hesitate to talk about or prepare our wills. We have become separated not only from death but also from God. In pre-technological civilizations, people asked questions about nature and catastrophe and death, which they assumed were all interconnected. But as these civilizations became more "sophisticated," they also often became more barbaric. God became an afterthought. America was founded on spiritual freedom, but where is that feeling about God and connection today?

What is *your* feeling about death? Can you write your thoughts about death in one sentence?

There are people who are ill but refuse to see a doctor for fear of what they might hear. When they are finally forced to go, perhaps by pain, if their condition turns out to be insignificant, they celebrate and wait for the next worry. People are content to be discontented.

If someone were to ask you, "What's the matter with you?" would you respond, "I'm going to die someday"? There are people who wake up every day scared to death because they do not know what they are facing. Heaven and Hell drive people crazy. "Well," they ask, as they get out of bed, "who's dying next?" Death can hold such a morbid fascination. One might think: "Will anyone remember me? Suppose no one lights candles for me." About the solitude of death, Andrew Marvell wrote:

> The grave's a fine and private place,
> But none, I think, do there embrace.[3]

According to the Upanishads, all matter is food. With this thought in mind, Sri Aurobindo said that "the eater eating is himself eaten."[4] We can see this in nature, but it also applies to us. There is a real sense of consumption. We see that our body, which contains the life force within us, consumes itself as it ages. The word *death* itself has the word *eat* within it—right in its belly, as it were. There is a relationship between food, eating, love, sex, devouring, and death. When a mother plays with her baby or young child, she will often pretend to be eating it. Love itself is a type of consumption. The Mother remarked upon this once when she saw a live rabbit placed in a cage as food for a snake. At first, the rabbit was terrified and trembling with fear, but then it became quiet and surrendered.

The question becomes: How do we get out of this circuitous trap of devouring ourselves? Food and eating are often related to personal psychological issues. Anorexia and bulimia are eating disorders: perverse forms of either abstinence or gluttony. In the latter case, one gorges and then rejects—not only food, but also love and beauty. There may well be a day when we will have a body that does not require material food, but that day is yet to come. When it arrives, all our energy will flow from breathing—although this will not be breathing as we know it now. Until that time arrives, food will continue to carry the pros and cons of love, warmth, friendship, satisfaction, energy, disease, pollution, waste, and death.

Desire

The life-death continuum has always been driven by *desire*, which permeates every aspect of our being. Desire has served its purpose by maintaining the life-death cycle in its endless pursuit of a heretofore indefinable goal. Various religions and spiritual disciplines have recognized this, but their remedy has been to deny enjoyment. Asceticism is a kind of mental surgery to cut desire out of our system. This radical approach ignores our fundamental roots. Enjoyment without attachment is a far better integrative approach. I enjoy what is given to me or not given to me.

Desire itself will fall away effortlessly as the Supramental Being manifests. Joy will become self-contained within our human form—that is, within the cells of the body, which will have qualities of the Divine, such as light, rapture, and freedom. Ultimately, to be human will mean to be divine, but in a physical body that has been transformed. This implies that death itself will no longer be necessary. As John Donne wrote in the seventeenth century, "Death shall be no more; Death, thou shalt die."[5]

The New Consciousness

Sri Aurobindo called the new consciousness that is now operational on Earth the Supramental Consciousness, or Supermind, or Truth Consciousness. The Mother often referred to it simply as the "new" consciousness. Until there is a critical mass of beings on Earth who embody the new consciousness, we will have to deal with the act and process of death. The new consciousness is progressive—that is, once it is established within us, its vibrational intensity increases as our cells and nervous system adapt to it.

Death Is Not an Escape

Meanwhile, we are ill prepared for death. We do not seem to realize that our acts and desires create inevitable consequences in the afterlife, just as they do in our everyday earthly existence. Death is not an escape. We do lose the burden of the body and its physical limitations, but we cannot escape our emotional and mental desires and attributes.

What happens if we have a bad dream or a nightmare? We rush back into the safe haven of our body and awaken. We do not have that safeguard when we die. It is not a question of punishment, but a natural consequence of cause and effect. If we are preoccupied with our desires, these must play themselves out when we leave our body.

We should be aware of the parts of our being and their actions when they withdraw permanently from our body at physical death. One view, as recounted by persons who have survived near-death experiences, is that when our heart stops beating and our brain waves cease, something in us, our soul, sees a brilliant light, as in a tunnel, and we go into a beatific realm, possibly meeting deceased friends and family members. The survivors only have a vague notion of what happens after that. Perhaps, eternal rest or sleep.

Parts of Being

To understand the process of death, we first must understand our own makeup. We call ourselves human beings, but what

comprises this beingness? According to Sri Aurobindo and others, although the terms may differ, we are comprised of *many*
beings, all superimposed on one another and of different grades
of energy and levels of development.

The being that is closest to our physical body is the *subtle
physical body*. It is not uncommon for people to see emanations of
this body as an energy field or "aura" around the physical body.

Next we have the *vital being*, which is comprised of our life
force, feelings, and emotional body. Our desires, which are never
totally fulfilled, reside in this subtle body.

Then we have our *mental being*. Our society has placed the
greatest importance on intelligence, but the normal or typical
state of mental activity is one of doubt, confusion, and illogic.
At death, these three subtle beings leave our physical body suc-
cessively. The first to leave is the subtle physical body, next the
vital being, and then the mental being.

Psychic Being

The last being to leave is the soul, or *psychic being*, an eternal
work-in-progress. The soul is fundamentally and paradoxically
one and the same in everyone, but also is absolutely unique for
each of us as it becomes a formed psychic being. It carries the
essence of our experiences of our many and varied life episodes
that had a divine quality to them, including kindness, unselfish-
ness, heroism, gratitude, compassion, and personal and impersonal love. The vital being also carries its own memories. The
issue of memory is very complex, since memories from past incarnations can come from different parts of one's being.

There is also a realm of cosmic consciousness that contains
all memories of the Earth and its inhabitants, which is separate
from any one person's memories. One would be extremely surprised by the extent of this computer-like data bank. Virtually
anything can be retrieved from cosmic consciousness, no matter
how trivial, if one has the ability to access it. Every e-mail we
send is recorded. Nothing is omitted.

Durga

Just as we have the freedom to say and do as we like, so others have that same freedom, so long as they don't interfere with our actions. Those "others" may be discarnate—that is, have a consciousness without a physical body. They are experiencing life in what we on Earth call death. If they incarnate, they will die to their life that we call death and be born into this life. While they are "dead," they can assimilate their past life, but they can make no further karmic progress. That can only be made while one is in a physical body, because it is only then that one can have a constant relationship or union with the Divine. The Mother discussed this idea in a conversation she had with the goddess Durga:

> This morning I had a visit from Durga. She pays me a visit every year, but this morning it was interesting because she explained to me her point of view, how she feels existence…. When she came last year, I told her…, "You fulfill your universal function very well, but you are missing something…." And I explained to her the meaning of being in conscious and attentive contact with the supreme Will. She understood. She understood and adhered, she said yes. And during the year she must have tried, because when she returned this morning, there was really a difference, especially a difference in the understanding, and she explained it to me. Then I spoke to her about the physical human nature and its infirmity, and she told me, "There is in this body something we—all of us up above—do not have and cannot have: the possibility of a constant Presence of and a constant contact with the Divine." She had never thought of it before! Only since a year ago. And she said it with such intensity—such intensity and understanding and meaning…. It was as though all human miseries instantly disappeared in front of this EXTRAORDINARY thing—the possibility of feeling in every cell the divine Presence.

It was really interesting. The morning was really interesting.

She stayed here while I was washing, and she told me, "See, you can do all this, and not for a minute, not for a second do you lose the contact with That, with the supreme wonder. And we who are full of power, without any of your petty miseries, any of your petty difficulties, we are so used to our way of being that we don't see the value of it, it's something obvious, almost inevitable." And she said *(Mother smiles)*, "We never think of the Divine, because we ARE the Divine.... So there isn't that will to progress, that thirst for ever better, ever more—we totally lack it."

It was really interesting. I am putting it into words (of course, she didn't speak to me in French!), but it was very simple, the contact was very simple *(gesture of inner exchange)*, and very natural, very spontaneous. At one point, I even asked her *(laughing)*, "Do you enjoy all this worship people give you?" She said no. "No, I don't care." She is too used to it, she doesn't care.[6]

The basic point here is that we on Earth have the capability to transcend our limitations and our egos, our separateness, while uniting with the divine essence within, and at the same time evolve to our own uniqueness. Up till now, death has been an integral part of this process, as it has allowed us to complete one episode and start another.

Balance

Part of our evolutionary process is to synchronize our various beings. Although usually synchronized, the physical, subtle physical, vital, mental, and psychic beings can each develop at different speeds on our spiritual journey. If we do not keep a reasonable balance between our five beings, we can run into trouble. If we try to move too fast on any one of the five levels, we can become physically, psychologically, or spiritually ill. Nature likes a status quo, or balance. When we try to change or progress, our being often rebels, tending to revert to its previous state. When we have a spiritual experience, we usually have a fallow period afterwards to allow our different beings to reharmonize.

In the spiritual path of evolution of our body and our consciousness, the body is the most resistant to change, lagging behind the other four beings. The body has the characteristic of apathy or laziness, a carryover from our ancestors in the animal world. Animals by nature are not workaholics. They do what is necessary to get their food, and that's it. When we feed our domesticated animals, they sleep even more.

The vital being is a difficult animal to tame, for it feeds on desire. Eventually, we must master the trio of money, power, and sex. They are mutually related, so that the excess of one has an impact on the others. There is no field where these are more prevalent than in politics.

Money, power, and sex have also been serious obstacles in the spiritual field. For centuries, the solution has been to take a vow of poverty, meekness, and chastity. That is the old order. We will discuss the new order in more detail later, but for the moment let us assume that the new order and the new being are in a fully developed state. At that point, the Supramental Being will have no need for money or wealth; will have unlimited divine power; will be in constant bliss without needing vital pleasures, although it will be able to experience and appreciate the joys of life; and will have no need for reproduction, because there will be an entirely different birth-death process.

While these ideas may seem extremely radical and beyond general comprehension, the Supramental Being will inevitably be the outcome of our new consciousness. Although it may take centuries for the Supramental Consciousness to fully manifest, we are already immersed in the process.

The practice that we can use to achieve mastery over money, power, and sex is to develop non-attachment to them. We enjoy them if we have them. If we don't, we still have enjoyment, for the Supramental Vibration will be established in our consciousness and in our body.

The issue of sex is a bit more difficult to deal with than the issues of money and power—especially in our culture, where we are constantly being sexually manipulated by advertising, films, television, and other broadcast and print media. Although sex is perfectly natural and healthy in ordinary life, it will become an obstacle at some point in our bodily transformation. Nevertheless, the worst thing anyone can do is to attempt to suppress the sexual urge. At some point in our spiritual journey in Integral Yoga, the sexual urge, like other addictions, will fall away by itself, if we have that aspiration.

Kicking the Habit

Years ago, I decided that I needed to stop smoking my pipe. I was smoking obsessively, and it was taking over my life. For example, I couldn't wait for dinner to be over so I could get to my pipe. For months I thought about stopping, but I was reluctant to give up what I thought was so much pleasure. Finally, a moment came when I knew it was time. I had had enough. The first thing I did was pray to the Mother for help. The very next day, I stopped without any withdrawal symptoms and never thought about it again. I'm sure I would have had much anguish if I had tried to stop prematurely without the right psychological and spiritual preparation.

When we are submerged in physical pleasures, we can see nothing else. But it is possible for us to have these pleasures, including sexual pleasure, without them having much, if any, impact on our consciousness. Some greater joy, called sublimation, has taken their place. As we grow up, we have to replace one pleasure with another, much as we pass from our tricycles to our bicycles. In the beginning, there is a great reluctance to give up what we have and know.

Self-Mastery

In all self-mastery, there is the realization of our freedom to do or not to do anything we please. We are no longer dependent upon some object or act or desire. We also recognize that beauty becomes a bigger part of our life. Compared to sexual pleasure, we get more enjoyment from music, painting, dance, architecture, and meditation. Something as simple as a sunset or a baby's smile can touch us profoundly. Furthermore, we automatically become kinder and more generous.

Many philosophers and poets have noted the relationship between sex and death, as in these lines from the sixteenth-century French poet Pierre de Ronsard (1524–1585), writing to his lover:

> Tomorrow, aching for your charms,
> Death shall take you in his arms
> And shatter your virginity.[7]

Procreation is part of the life-death cycle. We are created, we die, and we are reborn, ad infinitum. Inherent in the creation is death. When we are born out of the sex act, we are already preparing for death—not consciously at first, for we have a mistaken sense of immortality. We do have a strong relationship with immortality, but that has not as yet been transferred to our physical body. At present, immortality is only a state of consciousness.

Process of Death

How do we prepare for death? After we are physically dead, we die again and again over the next seven to eight days, as the various beings—subtle physical, vital, mental, and psychic— leave our physical body. Each departure is a death to our former life. It is during this period that we need help from our friends here. They should not grieve and hold us to this atmosphere, but rather become beacons of light as resource centers for our new journey. Instead of clinging to their memory of us and not wanting to let us go, they should celebrate our recent life and pray for us to have a safe and joyous journey.

When the Mother was asked how the news of death should

be received, especially by someone close to the departed, she replied:

> Say to the Supreme Lord: Let Thy Will be done; and remain as peaceful as possible. If the departed one is a person one loves, one should concentrate one's love on him in peace and calm, for that is what can most help one who has departed.[8]

Afterlife

As we lived our life, so shall we live on our journey in the afterlife. If we died in a state of emotional chaos, we will take that with us. And if we died in a state of bliss, we will take *that* with us. That is why the last thoughts and feelings that one has in this life are so important. They are not something that one can program at the last moment. They have to be lived.

We will have a harmonious journey in the afterlife if we achieved happiness, peace, and purpose in this life. Ideally, our actions, feelings, and thoughts were balanced. If they were not, then our afterlife can be quite unpleasant because we will attract disembodied thoughts and desires from the mental and vital realms. As I noted earlier, when we have nightmares we can escape by waking up. When we leave our body permanently, we do not have that option. That is why it is so important to achieve equanimity while living. It is also the reason for those left behind to give us some relief by offering joyful prayers rather than grief. Contrary to popular opinion, mourning ceremonies can be more of a hindrance than a help, obstructing us in our new process of assimilating our recent life episode.

If we have lived our last years in an addictive state, craving food, sex, drugs, money, power, or whatever, and feeling such negative emotions as anger, hatred, fear, jealousy, or greed, we are going to have some difficulty. Our misery will not be permanent, but we will have to dissolve our affinity to those things before we can find peace.

Suicide

Persons who have committed suicide will not find escape by dying. They will merely carry their unresolved issues into the afterlife with them. My younger brother, Don, committed suicide in 1990 at the age of fifty by deliberately taking an overdose of pills and alcohol. He had an incurable illness and had told me what he planned to do. As I mentioned earlier, both Surama and I had visions of him in a beautiful state of being, eight years after his passing. In Surama's vision, he was composing and playing music, which was a completion of what he had not fully accomplished while living here. Thus, it is possible to soften our karma in the afterlife as part of our assimilation of our previous life.

My Brother's Passing

When I first heard of my brother's illness, in August 1990, I was preparing for a trip to Pondicherry. When I arrived there, on September 4th, I was still very unnerved. On the 6th, still emotionally drained, I took a nap after breakfast. When I awakened, I knew that Don would be guided in some way by the Mother, to whom I had prayed that morning. Then I remembered how I had developed a rash around the time my mother had had a stroke. I seemed to be having the same kind of physical connection now to my brother. When I realized that, my anxiety lifted and I was able to get on with my life in India. I mention this because Don seemed to be assisted considerably in the afterlife, despite his suicide (a sin common to *all* religions), as evidenced by the dreams of him that Surama and I had years later.

No two journeys in the afterlife are exactly the same, but we know from persons who have undergone near-death experiences that there can be beauty in the transition. There is usually a brief momentary gap in consciousness at death. Often, just before dying, the person will experience peace and a sense of beauty. It is as though a certain part of their being has a vision of the other side, but we only hear about it from those who return. Most say that their earthly life was forever changed for the better. Perhaps, this is a divine intervention to give meaning to people who have never experienced beauty before.

But the journey in the afterlife is not all one of beauty. Much depends on our preparation beforehand: on how well we have fulfilled our purpose in life; on how well we have resolved our psychological issues and our cravings; on how attached we are to this physical life; and on the measure of inner peace that we have attained. These factors will all help to determine how smooth the transition will be.

Our Next Incarnation

At the moment of death, our soul will decide on its next incarnation, providing further evidence of the life-death continuum. The psychological state we are in at death will have a huge impact on our journey in the afterlife. If we have concentrated on the Divine through prayer, meditation, devotion, consecrated work, creativity, and beauty, we will be in the proper state of being at death. Our last thoughts will be of a sublime nature. There are no crash courses in which we can cram for the final exam at the last moment. But one contact or opening with our soul before passing on will prepare us for our next birth. This is why it is never wise to end our lives prematurely.

After we die, we go through a period of debriefing, which sometimes begins shortly *before* death, when we may see our life flash before our eyes. After physical death, the beliefs we have acquired while living will temporarily influence our journey, just as our belief system in life has an enormous impact on what we attract to us. In this sense, we take our memories with us for a while. If we believe in a hell and damnation, we are likely to have some experience of them, just as we will with a heavenly state. If we have no belief in an afterlife, we are *still* governed by certain laws and will go through a similar process.

Our life, our thoughts, and our feelings will be shown to us as if on a movie screen. Some lives may look like a bad movie. We will go over and over our life until we learn all the lessons that need to be learned. There are some beings who have led a particularly gruesome life and refuse to acknowledge their past deeds. It will take a long time for them to move on to the next stage.

Self-Realized Beings

For those who have achieved liberation while living, called "self-realization" by some, there is a choice whether to return to another earthly life to assist humankind or to move on to other realms of consciousness/existence. Of course, if our soul's journey is to transform the material world and our body, we will return until we complete that process.

There comes a point when we have assimilated our previous life experiences on Earth and are ready to repose in the soul world—a repose that is similar to sleep. However, this repose is not for an eternity. We will surely be reborn, although it may not come for hundreds of years. On the other hand, it may come almost immediately. It appears, for example, that children who die prematurely often reincarnate very soon, perhaps even into the same family. The situation for rebirth varies enormously, for each soul has a different destiny.

For most of us, the only part that is not eventually dissolved is the psychic being, which is immortal. However, if we have unified our vital and mental beings around the divine center during our lifetimes, they, too, will be immortal.

Dying Does Not Make Us Smart

In his commentary on the Isha Upanishad, Sri Aurobindo remarked that our afterlife depends on our development of consciousness while on Earth. If we persist in ignorance while alive, we will continue to be in darkness in the afterlife. As Sri Aurobindo put it:

> By departing from the physical life, one does not disappear out of the Movement, but only passes into some other general state of consciousness than the material universe.
>
> These states are either obscure or illuminated, some dark or sunlit. By persisting in gross forms of ignorance, by coercing perversely the soul in its self-fulfillment or by a wrong dissolution of its becoming in the Movement, one enters into

states of blind darkness, not into the world of light and of liberated and blissful being.[9]

On May 6, 1927, the Mother gave us insight on when to surrender to the Divine:

> One must know how to give one's life and also one's death, give one's happiness and also one's suffering, to depend for everything and in all things upon the Divine Dispenser of all of our possibilities of realization, who alone can and will decide whether we shall be happy or not, whether we shall live or not, whether we shall participate or not in the realization.
>
> In the integrality and absoluteness of this life, this self-giving, lies the essential condition for perfect peace, the indispensable foundation of constant beatitude.[10]

Notes

[1]Sri Aurobindo, *Birth Centenary Library*, vol. 17: *The Hour of God* (Pondicherry, India: Sri Aurobindo Ashram Press, 1972), p. 124.

[2]The Mother, *Collected Works of the Mother*, vol. 12: *On Education* (Pondicherry, India: Sri Aurobindo Ashram Press, 1976), pp. 82–92.

[3]Andrew Marvell, "To His Coy Mistress," in *Love Poems*, edited by Peter Washington (New York: Knopf, 1993), p. 37.

[4]Sri Aurobindo, *Birth Centenary Library*, vol. 18: *The Life Divine* (Pondicherry, India: Sri Aurobindo Ashram Press, 1972), p. 192.

[5]John Donne, "Divine Poems," in *Tudor Poetry and Prose*, edited by J. William Hebel et al. (New York: Appleton-Century-Crofts, 1953), p. 491.

[6]The Mother, *Mother's Agenda*, vol. 8: *1967*, ed. by Satprem (New York: Institute for Evolutionary Research, 1993), pp. 333–334.

[7]Pierre de Ronsard, "Corinna in Vendome," in *Love Poems*, edited by Peter Washington (New York: Knopf, 1993), p. 46.

[8]The Mother, *Collected Works of the Mother*, vol. 16: *Some Answers from the Mother* (Pondicherry, India: Sri Aurobindo Ashram Press, 1976), p. 416.

[9]Sri Aurobindo, *Birth Centenary Library*, vol. 12: *The Upanishads* (Pondicherry, India: Sri Aurobindo Ashram Press, 1972), p. 77.

[10]The Mother, *Collected Works of the Mother*, vol. 1: *Prayers and Meditations* (Pondicherry, India: Sri Aurobindo Ashram Press, 1976), p. 374.

12

Beauty

That which we are seeking through beauty is in the end that which we are seeking through religion, the Absolute, the Divine.

—*Sri Aurobindo*[1]

The appreciation of beauty was encouraged by the ancients and was an integral part of early religions. According to Hindu teachings, each prior civilization revealed one special aspect of the divine manifestation and was then dissolved. In the present manifestation—the seventh and last—the power and form of *Ananda* will reach full flowering. Beauty is an integral part of this *Ananda*.

Strangely enough, beauty is foreign to our modern consciousness. For the last several centuries, Western culture has emphasized the development of the mind, putting beauty in the back seat. Architecture, for example, emphasizes economics and utilitarianism as the dominant and guiding principles. "Form follows function" is the rule. Our appreciation of beauty has become secondary and superficial.

When Rollo May tried to promote his excellent book *My Quest for Beauty* on television talk shows in the mid-1980s, he was told by various people in the business that the American public had no interest in beauty. At first he disagreed, but after his book tour he had to concur.

In a book review in December 1999 of Elaine Scarry's *On Beauty and Being Just*, Kenneth Baker begins:

> Beauty has been in disrepute for at least a generation. Harvard professor of aesthetics Elaine Scarry is the latest of several writers to try and rehabilitate it.[2]

I myself did not grow up with beauty, since I was reared in an industrial area in a working-class environment in the Midwest. It was not a part of my Protestant upbringing, and, in fact, I cannot recall ever discussing it. Everything was geared to physical and economic survival. I had very little exposure to the arts. But since then, beauty has been brought into my life in innumerable ways, both inner and outer.

Einstein

Interestingly, Albert Einstein gave pre-eminence to beauty over everything else in life. At a gathering at a private home in New York City in the 1950s, after an evening of chamber music by Bach, Dr. Einstein asked a young man sitting nearby if he had enjoyed the music. When the young man said that he was unfamiliar with Bach, Dr. Einstein took him upstairs for an introduction to musical appreciation, from Bing Crosby to Enrico Caruso. At the end, they finally listened to some Bach. When they returned to the party, the hostess was indignant at the absence of her distinguished guest. Dr. Einstein said he was sorry, but he and his young friend had been engaged in the greatest activity of which man is capable: opening up yet another fragment on the frontier of beauty.

What youths see and hear has tremendous influence on them. The infusion of beauty at a young age is essential. In the 1960s and 1970s, it was awkward to mention "love" and "God," but now those topics are beginning to permeate everywhere. The walls of resistance are breaking down. When Princess Diana was killed in the summer of 1998, there was an overwhelming display of grief and love. The "Queen of Hearts" had opened up the hearts of millions through her life and death. Her love and beauty were contagious, but not fully recognized until her tragic death.

Rollo May on Beauty

Many of us are anaesthetized to beauty, perceiving it as either embarrassing or insignificant. Nothing conveys this better than a session that Dr. May had with one of his clients, who arrived saying she was weary and didn't have much to talk about. Nevertheless, she reluctantly agreed to try free association—that is, to say whatever came into her mind. Following are a few excerpts from Dr. May's summary of the hour:

> "The first thing that comes to me, I stopped my car on the way here to look at the twilight. It was just beautiful, the purple hues with the green hills behind them...it is the most beautiful time of day.... I don't believe in a God, at least in a personal God, there is so much evil in the world, it makes it so pointless. But when I see such beauty, I can't believe it is by accident. The poets in the country I came from speak of this time of day when they are writing the most important things—when they write of love and so on.
>
> "In the twilight I used to go to the beach all alone, it was lovely.... This time of day would be a good time to die, a good time to be alone.... I should have been a poet [smiling].... This time at twilight doesn't last long.... It seems to say something about true love—it can't be actualized. [Silence]
>
> "I would like to die at this time.... It is so

peaceful here in your office…. I keep noticing the beauty outside the window…. My mother called from [another country]…called all the way to tell me she had a cold…. That ruins the beauty…. My mother always wanted me to notice the beauty…to enjoy the world.

"The bay is so beautiful…. I stop each time I drive toward the bridge…. San Francisco seems unreal, like a *fata morgana*…. I am part of it…it feels so good, I want to melt into it."

At the end of the hour, I asked her how she felt. "Somewhat relaxed…like when I go to a good movie. My friends want to talk about it, but not I…. This scene here [looking out my windows] is pure beauty." She then expressed her fear that she had said nothing today, maybe it was all superficial talk. I assured her that no topics could be more important than beauty, God, death. I added that I thought it was the most profound hour we had ever had.

This person is like the majority of people in our western culture: we suppress our feelings of beauty; we are shy about them, they are too personal. We talk about "the view," anything to avoid the personal statement. And if we do let out such feelings, we apologize for them.[3]

Beauty purifies and liberates the soul. Beauty is above knowledge and ultimately transcends emotion. We have to establish some equality or equilibrium in our consciousness to receive it. We cannot receive beauty while we are preoccupied with other tasks. Beauty is not just another distraction.

Beauty in India

I had to be initiated into the mysteries in order to prepare myself to receive beauty. Prior to my arrival in India in late 1973, I had not given beauty much thought. My first three weeks at the Sri Aurobindo Ashram were very unsettling. I realize now that I was being tested. I had to quiet down internally and become peaceful in order to receive anything.

In the West, we are action-oriented. When I am in India, however, I am pulled inward, as though my inner being is opened up. I can also feel and see this happening in those around me. One can go spontaneously into the inner depth of one's being only after one has made a transition. I have found that we are so outward-oriented in America, with our minds racing all the time, that when we enter an environment like India, we need to reverse our consciousness. It is like going through a detox program. We have to "dry out" or empty ourselves of the external and just "be." In my travels to India, I have gone through this transition innumerable times, and now it is easy for me to adjust. I have found that we develop a kind of protective shell around us in the West because we are bombarded with so many stimuli. But this shell also numbs us and restricts our souls or psychic beings from coming forward.

Pondicherry

Beauty helps us to transcend these limitations and to purify us as we begin to establish some inner peace. It was in this state of consciousness that I had my first real connection with music. Surama and I were on the verandah of the Sri Aurobindo Library one balmy evening. As the breeze rustled the palm trees, I could hear the ocean from the Bay of Bengal crashing against the boulders on the shore. There was a beautiful orange-colored full moon. The lights were turned out as we sat on the tile floor. Vivaldi's *Four Seasons* was playing on the sound system. This was my first true experience of receiving the beauty that we find in music.

After the program, Surama said to me, "You know that kundalini current coming up the spine that you've talked to me about? Well, I just felt it while listening to this music." We both felt that this was a transcendent moment.

Jeanne Korstange, a devotee of Sri Aurobindo, related her experience of beauty in the following way:

All of us have memories of beauty…. I think immediately of those breathtaking moments when I've walked into Mother Nature at her heights of perfection. There was the clear, cold night when the stars seemed close enough to reach and touch as I ascended the hill in Darjeeling for a view of Kanchenjunga. I've had the delight of going to the beach in Auroville on a full moon night and seeing the phosphorescent lights dance on the waves…. I have my collection of photos which have attempted to capture sunsets, rainbows, mountains, dew drops on roses, or shell fish on rocks. I have rocks and pebbles from the beaches of Maine, and driftwood from Lake Michigan, and Clay Babies from Vermont. All of these things were a passing moment, a fleeting glimpse of "the soul behind, the self and spirit."[4]

David Abram, author of *Spell of the Sensuous*, gives more relevance to beauty than to logic and science:

There is something about the experience of being inside the world, being radically imbedded or situated in the depths of the blooming, buzzing field of life. Really immersed in its depths. That's what it is about for me. The culture, the civilization into which I was born, keeps tearing me away from the mystery, keeps forcing me to ponder the world, or to calculate it, as though I were outside looking in. Science keeps trying to figure out the world, which to me is ludicrous. Beauty is too big for us to ever figure out. Logic itself, and the logic that we might apply to come up with an understanding or explanation of beauty, that logic has been created out of beauty.

Beauty drives evolution. Moves evolution. It is the motivation underlying survival, underlying reproduction. Why does life seek to perpetuate itself, if not because it is enjoying being alive? What is that enjoyment about? It is the deliciousness of experience. It is beauty. Beauty drives evolution from the smallest, simplest, single-celled entity on up to us. Beauty was there prior to any explanation we can provide.

Beauty is deeply linked to eros, that impulse that drives and motivates and draws, that keeps pulling life out of itself to shape-shift into ever new forms. And what is eros if not that pleasure and astonishment with that which is not oneself? So logic, or rational logical reasoning, can never fully explain beauty, because beauty is the larger context. Beauty is that which ultimately explains logic.[5]

Rama and Sita

Beauty is expressed through love, and love through beauty. The Hindu poet Tulsidas described the love at first sight that occurred between the Indian gods Rama and Sita:

> Bringing Rama to her heart along the path of the sight,
> Sita closed the doors with her winking.[6]

N. Sri Ram commented on the importance of beauty:

Beauty is the creation of Life, which flows into a form and impresses it with the Truth which is at the very source of that flow.

That which is wholly beautiful has an absoluteness which is the sign and seal of the hidden Divinity.

Beauty is ever a perfect adjustment. That which is beautiful—a poem, a place of architecture, a melody, a flower—has a unity, a center of origin whence is its inspiration.

There is such a thing as a stairway of beauty, a progressive appreciation and sense of the beautiful. Taste has to evolve and reach maturity and refinement.

Beauty, not as an abstract principle but in its endless rendering, is the language of God; it translates the infinite, subjective truth into its appropriate object expression.

The law of Beauty is the law of the Spirit in manifestation; it is the Law of the self-relation of the One to the many.[7]

Universal Beauty

The Mother also emphasized the importance of beauty, noting that one must elevate one's consciousness to experience universal beauty:

In the world of forms, a violation of Beauty is as great a fault as a violation of Truth in the world of ideas. For Beauty is the worship Nature offers to the supreme Master of the universe; Beauty is the divine language in the forms. And consciousness of the Divine which is not translated externally by an understanding and expression of Beauty would be an incomplete consciousness.

But true Beauty is as difficult to discover, to understand, and above all to live as any other expression of the Divine; this discovery and expression exact as much impersonality and renunciation of egoism as that of Truth or Bliss. Pure Beauty is universal, and one must be universal to see and recognize it.[8]

Sri Aurobindo and the Mother held beauty to be the pinnacle of divine expression on Earth. In the Vedanta, the highest trinity of the Supreme is conceived as pure existence, pure consciousness-force, and pure *Ananda*. The expression of *Ananda* is individualized as love, joy, and beauty, and the one characteristic throughout is harmony. Sri Aurobindo uses the term *delight* or *all-delight* as synonymous with *Ananda*.

Beauty in matter is the most visible and readily accessible evidence of the Divine and its manifestation. We are part and parcel of this unfolding, and it is our task to reveal or uncover the beauty that is both outside us and inside us—in our soul and ultimately in our cells. Eventually, we must see the beauty in every form, even the ugliest and most hideous. As Kabir wrote:

> Since I got the vision of the Lord, my consciousness does not turn inwards.... I behold the beautiful form of the Lord everywhere. In the centre of all forms stands the Formless, yet ineffable is the beauty of the "Form."[9]

It is evident that if we have this potential to discover beauty we will meet resistance, for the adverse forces do not want this to occur. Resistance by the hostile forces is everywhere, for they embrace the ugly. We know the level of our transcendence by our experience of the beautiful. This is not to be construed as mundane pleasures but as beauty that is self-revealing—without shadows, as it were. The closer we get to Spirit, the closer we get to our inner essence. As Sri Aurobindo said, "The eater of the honey of sweetness who is seated in the soul of man extends himself through the universe."[10]

Upanishads

The Upanishads unified beauty, truth, and power. It was to this union that Sri Aurobindo was referring when he said, "Beauty shall walk celestial on the earth."[11] *Ananda* and beauty are inseparable. As Sri Aurobindo said:

> Beauty is Ananda taking form—but the form need

not be a physical shape. One speaks of a beautiful thought, a beautiful act, a beautiful soul....
What we speak of as beauty is Ananda in manifestation; beyond manifestation beauty loses itself in Ananda or, you may say, beauty and
Ananda become indistinguishably one.[12]

A day will come, according to Sri Aurobindo, when we will
see a new beauty: "Supramental beauty is the highest divine
beauty manifesting in Matter."[13]

The appreciation of beauty is a progressive journey from
beauty of the senses to universal beauty, and ultimately to the
highest divine beauty, which will manifest in matter and the body
itself. There is an outer beauty and a beauty of the inner being
and inner worlds.

Rasa

Sri Aurobindo defined *rasa* as concentrated taste, a spiritual
essence of emotion. The meaning can be more easily understood
as the liquid flow, or sap of delight, that keeps trees alive. The
rasa transforms itself into flowers that morph into fruit. We experience the *rasa* through the fruit. The *rasa* is the mind's understanding of beauty. If we can identify with the inner essence or
rasa of the tree, we can experience the beauty of the tree in its
form. But we can also identify with the *rasa* through the fruit of
the tree, which gives us an egoistic enjoyment that can be
transcended to a universal level when we get closer to the
origin of delight.

Miracles

Outer beauty can be described as horizontal—that is, it is
beauty on the physical plane. The subtle worlds or dimensions
of consciousness can also have a beauty that is experienced by
the inner being. Occasionally, there are crossovers from the subtle
or nonphysical world to our physical world, which we call
miracles. These visions usually give a luminous impression of
beauty whereby one feels transcended. There can be an impact

that reaches one's soul to the point of transformation. Most often, though, these visions are on the inner plane with eyes closed. Sri Aurobindo said of this transforming journey:

> The bliss must be pure and unalloyed, unalloyed by self-regarding emotions, unalloyed by pain and evil. The sense of good and bad, beautiful and un-beautiful, which afflicts our understanding and our senses, must be replaced by *akhanda rasa*, undifferentiated and unabridged delight in the delightfulness of things, before the highest can be reached. On the way to this goal, full use must be made of the lower and abridged sense of beauty which seeks to replace the less beautiful by the more, the lower by the higher, the mean by the noble.[14]

Power of Faith

On the way to the goal, the Mother said:

> One's attitude is extremely important, even one's outer attitude. People do not know just how important faith is, how faith is miracle—the creator of miracles. For if at each moment, you expect to be uplifted and drawn towards the Divine, He will come and lift you, and He will be there, very near, nearer and nearer.[15]

Tagore

Our perception of beauty needs to mature, for life is not what it appears. The great Bengali poet Rabindranath Tagore contrasted his experience of beauty on the Ganges with what was seen by the helmsman:

> One day I was out in a boat on the Ganges. It was a beautiful evening in autumn. The sun had just set; the silence of the sky was full to the brim with ineffable peace and beauty. The vast expanse of

water was without a ripple, mirroring all the changing shades of the sunset glow. Miles and miles of a desolate sandbank lay like a huge amphibious reptile of some antediluvian age, with its scales glistening in shining colours. As our boat was silently gliding by the precipitous river-bank, riddled with the nest-holes of a colony of birds, suddenly a big fish leapt up to the surface of the water and then disappeared, displaying on its body all the colours of the vanishing sky. It drew aside for a moment the many coloured screen, behind which there was a silent world full of joy. It came up from the depths of its mysterious dwelling with a beautiful dancing motion and added its own music to the silent symphony of the dying day. I felt as if I had a friendly greeting from an alien world in its own language, and it touched my heart with a flash of gladness. Then suddenly the man at the helm exclaimed with a distinct note of regret, "Ah, what a big fish!"[16]

When we view life from the more common egocentric point of desire (called desire-soul or false soul), we distort or limit our perception of beauty. The clash between desire and an attached response was expressed by Lord Byron: "Who can view the ripened rose nor seek to wear it?"[17] A similar thought is expressed in a Chinese Proverb: "A thorn defends the rose, harming only those who would steal the blossom."

Silence

To go deeper in our experience of beauty requires, even demands, an inner peace and quietude similar to having a spiritual experience through meditation. We may have a glimpse of beauty or a soul-experience, but we cannot contain it for long without this foundation of inner silence. We have not yet learned to receive. If we are always seeking, always looking outside ourselves, there is no way we can receive until we make an offering and surrender to that supreme silence.

Western society is not conducive to that, and in fact often does not condone it. We run from the silence. We purposely keep every moment of the day filled with something. This addiction to noise and activity has to be broken so that we can consciously choose to be active or at rest in repose. Once we achieve that, the action and the repose, they can be integrated and we can be active in the silence. This is very difficult to do in the West.

I have been attempting this kind of integration since 1974. I have found that to be active—working in a business, driving an automobile, being social—requires a great deal of conscious effort and commitment. My particular path is to retreat to India every few years so that the divine conscious-force can be permanently stationed in my body. This has had a tremendous stabilizing influence on me, so that I seldom feel alone or alienated or depressed. Each individual has to choose his or her own method or approach. The ways are countless, but it helps immeasurably if one can first realize one's psychic being. The heroic Helen Keller, who was both blind and deaf, said that the most beautiful things cannot be seen or touched, but must be felt with the heart.

Relaxation

We know from personal experience that pain is increased at the dentist's or doctor's office if we tense up. The Mother talked about this contraction and how its release can lead to a greater receptivity to beauty:

> You may have noticed in the different parts of your being, when something comes and you do not receive it, it produces a stiffening—something hardens in the vital, in the mind or in the body. There is a clenching, and this tension hurts—the first thing to do, then, by force of will, is to relax this clenching.... You must learn how to "let go...." This process of relaxation of tensions may be differently applied in the mind, in the vital, or

in the body, but logically it is the same thing. You can enlarge your consciousness as vast as the earth and even the universe. When you do that, you become truly receptive.[18]

Beauty comes in many different shapes and forms, as was elucidated by Sri Aurobindo:

> When [the soul] can get the touch of this universal, absolute beauty, this soul of beauty, this sense of its revelation in any slightest or greatest thing, the beauty of a flower, a form, the beauty and power of a character, an action, an event, a human life, an idea, a stroke of the brush or a chisel or a scintillation of the mind, the colors of a sunset or the grandeur of the tempest, it is then that the sense of beauty in us is really, powerfully, entirely satisfied. It is in truth seeking, as in religion, for the Divine, the All-Beautiful in man, in nature, in life, in thought, in art; for God is Beauty and Delight hidden in the variation of his masks and forms. When, fulfilled in our growing sense and knowledge of beauty and delight in beauty and our power for beauty, we are able to identify ourselves in soul with this Absolute and Divine in all forms and activities of the world and shape an image of our inner and our outer life in the highest image we perceive and embody the All-Beautiful, then the aesthetic being in us who was born for this end has fulfilled himself and risen to the divine consummation. To find highest beauty is to find God; to reveal, to embody, to create as we say, highest beauty is to bring out of our souls the image and power of God.[19]

Anne Frank

Beauty can be poignantly manifested in people—especially

those who are heroic and demonstrate forgiveness of their oppressors. This point was beautifully revealed to us through the life of Anne Frank, who hid from the Nazis during World War II. When Anne and her family were betrayed, they were sent to a concentration camp, and, of the eight family members, only her father survived, who had her diary published. In the depths of her ordeal, Anne had written the following words:

> I feel the beauty of nature and the goodness of the people around me. Every day I think what a fascinating and amusing adventure this is! With all that, why should I despair?[20]

Although we have yet to experience sustained harmony on Earth, there is every reason to believe that it will come with the continued manifestation of the Supermind. Sri Aurobindo said about this:

> Harmony is the natural rule of the spirit, it is the inherent law and spontaneous consequence of unity in multiplicity, of unity in diversity, of a various manifestation of oneness. In a pure and blank unity, there could be indeed no place for harmony, for there is nothing to harmonize; in a complete or a governing diversity, there must be either discord or a fitting together of differences, a constructed harmony. But in a gnostic unity in multiplicity, the harmony would be there as a spontaneous expression of this unity.[21]

Divine Mother as Shakti

In Indian thought, the Supreme Being creates or manifests the universe through a power called the *Shakti*, or Divine Mother, who has four main powers or attributes. One of these is beauty, which has been given the name Mahalakshmi, from *Maha*, "great," and *lakshmi*, "beauty." The characteristics of beauty include harmony, vividness, opulence, and grace. These qualities will manifest more and more as we proceed from disorder to order, from disharmony to harmony.

We have seen in previous chapters that the cards are stacked against us in our quest for peace and harmony. There are obstacles everywhere, even in matter itself. Literature is replete with happy endings, but that may be all wishful thinking. There is no factual basis for believing that life is *not* a mixed bag of suffering and joy. Beginning in 1956, the new consciousness has been manifesting gradually, until today numerous individuals and groups are declaring that we are approaching a period of unprecedented spiritual transcendence here on Earth. That is also the main thrust of this book.

All people—even those without any conscious spiritual aspiration—generally try to achieve some balance in their minds and emotions. We all want to have some equilibrium or equality of being. This becomes critical as we prepare to receive the golden light in our consciousness and in our body. The consciousness-force is available to everyone, but not everyone is prepared to receive it.

Hour of God

Sri Aurobindo alerted us to the new consciousness in his declaration called "The Hour of God," which is even more timely today than when he uttered it decades ago:

> There are moments when the Spirit moves among men, and the breath of the Lord is abroad upon the waters of our being; there are others when it retires, and men are left to act in the strength or the weakness of their own egoism. The first are periods when even a little effort produces great results and changes destiny; the second are spaces of time when much labor goes to the making of a little result. It is true that the latter may prepare the former, may be the little smoke of sacrifice going up to heaven which calls down the rain of God's bounty.

Unhappy is the man or the nation which, when the divine moment arrives, is found sleeping or unprepared to use it, because the lamp has not been kept trimmed for the welcome, and the ears are sealed to the call. But thrice woe to them who are strong and ready, yet waste the force or misuse the moment; for them is irreparable loss or a great destruction.

In the hour of God, cleanse thy soul of all self-deceit and hypocrisy and vain self-flattering that thou mayst look straight into thy spirit and hear that which summons it. All insincerity of nature, once thy defense against the eye of the Master and the light of the ideal becomes now a gap in thy armor and invites the blow. Even if thou conquer for the moment, it is the worse for thee, for the blow shall come afterwards and cast thee down in the midst of thy triumph. But being pure, cast aside all fear; for the hour is often terrible, a fire and a whirlwind and a tempest, a treading of the winepress of the wrath of God; but he who can stand up in it on the truth of his purpose is he who shall stand; even though he fall, he shall rise again; even though he seem to pass on the wings of the wind, he shall return. Nor let worldly prudence whisper too closely in thy ear; for it is the hour of the unexpected.[22]

Harmony and Resistance

Harmony is the natural rule of the spirit. It just hasn't had the opportunity to manifest in its fullness. That time is coming, but it is difficult. There is resistance throughout humanity and nature. When the Mother was asked if the disasters and catastrophes in nature are the consequences of a discordant and sinful humanity, she replied:

Perhaps the truth is rather that it is one and the same movement of consciousness that expresses itself in a Nature ridden with calamities and catastrophes and in a disharmonious humanity. These two things are not cause and effect, but stand on the same level. Above them there is a consciousness which is seeking for manifestation and embodiment upon earth, and in its descent towards matter it meets everywhere the same resistance, in man and in physical Nature. All disorder and disharmony that we see upon earth is the result of this resistance. Calamity and catastrophe, conflict and violence, obscurity and ignorance—all ills come from the same source. Man is not the cause of external Nature, nor external Nature the cause of man, but both depend on the same one thing that is behind them and greater, and both are part of a perpetual and progressive movement of the material world to express it.[23]

A miracle simply replaces a vibration of disharmony with harmony, whether an illness is cured, an accident averted, or a catastrophe prevented. Our faith can bring about grace and harmony. The Mother declared:

It is in this creation, in this universe, that the perfection of a divine world can be manifested— what Sri Aurobindo calls the Supramental. Equilibrium is the essential law of this creation, and that is why perfection can be realized in the manifestation.[24]

Superman Consciousness—Divine Harmony

We can have peak experiences of this beauty and harmony, such as when Surama and I experienced the beauty of Vivaldi's music under the brilliant moon and swaying palm trees. Everyone wants to make these experiences continuous and permanent. I had a taste of this supreme harmony in Pondicherry in the early 1990s. I was sitting near the main Ashram dining room, conversing with a woman at a table by the small pool. There was a crowd gathered for the darshan of February 21, celebrating the Mother's birthday. I had been at the ashram for a month or so and felt relaxed and at peace. Suddenly, I noticed that the "atmosphere" had changed. It was quite subtle, but radiated with peace, harmony, good will, and joy.

The Mother called this manifestation the Superman Consciousness, but this phrase does not do it justice. The consciousness was external to me—that is, it was outside of me. I did not say anything to my companion, but continued the conversation until I returned to my residence to prepare for the trip home via Madras. I had gone through this ritual many times before, usually taking my suitcase to the waiting taxi and leaving, as Sri Ramakrishna once said, like a wandering minstrel after doing my song and dance, never more to be heard from again. But this time the permeation of divine harmony followed me, and people appeared from everywhere. There was a small crowd when I departed, which made me feel like royalty. That was my first experience of the "supreme" consciousness in the physical atmosphere. The feeling of this Divine Presence in the atmosphere is remarkably similar to the feeling in the supramentalized region of the subtle physical. That consciousness will ultimately bring peace on Earth when we are prepared to receive it. Sri Aurobindo wrote about this in a poem called "Descent":

> All my cells thrill swept by a surge of splendor,
> Soul and body stir with a mighty rapture,
> Light and still more light like an ocean billows
> Over me, round me.
>
> Rigid, stone-like, fixed like a hill or statue,
> Vast my body feels and upbears the world's weight;
> Dire the large descent of the Godhead enters
> Limbs that are mortal.
>
> Voiceless, thronged, Infinity crowds upon me;
> Presses down a glory of power eternal;
> Mind and heart grow one with the cosmic wideness;
> Stilled are earth's murmurs.

Swiftly, swiftly crossing the golden spaces
Knowledge leaps, a torrent of rapid lightnings;
Thoughts that left the Ineffable's flaming man-
sions,
   Blaze in my spirit.

Slow the heart-beats' rhythm like a giant
hammer's;
Missioned voices drive to me from God's door-
way
Words that live not save upon Nature's summits,
   Ecstasy's chariots.

All the world is changed to a single oneness;
Souls undying, infinite forces, meeting,
Join in God-dance weaving a seamless Nature,
   Rhythm of the Deathless.

Mind and heart and body, one harp of being,
Cry that anthem, finding the notes eternal,—
Light and might and bliss and immortal wisdom
   Clasping for ever.[25]

Beauty and the Beast

 Beauty is experienced on different levels. Even on a universal plane, all is not reduced to a common level. But how do the
ugly and the hideous correspond to our concept of beauty and
transformation? Here is one of the best-known stories illustrat-
ing these apparent opposites:

  Beauty ("la Belle") is the youngest and favorite
  daughter of a merchant, who suffers reverses. He
  sets out on a journey in the hope of restoring his
  shaken fortunes. Unlike her sisters, Beauty asks
  him to bring her back only a rose. The journey
  proves a failure, but on his return, in the beautiful garden of an apparently uninhabited palace,
  he plucks a rose for Beauty. The Beast, an ugly

monster to whom the palace belongs, threatens him with death as the penalty for his theft unless he gives him his youngest daughter. Beauty sacrifices herself and goes to the Beast's palace and lives there. She is gradually filled with pity and affection for the Beast and finally consents to marry him, whereupon he turns into a beautiful prince, having been released from a magic spell by her virtue and courage.[26]

This story reveals the release of inner beauty by one's love and self-giving, which indicate a transcendence of the mind. From one universal standpoint, we have devolved into the hideous, and our task is to transform ourselves into a glorious and resplendent golden light of truth. The possibility to achieve this has been hidden from us and is only now coming to light. This is the purpose and the function of the Supramental Consciousness.

Rainbow, the Hippie

I had my own experience with a beauty and beast called Rainbow, who was a homeless hippie poet with annoying nervous mannerisms. He constantly interrupted, even monopolized, the conversation in a small circle of people studying Sri Aurobindo's teachings. When he finally became quiet, I discovered the beauty of his soul that had been waiting to emerge. He was radiant—a perfect example of beast and beauty existing side by side. The support of the group and Rainbow's surrender to the process allowed the beauty of his soul to manifest, and he felt it. Sri Aurobindo said of this kind of transformation:

> When I had the dividing reason, I shrank from many things; after I had lost it in sight, I hunted through the world for the ugly and the repellent, but I could no longer find them....
>
> God had opened my eyes; for I saw the nobility of the vulgar, the attractiveness of the repellent, the perfection of the maimed, and the beauty of the hideous.

> I knew my mind to be conquered when it admired
> the beauty of the hideous, yet felt perfectly why
> other men shrank back or hated.
>
> To feel and love the God of Beauty and Good in
> the ugly and the evil, and still yearn in utter love
> to heal it of its ugliness and its evil, this is real
> virtue and morality.[27]

By purifying our vital and mental beings, we can enter into the Supreme Beauty and Love beyond all our mental attributes of ugliness and beauty. There is a supreme truth that transcends both.

Ugliness

Some choose not to perceive ugliness, so that it does not exist for them. This is a negative attitude that does not transform life here on Earth. A positive approach would be to reject the hideous and transform it by bringing down the power of beauty and *Ananda* into contact with what the Mother called the "deformation and the disguise, in such a way that little by little this deformation and disguise will be transformed by the influence of the Truth that is behind."[28] At another time, the Mother stated: "Our aim is not to accept these things and enjoy them, but to get rid of them and create a life of spiritual beauty and perfection. That cannot be done so long as we accept these uglinesses."[29]

Again, we must proceed in our evolutionary process as if nothing is what it appears. There is a key available to us to reveal the truth of our being, which can burst into a dazzling shower of light and beauty and joy and love. That is the key to our heart, our psychic being, which then opens us up to more possibilities.

Essence of the Cherry Tree

Through an inner identification with the vibration of a flower, the Mother was able to get an impression of its quality, which she translated into a thought. She collected these impressions, not only for numerous flowers but also for the many shades and colors of the same flower. Here the Mother is speaking about the inner essence of cherry trees:

> Thus hast thou made thyself one with the soul of the cherry-trees, and so thou canst take note that it is the Divine who makes the offering of this flower-prayer to heaven.[30]

The Mother refers below to the pattern of the psychic being in evolution, which began in plant life. This psychic or soul essence in the flower expresses itself to us as beauty:

> As soon as there is organic life, the vital element is there, and it is this vital element that gives to flowers the sense of beauty. It is not perhaps individualized in the sense we understand it, but it is a sense of the species, and the species always tries to realize it. I have noticed a first elementary psychic vibration in plant life, and truly the blossoming of a flower is the first sign of the psychic presence. The psychic individualizes itself only in man, but it existed before him; only it is not the same kind of individualization, it is more fluid and manifests as force or as consciousness rather than as individuality. Take the rose, for example; its great perfection of form, color, and smell expresses an aspiration and is a psychic gift. Look at a rose opening in the morning with the first contact of the sun—it is a magnificent self-giving aspiration.[31]

Receptivity in Flowers

We are not often receptive to the forces of higher consciousness, even those of us who pray for it. We both seek and block the response at the same time. The Mother circumvented this lack of receptivity in a roundabout fashion by means of flowers.

There are other recorded instances when she transmitted her force to someone through his or her cat. Ironically, we may be more open and loving to our pets than to the Divine. The Mother often gave flowers to disciples, one of whom asked her about the significance of this:

> *When you give us a particular flower, do you give us a chance of acquiring that quality or virtue?*

> When I give flowers, it is always along with the capacity they represent. Each one receives according to his receptivity. I can transmit a state of consciousness more easily to a flower than to a man: it is very receptive, though it does not know how to formulate its experience to itself because it lacks a mind. But the pure psychic consciousness is instinctive to it. When, therefore, you offer flowers to me, their condition is almost always an index to yours. There are persons who never succeed in bringing a fresh flower to me—even if the flower is fresh, it becomes limp in their hands. Others, however, always bring fresh flowers and even revitalize drooping ones. If your aspiration is strong, your flower-offering will be fresh. And if you are receptive, you will also be easily able to absorb the message I put in the flowers I give you. When I give them, I give you states of consciousness; the flowers are the mediums, and it all depends on your receptivity whether they are effective or not.

> *Why do you generally give red roses to men, light-colored roses to women, and different colors to the little boys and girls?*

> It is because red roses give an impression of force, and light-colored roses an impression of charm and sweetness.
> There are too many reasons for me to speak

about them. And truly speaking, there are many exceptions, according to the character of the people.[32]

Opening

When the Mother was asked the best way to open oneself to the deep influence of flowers, she replied:

> Love of flowers is a valuable help for finding and uniting with the psychic [that is, the soul].
>
> When you are receptive to the psychic vibration, that puts you in a more intimate contact with the psychic in your own self.[33]

When asked how to develop our consciousness with plants and flowers, she responded:

> First you must learn to be silent, then note carefully what happens in the consciousness.[34]

The Divine as Comforter

The Mother spoke about our personal relations with others as contrasted with our love for the Divine:

> Since we have decided to reserve love in its full splendor for our personal relation with the Divine, we shall, in our relation with others, replace it by a whole-hearted, unchanging, constant, and egoless kindness and goodwill. It will not expect any reward or gratitude or even recognition. Whatever the way others treat you, you will not allow yourself to be carried away by resentment: and in your pure unmixed love for the Divine, you will leave Him the sole judge as to how He is to protect you and defend you against the misunderstanding and bad will of others.
>
> Your joys and your pleasures you will await

from the Divine alone. In Him alone you will seek and find help and support. He will comfort you in all your pain, lead you on the path, lift you up if you stumble, and if there are moments of faintness and exhaustion, He will take you in His strong arms of love and wrap you in His soothing sweetness.[35]

Signicance of the Rose

The Mother listed the significance of the various shades of the rose as follows:

Rosa
Rose

LOVE FOR THE DIVINE
The vegetal kingdom gathers
together its most beautiful
possibilities to offer them to
the Divine.

Rosa
white roses tinged pink

AFFECTION FOR THE DIVINE
A sweet and confident
tenderness that gives itself
unfailingly to the Divine.

Rose
bicolored roses

BALANCE OF THE NATURE
IN THE LOVE FOR THE DIVINE
Passive and active, calm and

ardent, sweet and strong,
silent and expressed.[36]

Art

In shifting from natural to man-made beauty, the Mother said, "Art is nothing less in its fundamental truth than the aspect of beauty of the Divine manifestation."[37] the Mother emphasized the importance of art in becoming conscious:

> The discipline of Art has as its center the same principle as the discipline of Yoga. In both the aim is to become more and more conscious; in both you have to learn to see and feel something that is beyond the ordinary vision and feeling, to go within and bring out from there deeper things.[38]

The work of masterful artists can put us in touch with sublime beauty. Perhaps that is why we revere artists and are even in awe of the creative faculty. According to integral yogi A. B. Purani, "Thus the spiritual seeker, the poet, and the artist all seek the same Reality, and at times by very similar methods."[39]

Art is a means of expression and not an end in itself. Beauty reveals itself, depending upon our intent. For the ordinary person, the experience of beauty is quite limited. In fact, most people don't allow beauty in. We don't make space for it. If we were to concentrate on a flower or a person, we could begin to experience their inner beauty. Universal beauty is not revealed to us without aspiration and without a state of calm and stillness.

To perfectly educate the soul, one should experience art, poetry, and music. Sri Aurobindo said of this:

> Poetry raises the emotions and gives each its separate delight. Art stills the emotions and teaches them the delight of a restrained and limited satisfaction.... Music deepens the emotions and harmonizes them with each other.[40]

In the twentieth century, we were exposed to an extraordinary variety of artistic styles in art, poetry, and music—some of which were offensive to the senses of some people. The intense infusion of different modes of expression indicates preparation for a change in the world. Rollo May said that the artist has two functions:

> In the times of the creation of symbols, the function of the artist is to *create new order.* In times of excessively rigid symbols, in contrast, the function of the artist is to *create chaos.* This latter is the challenge facing modern artists. The artists are concerned with form and the breaking up of mis-used form. This is not only of the professional artist but of the artist in each of us.[41]

Chaos

Can there be any doubt that the last century was a period of chaos? However, the Mother said that chaos is a necessary function of transformation:

> O divine Master, let Thy light fall into this chaos and bring forth from it a new world. Accomplish what is now in preparation and create a new humanity which may be the perfect expression of Thy new and sublime Law.[42]

We must look beyond chaos to see what it is leading to. The Mother described the role of Sri Aurobindo in that process of transformation as follows:

> Sri Aurobindo has come to announce to the world the beauty of the future that will be realized. He has come to bring not a hope but the certainty of the splendor towards which the world is moving.
>
> The world is not an unfortunate accident; it is a miracle moving toward its expression.[43]

Real Beauty

We are at a disadvantage in the West because the importance of beauty has been hidden from us. I feel that I am just beginning to appreciate it. Think for a moment about your own response to beauty. How do you express it? Is it captivating? Does it cast a spell over you to the point where you are enthralled? A. B. Purani says this "is not the nature of the experience of pure beauty. When one feels: 'beauty liberates me, beauty raises me to the Infinite,' then he has come in contact with the real thing."[44]

We need preparation to truly experience beauty; our emotions and thoughts have to quiet down. We must become open to beauty to let it in. The more our psychic being opens, the more we experience beauty. The more we experience beauty, the more our psychic being opens.

Rollo May said that beauty saved his life after his trip up the mountain. Sri Ramakrishna, as a young boy, had a transfiguring experience when he saw a flock of white cranes flying overhead against a background of dark clouds. The beauty of the scene transfixed him, so that neighbors had to call his parents to carry him in from the field.

Once I had a tenant, Judith, who became unbearable with her incessant demands and complaints. Needless to say, we were relieved when her lease was up. A few years later, I was in a local drugstore when I heard the words, "Hi, remember me?" It was Judith. I was amazed to see in her a beauty that I hadn't seen before. She was bright and cheerful, although I soon learned that she had contracted lung cancer, which is fatal in 95 percent of the cases. She had been in remission for more than three years and had learned to let go of everything. She said that she had no assurance that the cancer would not return, but it really didn't matter that much now, because she had finally learned how to live. I never saw her again, but her transformation to a beautiful person was remarkable. As we get nearer to absolute *Ananda*, we get closer to greater joy. As John Keats wrote:

> Beauty is truth, truth beauty—that is all
> Ye know on earth, and all ye need to know.[45]

Notes

[1] Sri Aurobindo, *Birth Centenary Library*, vol. 15: *Social and Political Thought* (Pondicherry, India: Sri Aurobindo Ashram Press, 1972), p. 135.

[2] Kenneth Baker, "Book Review," *San Francisco Chronicle*, November 28, 1999.

[3] Rollo May, *My Quest for Beauty* (Dallas: Saybrook, 1985), pp. 21–22.

[4] Jeanne Korstange, "Sri Aurobindo and the Mother on Beauty," *Collaboration*, Fall 1986, p. 3.

[5] Rod MacIver, "Gordon Orions and David Abrams, On Red-Winged Blackbirds and on Beauty," *Heron Dance*, 24 (1999), 32–33.

[6] A. B. Purani, *On Art: Addresses and Writings* (Nargol, India: Nava Sarjan Society, 1965), p. 102.

[7] N. Sri Ram, "Thoughts for Aspirants," *For the Love of Life*, 12 (April 1986), 38.

[8] The Mother, *Collected Works of the Mother*, vol. 1: *Prayers and Meditations* (Pondicherry, India: Sri Aurobindo Ashram Press, 1976), p. 349.

[9] Quoted here from Purani, *On Art*, pp. 93–94.

[10] Sri Aurobindo, *Birth Centenary Library*, vol. 9: *The Future Poetry* (Pondicherry, India: Sri Aurobindo Ashram Press, 1972), p. 238.

[11] Sri Aurobindo, *Birth Centenary Library*, vol. 28: *Savitri* (Pondicherry, India: Sri Aurobindo Ashram Press, 1972), p. 346.

[12] Sri Aurobindo, *The Future Poetry*, p. 491.

[13] Sri Aurobindo, *The Future Poetry*, p. 491.

[14] Sri Aurobindo, *Birth Centenary Library*, vol. 17: *The Hour of God* (Pondicherry, India: Sri Aurobindo Ashram Press, 1972), p. 238.

[15] The Mother, *Mother's Agenda*, vol. 1: *1951–1960*, ed. by Satprem (New York: Institute for Evolutionary Research, 1979), pp. 118–119.

[16]Quoted here from Purani, *On Art*, pp. 94–95.

[17]Quoted here from Purani, *On Art*, p. 99.

[18]The Mother, *Flowers and Their Messages* (Auroville, India: Auropress Trust, 1973), p. 83.

[19]Sri Aurobindo, *Social and Political Thought*, p. 135.

[20]Anne Frank, *The Diary of a Young Girl* (New York: Doubleday, 1995), p. 281.

[21]Sri Aurobindo, *Birth Centenary Library*, vol. 19: *The Life Divine* (Pondicherry, India: Sri Aurobindo Ashram Press, 1972), pp. 1040–41.

[22]Sri Aurobindo, *The Hour of God*, p. 1.

[23]The Mother, *Words of the Mother* (Pondicherry, India: Sri Aurobindo Ashram, 1949), pp. 59–61.

[24]The Mother, "Questions and Answers on Thoughts and Aphorisms," *Bulletin of the Sri Aurobindo International Centre of Education*, August 1961, p. 109.

[25]Sri Aurobindo, *Birth Centenary Library*, vol. 5: *Collected Poems* (Pondicherry, India: Sri Aurobindo Ashram Press, 1972), p. 563.

[26]Margaret Drabble, ed., *The Oxford Companion to English Literature*, 5th ed. (New York: Oxford University Press, 1985), p. 76.

[27]Sri Aurobindo, *The Hour of God*, pp. 81, 84.

[28]The Mother, "Questions and Answers on Thoughts and Aphorisms," *Bulletin of the Sri Aurobindo International Centre of Education*, February 1961, p. 89.

[29]The Mother, "Sri Aurobindo—His Life and Work," *Bulletin of the Sri Aurobindo International Centre of Education*, August 1962, p. 103.

[30]The Mother, *Flowers*, p. ix.

[31]The Mother, *Flowers*, p. viii.

[32]The Mother, *Flowers*, p. xvii.

[33]The Mother, *Flowers*, p. xi.

[34]The Mother, *Flowers*, p. xiv.

[35]The Mother, *Flowers*, p. 164.

[36]The Mother, *Flowers*, pp. 164–165.

[37]The Mother, "Art," *Bulletin of the Sri Aurobindo International Centre of Education*, February 1961, p. 126.

[38]The Mother, "Art," p. 116.

[39]Purani, *On Art*, p. 28.

[40]Sri Aurobindo, *The Hour of God*, pp. 245–246.

[41]May, *My Quest for Beauty*, p. 161.

[42]The Mother, *Prayers and Meditations*, p. 205.

[43]The Mother, *Prayers and Meditations*, p. 205.

[44]Purani, *On Art*, p. 96.

[45]John Keats, "Ode on a Grecian Urn," in *John Keats: Complete Poems*, edited by Jack Stillinger (Cambridge: Harvard University Press, 1982), p. 283

Part
Three

13

Psychic Being
—Work in Progress

*In the soul, the individual
and the Divine are eternally
one; therefore, to find one's
soul is to find God; to identify with one's soul is to unite
with the Divine.*

—The Mother[1]

The concept and practice of living fully and simultaneously
in the external or material world and the subjective soul world
could not be more significant in our lives. Only the soul world
provides us with the very core or truth of our being. Most people
live in the objective world rather than the inner one. Of course,
the soul world always has an influence on our outer lives, but
that influence is often so filtered and diluted that its effect is a
fraction of what it could be.

Preceding each incarnation or life episode, our psychic being lays out the general lines for our life experiences, determin-

ing what we want to accomplish—that is, our mission in life. It is difficult to see this playing itself out from day to day, but in retrospect a pattern or trend is evident. However, the soul-enriching moments may be few. Here is an exercise to gain some overall perspective for your soul experiences:

✪

Sit comfortably and try to look at your life all at once—that is, gather its essence. See what images rise up in your consciousness. There will likely be only a few, even if you are a senior citizen. These are the true moments of your life, which give the most substance to your psychic being and endure eternally.

✪

Development of Psychic Being

These numinous experiences (some may be quite simple) contribute to our eternal character. It is somewhat like our childhood development, but a new luminous child is being formed internally (that is, on another level of consciousness), which will have far-reaching implications. Our psychic being draws to it people and events that will help fulfill its mission in life. The choices we make determine if we will fulfill our goals in this lifetime. It is this psychic being that survives bodily death and comes back to take a new physical body and continue its evolution.

Because most people live in the objective world, there is an imbalance between their inner and outer worlds, and that is what causes virtually 100 percent of our misery, problems, and suffering. What can we do about it without going into a monastery or into denial about life? How can we lead a full and productive life by participating in the material world while also fulfilling our inner needs?

Foundation

The external world is constantly pulling us out of our inner focus. This pull has served a purpose in the evolution of humanity to maintain the status quo, in which there is very little change in consciousness from one generation to the next. Reason has served us well in the past, but now we are ready for the next leap. We have our personal or individual evolution, but there is also evolution on a grander scale. The evolution of the mind has reached its fulfillment; it has gone about as far as it can. We are now ready in the twenty-first century to move into an overt spiritual evolution that is unprecedented on a collective basis. The realization of the psychic being is a major step in this process and serves as the foundation for further spiritual development.

Central Being

Nothing in our lives is more important than the discovery of our psychic being, and perhaps nothing is more misunderstood or neglected. The genius of Sri Aurobindo is in part due to his comprehensive vision and his synthesis of the innumerable parts of being and planes of consciousness. He provided a continuity and purpose or integrality to the evolution of consciousness. One of his fundamental concepts was what he called the "central being," which comprises the soul, the psychic being, and the *jivatman*. The soul is the unformed essence of the Divine, which life experiences shape into the psychic being. Both the soul and the psychic being are located physically behind the heart but within the subtle body. The *jivatman*, which is stationed above the head, is the immutable divine presence presiding over our soul's life episodes without participating directly in life itself. The *jivatman* projects its consciousness into our mental being, vital being, physical being, and psychic being, each of which is called in Sanskrit a *purusha*, which means a true or conscious being that is a witness and support of the forms and works of nature.

Continuity of Life

Every human being began existence as a tiny spark of the Divine. As the Mother stated:

> It begins in the mineral, it is a little more developed in the plant, and in the animal there is a first glimmer of the psychic presence.[2]

Most people misconceive what the soul really is, confusing it with the vital being, which rules most people's intense contacts with events, things, and other people. We may say that a certain individual has "soul," by which we mean a passion for life, but this is characteristic of the vital being, not the psychic being. The vital vibration is more easily perceived than the vibration of the soul. Nevertheless, it is possible for one to have an intense vibration of the soul and virtually no vital vibration. As the Mother said:

> Some people are full of a very pure, very high, very selfless psychic love, and yet they know nothing about it and think they are cold, dry, and without love because this admixture of vital vibration is absent. For them love begins and ends with this vibration.[3]

When the psychic being matures to a fully individualized state, the qualities inherent in it are released and can become fully operational in our daily lives. Although the soul's influence is always active, its action is slow and diluted when it is hidden.

Qualities of the Soul

I divide the qualities of the soul into seven categories. The first is a feeling of joy and happiness that spontaneously emanates from our being and at times even moves us to tears of joy— as, for example, when we see a baby. This joy is an expression of what Sri Aurobindo calls the "delight-soul in the universe."[4]

Second, co-existing with this joy, is love, even divine love, because through our soul we have identified with the divine consciousness. This love, which flows spontaneously, is not demanding and does not insist upon a response.

Third, this love is unselfish and generous. We give freely of ourselves for the divine work in the world. We have compassion for all life and express our gratitude for our relationship with the Divine. Compassion and gratitude manifest when the psychic being is active in life.

Fourth, along with the joy and love inherent in *Ananda* (bliss) is beauty and the nobility of life. The expression of this beauty and nobility is quiet—not demonstrative, as it can be in the expression of the vital. The psychic being is rich in substance and has a full sweetness, but is not cloying.

Fifth, the emergence of the psychic being gives us a calm and peace as well as a kind of inner freedom. We do not feel constricted and boxed in. We are better able to face difficulties with this inner knowledge, which enables us not to be troubled.

Sixth, this true knowledge, often experienced initially as light, gives us a feeling of Oneness and connectedness with all life forms. We feel as if we have lived for an eternity. We develop an intuitive knowledge that cannot give reasons for knowing, but all the same we know.

Seventh, the soul exhibits qualities of sincerity, perseverance, will, and strength. Our purification or cleansing leading up to the emergence of the psychic being allows sincerity in our actions. We develop a capacity to endure all hardships.

Becoming Conscious

About uniting with our soul, the Mother said:

> If one is able to consciously unite with one's psychic being, one can always be in this state of receptivity, inner joy, energy, progress, communion with the divine Presence. And when one is in communion with That, one sees it everywhere, in everything, and all things take on their true meaning.[5]

Critical Emergence

At the critical moment one's psychic being rushes forth with an explosive, illuminating and dazzling light. The Mother said the psychic experience invariably occurs in this manner. She had never seen any one have a gradual emergence.

This emergence or "bringing forth the psychic being" as Sri Aurobindo called it is a transfiguring experience. One has a reversal of consciousness where life is never the same again, that is, one has touched the Divine.

Liberation

When one has made definitive contact with the psychic being, one is liberated and can choose whether or not to be born again. A decisive moment in one's evolution has been reached. As the Mother said:

> When one enters consciously into contact with one's soul and the union is established, it is over, it can no longer be undone, it is something permanent, constant, which resists everything, and which, at any moment, if referred to, can be found.[6]

Progress can only be made here on Earth, for, as the Mother stated, "it is only upon Earth that you will find the psychic being. The rest of the universe is formed in quite a different way."[7] There may, however, be a type of passive progress made in the afterlife, but it is merely remedial, cleaning up loose ends or fulfilling what was not accomplished in the prior life—as in the case of my late brother Don, whom Surama saw composing music to complete his previous incarnation.

The individuation of our psychic being has a greater significance than just our personal development or release. As the Mother said:

> It is only upon Earth that the psychic life begins, and it is just the process by which the Divine has

awakened material life to the necessity of rejoin-
ing its divine origin.[8]

The Search

Sri Aurobindo said that there are a thousand ways to reach
the Divine. Each approach has its own experiences and ramifi-
cations. Often the search begins with unrest, dissatisfaction, and
an emptiness that nothing seems to assuage. Then we may meet
someone, or read a book, or hear a talk that puts us on a new
track. One thing leads to another, and we have a breakthrough.

The Godhead

In my own case, I found a new track in my spiritual path in
1969. When I first went to India in 1973 and had an illumination
of my soul, I spontaneously thought of the Mother because my
consciousness was already turned toward her. I know of another
devotee in India who had a soul-encounter with Krishna. A Christian mystic would likely have a similar experience with Jesus.
God actually has no name, but we identify with him or her, depending on our religious or spiritual persuasion. The various
spiritual personalities merge into one Godhead, just as all the
divine qualities—including love, knowledge, power, joy and
peace—are fundamentally one. The division is necessary for the
play in our own evolution. The antithesis of what the spiritual
figure represents comes into being when we make that figure
exclusive to our belief and deny the validity of other beliefs. If
we wish to avoid speaking from a divided consciousness, we
can impose no limitations on how the Godhead can represent
itself.

On this point, there is an instructive story about Ramakrishna
and one of his disciples. One day, a Christian was preaching about
Christ from the steps of a temple in India. Ramakrishna's disciple publicly berated the Christian for this blasphemy and later
proudly told Ramakrishna what he had done. Ramakrishna was
furious and ordered the disciple never to do that again. "Don't
you know," he said, "it was I who was speaking through the
Christian?"

Avatars

Sri Aurobindo believed that avatars come at critical moments in history to fulfill specific missions. Ramakrishna, for example, synthesized most of the religious approaches to the Divine in Hinduism, Islam, and Christianity through his own inner practice. After him, the next stage of evolution was ready to commence. Sri Aurobindo and the Mother's mission was to take the evolution of consciousness to the next level—the Supermind or Supramental Consciousness. The first major goal in this process is to realize the psychic being, which becomes the foundation for the next stage of the transformation. While this is the preferred sequence, the spiritual process may proceed differently. Realization of the Divine through the psychic being is regarded, however, as the safest method of transformation.

Some years ago, there was an authority on nutrition by the name of Paavo Airola, who conceived an "optimum diet." That is, people who wanted to achieve optimum health would have to follow his diet completely. On the other hand, individuals who scaled back on the diet would still receive benefits, but not as much.

A Global Action

The complete spiritual path relating to a divine life on Earth is not for everyone, especially the path proposed by Sri Aurobindo and the Mother. But, like it or not, the new consciousness is having a universal impact because a global spiritual consciousness has manifested. The effect on each individual will depend on that person's receptivity to the force at work now, whether or not he or she practices a spiritual discipline. The new consciousness is bringing startling changes on an individual and global level. We are at the point where no one is immune from the Supramental force. We can progress with relative ease if we aspire to union with the Divine and surrender to it. This presupposes that we make a conscious effort to unite with the psychic being. This then becomes our spiritual discipline, which is known in India as yoga. Integral Yoga is not a religion, nor does it have rituals, dogmas, or gurus. I believe that even agnostics and atheists can practice the Yoga of Transformation if they have a sincere aspiration to find the truth of their being and are receptive to that realization.

All Created Equal

Now is the moment of truth. The deciding factor in our divine realization is our sincerity to find that truth and act upon it. Brushed aside, in this personal endeavor of union with the Divine, are all issues of race, gender, age, religion, intelligence, wealth, power, and success. That is, everyone is now on an equal footing. It is the essence of being created equal. We are at once alone, but only in appearance, and with the opportunity to be one with all beings and planes of existence in the march toward transformation of matter.

Importance of Intention

How do we accomplish this transformation? Many, if not most, people are perplexed when they take up this path of self-knowing. Each individual is unique and finds his or her own way, which is the utmost test of sincerity. There is no entrance exam. All it takes is a simple aspiration. The Divine is waiting for our response, knows our every thought, feeling, and act, and is closer to us than we can possibly imagine. We can concentrate on our heart area and aspire for that tiny flame there to grow and consume our nature. We can offer or surrender all of our thoughts, feelings, and acts to the Divine. We can start with a few minutes of concentration in the morning and evening. Our intention means everything, and the Divine is waiting for the slightest opening for us to give our consent. But the necessity of our consent has been augmented by the advent of the Supramental on a global scale. Our psychic being will guide us if we ask.

Simplicity

The process is so simple that people cannot believe it. Our minds want to complicate everything. The path becomes difficult because of all the baggage we bring with us. It helps enormously to speed up the process if we have done some work of purification so that we have a reasonable measure of quiet in our minds and emotions. If we are disturbed by so many conflicting thoughts and feelings that we cannot sit quietly and feel peace and equanimity for twenty minutes, then we have an indication of the work we need to do. The point of our suffering indicates the point of our weakness. On the other hand, if we have been successful in life, by whatever terms we care to measure that, and are content and self-satisfied, we are likely never to begin the search. Many, after reaching that level of apparent success, still feel empty and unfulfilled and wonder why. That is a good start in the quest, for there are innumerable ways that we glaze over our feelings of separation and the underlying sense of feeling unfulfilled.

Education

Our education as young children is woefully inadequate. We can help our children immeasurably by being alert to their inner process and creating an environment that facilitates their inner growth. The Mother wrote about this:

> Even a fleeting idea in a child, at a certain moment in its childhood when the psychic being is most in front, if it succeeds in penetrating through the outer consciousness and giving the child just an impression of something beautiful which must be realized, it creates a little nucleus, and upon this you build your action.[9]

Sooner or later, we all must build our nucleus, which means we must become conscious of our divine spark within and build upon that. It is not a process for which we need training, but rather evolves from our life experiences. We can accelerate the process by concentrating on the heart center. This involves rejecting everything that is not conducive to our growth. If we listen carefully to our psychic being, it will give an indication of what to do. It will guide us if we let it, but some people choose to ignore it. Again, one requires a measure of sincerity.

Feeding the Inner Flame

Here is one guided-imagery exercise that I have found helpful:

❖

Sit comfortably with your eyes closed and visualize a small flame in your heart area (just behind
the physical heart). You can also imagine the
flame, feel it, sense it, or just know it's there. Put
your thoughts, one by one, into the flame as you
would put paper into a fire. Each time you put a
thought into the flame, it will grow higher and
higher. After a couple of minutes, begin putting
your feelings and emotions into the flame with
whatever comes to mind. Each time the flame
grows higher towards the top of your head. Then
put any feelings or sensations from your body,
any discomforts, or illness into the flame. See if
you can get the flame to go up and out the top of
your head. Become quiet and quietly observe for
a few minutes. This is an exercise in purification
and aspiration.

Now let the aspiration go and just sit quietly
in a receptive manner. Visualize yourself as an
open book with blank pages, letting light, love,
power, and peace descend into you. This is an
exercise in surrender. It is very passive and the
complement of aspiration.

❖

Aspiration—Surrender

If we aspire all of the time, there is no room to be receptive.
Conversely, if we are in a passive and surrender mode all the
time, there is no fire, no spark. We become inert. Of the two
modes, spiritual seekers are more likely to be passive than to
aspire. A balance is needed between the two until they ultimately
become one. Like any of our learning endeavors, this is a progressive practice. Anyone who is interested in spiritual growth
has some spark of aspiration. To become more conscious, whether
by yoga or some other practice or discipline, is to fan the flame
and accelerate our growth so that we can do in a few months or

years what usually takes several lifetimes. The key is the intensity of our aspiration.

One of the best accounts on aspiration concerns Ramakrishna, who said that our aspiration must become like a drowning person gasping for air. Of course, he was exceptional, but we can learn something from his example because he practiced what he preached.

In this active-passive attitude, first we aspire or grasp for some unknown inspiration, and then we switch and receive. This is very much akin to the creative process. When we are trying to solve a problem, remember a name, or become inspired to write, we are aspiring. In ordinary life, it often happens that we receive answers to our questions while we are asleep or in some other passive and receptive mood when we have stopped thinking about the issues. Friedrich Nietzsche said about this process:

> Something profoundly convulsive and disturbing suddenly becomes visible and audible with indescribable definiteness and exactness. One hears—one does not seek…. There is an ecstasy whose terrific tension is sometimes released by a flood of tears, during which one's progress varies from involuntary impetuosity to involuntary slowness…. Everything occurs quite without volition, as if in an eruption of freedom, independence, power, and divinity.[10]

Another practice of self-discovery is to offer our work to the Divine. The offering can be quite ordinary, even some kind of housework or other mundane task. In our spiritual quest, the offering can be an attitude toward, a thought about, or remembrance of the Divine.

Creativity, Art and Yoga

According to many artists, the creative act is not a mental phenomenon but rather something that occurs through work itself. Selden Rodman, a poet, states:

> I've talked to many great painters, as well as po-
> ets, who say that their greatest works are as a re-
> sult of working, not as a result of anything of
> which they had a complete vision to begin with,
> or even more than just the germ of an idea.[11]

With some artists, work is a compulsion. They must literally work to maintain their sanity. Robert Engman, a sculptor, says of his creative work:

> I have to keep working. Vacations are not good
> for me. I take my family on vacations, but I have
> to work just the same. The place has changed,
> that's all. Whenever I don't work with consis-
> tency, I'm impossible to live with. I'm not kind to
> my family. I get wrapped up in all sorts of com-
> plications…. When I work I'm straight. When I
> get distracted I start to question everything. I
> don't know how my inspiration is triggered. All
> I know is that I have to hammer away at it all the
> time for a good portion of each day.[12]

Although Engman's attitude may be extreme, his emphasis on work has its place. However, the ideal state is to be at peace with oneself, whether or not one is working.

Arthur Koestler, penetrating thinker and author, equated creativity with a mental act in a way that resembles our attempts to merge with the truth of our being:

> The creative act, by connecting previously unre-
> lated dimensions of experience, enables [one] to
> attain to a higher level of mental evolution. It
> is an act of liberation—the defeat of habit by
> originality.[13]

Henry Miller, the novelist, described the surrender or abandonment of the will in the creative process:

> One gets nearer to the heart of truth, which I suppose is the ultimate aim of the writer, in the measure that he ceases to struggle, in the measure that he abandons the will. The great writer is the very symbol of life, of the non-perfect. He moves effortlessly, giving the illusion of perfection, from some unknown center which is certainly not the brain center but which is definitely a center, a center connected with the rhythm of the whole universe and consequently as sound, solid, unshakable, as durable, defiant, anarchic, purposeless, as the universe itself. Art teaches nothing, except the significance of life. The great work must inevitably be obscure, except to the very few, to those who, like the author himself, are initiated into the mysteries.[14]

James Joyce, the great Irish writer, caught the essence of the formation of the psychic being:

> Welcome, O life! I go to encounter for the millionth time the reality of experience and to forge in the smithy of my soul the uncreated conscience of my race.[15]

Life as Art

In talking about the soul, one is invariably faced with the overriding perplexity of life and our need to be creative. A dancer from India named Shanta Gandhi once said to Studs Terkel, the writer, as she thought about starvation in Bangladesh: "I'm afraid that art is very, very pale company compared to real life sometimes. Very pale indeed." To this, Terkel later commented that perhaps life *is* an art form.[16] What makes life an art form is that the psychic being is created from life. It is each individual's supreme creation molded out of the essence of life itself.

We reach a silence in our being when we have integrated aspiration and surrender into a natural flow. At that point, there is simultaneously movement and no movement. This paradox is a great mystery, reminding one of the parts of the atom, which at one moment are particles and at another moment are waves, neither of which are predictable.

Necessity of Silence

T. V. Kapali Sastry, an integral yogi, said that silence is behind everything and serves to prepare the necessary opening to the Lord:

> Man awakens to deeper strata of being where there is a happy silence, where he begins to feel that there is his true centre. And in the silent chamber of the heart he discovers that flame of aspiration towards the Divine which has been so long lying latent, slumbering, but now, under conditions more congenial to its rise, has got well-kindled, awakened, and leaps up to a growing flame. Silence in the mind and life-parts is the most indispensable condition for this flame to be increasingly active. The flame is smothered in its enveloping smoke of desires, passions, and restless movements.[17]

Difficulties

To establish the inner silence, we must first encounter the obstacles and conflicts within. Each negativity is a means for growth, representing a positive potential that must be expressed. The Mother remarked about difficulties:

> The nature of your difficulty indicates the nature of the victory you will gain, the victory you will exemplify in Yoga. Thus, if there is persistent selfishness, it points to a realization of universality as your most prominent achievement in the fu-

ture. And, when selfishness is there, you have also the power to reverse this difficulty into its opposite, a victory of utter wideness.

When you have something to realize, you will have in you just the characteristic which is the contradiction of that something. Face to face with the defect, the difficulty, you say, "Oh, I am like that! How awful it is!" But you ought to see the truth of the situation. Say to yourself, "My difficulty shows me clearly what I have ultimately to represent. To reach the absolute negation of it, the quality at the other pole—this is my mission."

Even in ordinary life, we have sometimes the experience of contraries. He who is very timid and has no courage in front of circumstances proves capable of bearing the most!

To one who has the aspiration for the Divine, the difficulty which is always before him is the door by which he will attain God in his own individual manner: it is his particular path towards the Divine Realization.

There is also the fact that if somebody has a hundred difficulties, it means he will have a tremendous realization—provided, of course, there are in him patience and endurance and he keeps the aspiring flame of Agni burning against these defects.

And remember: the Grace of the Divine is generally proportioned to your difficulties.[18]

Creating From the Essence

We are indeed created in the image of God, but it is an evolving image. We start as a tiny spark and grow over numerous lifetimes into a glorious, luminous being. It is possible to see this new being in an inner vision. It is utterly magnificent, but also different for each person when fully formed. In this sense, we are all artists and can create the most beautiful works of art possible. We are all created equal with the divine essence, but it is up to us to develop and mold that essence through our experiences in life that give it its uniqueness.

Reorganization

The creative act continues even after the psychic being comes forward, which is first initiated through our own effort, but ultimately emerges by grace. The dysfunctional family of mental, vital, and physical beings, each acting independently, is gradually brought under direct guidance by the radiance of the emerged psychic being—that is, the psychic being can now begin to realize its true function by organizing or unifying these three beings around itself.

Empowered by the Gods

For some aspirants at a certain advanced stage, the psychic being can be widened or empowered to reach a complete value. There are beings (called Gods) in the farthest reaches of consciousness (called Overmind by Sri Aurobindo) who can merge with the formed psychic being. This gives a wider consciousness and a grander scope and knowledge to the psychic being. The gross physical body of the transformed individual will often appear much larger than its physical being to persons who are perceptive enough. People can then receive benefits from the enhanced psychic being just from its presence.

Facilitation

The significant illumination or the psychic change of one's being can be facilitated by a Supramental Consciousness that proceeds through the soles of one's feet upward through the body (actually the subtle body) and out the top of the head. The light then reverses and courses down through the body. This process is considered highly beneficial, since it allows the recipient to resume activities quickly rather than be bedridden for several days in order to assimilate and recuperate. For continued work in the world this assumes that the psychic being wants to continue to carry on the divine work, and the person has given his or her consent. The Mother said that nine out of ten integral yogis choose to return for the work.

This action of the divine light establishes a constant connection between the "head" and "heart," or mind and psychic being. The "head" has been opened to receive the direct influence of the *jivatman*, and one can automatically communicate nonverbally with others from either the "head" or the "heart."

Three Approaches

All of this may sound like a Herculean effort, and it *is*, but there is a divine will and intelligence that oversees and completes the work for us. Initially, the aspirant has to make some effort and consent and surrender to the divine will. No special esoteric or occult knowledge is required. However, occult knowledge can facilitate the process, and intellectual effort can give precision to it. But the indispensable way to achieve transformation is through the spiritual approach, which includes aspiration and surrender.

The fire of aspiration in the center of our being is the result of a divine force working through it. This force is also, as Sri Aurobindo says, "the fire of aspiration, purification, and Tapasya [spiritual effort] which comes from the psychic being. It is not the psychic being, but a power of the psychic being."[19] Each of us has the potential to become conscious of this fire, thereby setting it into action by conscious aspiration.

Spiritual Approach

The spiritual approach to transformation makes one open to supreme love, consciousness, and power. This identification, according to the Mother, makes all the cells in one's body capable of receiving and expressing the Supramental Consciousness.

Occult and Intellectual Approach

The occult approach to transformation brings in the detailed knowledge of all the powers and personalities in the intermediary worlds, where the gods in the Overmind can descend into the receptive psychic being. The intellectual approach to transformation reduces approximation and gives a more detailed procedure and a more direct and precise action. As Sri Aurobindo said, "I think I can say I have been testing day and night for years upon years more scrupulously than any scientist his theory or his method on the physical plane."[20]

In correspondence in 1935 with Nirodbaran, one of his disciples, Sri Aurobindo said, "Now I have got the hang of the whole hanged thing—like a very Einstein, I have got the mathematical formula of the whole affair (unintelligible as in his own case to anyone but myself) and am working it out figure by figure."[21]

No Special Training Needed

Anyone can go through this process without special training or spiritual knowledge if one has sufficient aspiration and receptivity. The Bhagavad Gita states, "As men approach Me, so I accept them to my love; men follow in every way my path."[22]

Our lengthy evolution over countless lives reaches its first climax or realization with the emergence of our center of truth, the psychic being. This is achieved in part by meditation and prayer through a purification and concentration of our life by faith, sincerity, aspiration, surrender, and rejection of impure thoughts, feelings, and acts. The psychic being comes forward by grace, and our inmost soul has a direct and transforming influence and guidance in our life.

Unification

Our lower or outer nature of mental, vital, and physical beings becomes unified over a period of time around the psychic being through its radiating influence. Our inner and outer beings are in harmony, and this aspect of our new creation is complete to the extent that we can continue our journey of the soul if we so choose. Some psychic beings may reach further completion by merging with a descent of an Overmind being or godhead that brings a wider consciousness and greater power. This enhanced psychic being serves as a sort of relay station to others on the spiritual path and can send emanations to them.

The poet saint-ramprasad implores us:

O my man, you do not know how to till!
If you knew! Oh, you have such a piece of land—
This human life of yours!
You could have reaped gold from it.[23]

Notes

[1]The Mother, *Collected Works of the Mother*, vol. 16: *Some Answers from the Mother* (Pondicherry, India: Sri Aurobindo Ashram Press, 1976), p. 229.

[2]The Mother, *Collected Works of the Mother*, vol. 4: *Questions and Answers, 1950–1951* (Pondicherry, India: Sri Aurobindo Ashram Press, 1976), p. 143.

[3]The Mother, *Collected Works of the Mother*, vol. 15: *Words of the Mother* (Pondicherry, India: Sri Aurobindo Ashram Press, 1976), p. 345.

[4]Sri Aurobindo, *Birth Centenary Library*, vol. 21: *Synthesis of Yoga* (Pondicherry, India: Sri Aurobindo Ashram Press, 1972), p. 708.

[5]The Mother, *Collected Works of the Mother*, vol. 8: *Questions and Answers, 1956* (Pondicherry, India: Sri Aurobindo Ashram Press, 1976), pp. 305–306.

[6]The Mother, *Collected Works of the Mother*, vol. 7: *Questions and Answers, 1955* (Pondicherry, India: Sri Aurobindo Ashram Press, 1976), p. 264.

[7]The Mother, *Questions and Answers, 1950–1951*, p. 164.

[8]The Mother, *Questions and Answers, 1950–1951*, p. 164.

[9]The Mother, *Questions and Answers, 1950–1951*, p. 255.

[10]Friedrich Nietzsche, "Composition of *Thus Spake Zarathustra*," in *The Creative Process: A Symposium*, edited by Brewster Ghiselin (New York: Mentor, 1952), p. 202.

[11]Selden Rodman, "Poetry," in *The Creative Experience*, edited by Stanley Rosner and Lawrence E. Abt (New York: Dell, 1970), p. 327.

[12]Robert Engman, "Sculpture," in *The Creative Experience*, edited by Stanley Rosner and Lawrence E. Abt (New York: Dell, 1970), p. 351.

[13]Arthur Koestler, *The Act of Creation: A Study of the Conscious and Unconscious in Science and Art* (New York: Dell, 1964), p. 96.

[14]Henry Miller, "Reflections on Writing," in *The Creative Process: A Symposium*, edited by Brewster Ghiselin (New York: Mentor, 1952), p. 181.

[15]James Joyce, *A Portrait of the Artist as a Young Man* (New York: Viking, 1963), p. 253.

[16]Studs Terkel, "Interview," *San Francisco Chronicle*, May 29, 1977.

[17]T. V. Kapali Sastry, *Sadhana* (Pondicherry, India: Dipti Publications, 1976), p. 20.

[18]The Mother, *Collected Works of the Mother*, vol. 3: *Questions and Answers* (Pondicherry, India: Sri Aurobindo Ashram Press, 1976), p. 143.

[19]Sri Aurobindo, *Birth Centenary Library*, vol. 24: *Letters on Yoga* (Pondicherry, India: Sri Aurobindo Ashram Press, 1972), p. 1120.

[20]Sri Aurobindo, *Birth Centenary Library*, vol. 26: *On Himself* (Pondicherry, India: Sri Aurobindo Ashram Press, 1972), p. 469.

[21]Kireet Joshi, *Sri Aurobindo and the Mother: Glimpses of their Experiments, Experiences, and Realisations* (Delhi: The Mother's Institute of Research, 1996), p. 89.

[22]Maheshwar, ed., *Bhagavad Gita in the Light of Sri Aurobindo* (Pondicherry, India: Sri Aurobindo Ashram Trust, 1985), p. 66.

[23]Nolini Kanta Gupta, *Collected Works*, vol. 6: *Sweet Mother* (Calcutta: Nolini Kanta Gupta Birth Centenary Celebrations Committee, 1989), p. 251.

14

The Microcosm

My own life and my Yoga have always been, since my coming to India, both this-worldly and other-worldly, without any exclusiveness on either side.

—*Sri Aurobindo*[1]

I believe I first heard about the "real world" when I was in college. "When you get out in the *real world*," said the professors, "it won't be book stuff anymore. It will be the way things *really* work."

When I was in army basic training at Camp Chaffee, Arkansas, in 1954, and later, when I was serving in Alaska, the *real world* phrase came up often. But the "real world" was always *somewhere else*. What were these other compartments of life that were the "real world"?

I discovered later that this "real world" is about money, power, work, and making a living. This world is actually a good training ground, because it teaches us to be realistic. If my ideas don't work, or if my business is losing money, I won't continue in the same vein if I have any sense.

The Mother liked her materialistic upbringing. It gave her a foundation that she felt was absolutely essential for later delving into other levels of reality without going off into flights of fancy.

Our Perception Is an Illusion

For most of us, reality consists of what we can experience through the senses. We think of everything else as supernatural stuff with no basis in reality. Science has proved that our perception of matter is an illusion (Maya), for matter is mostly 99% space with the appearance of solidity created by the rapid movement of atoms and subatomic particles. At the age of fourteen, when the Mother first heard this scientific pronouncement, she said, "If it's like that, then nothing is true!"[2]

Scientists continue to search for the origin of reality in subatomic particles. But how can one quantify pure consciousness? Nevertheless, science has made great inroads into the inner nature of reality through quantum mechanics. Most scientists are not concerned with consciousness per se. Sri Aurobindo and the Mother, on the other hand, explored the true nature of matter from the standpoint of yoga and consciousness.

What Is Real?

Matter, energy, and consciousness are inseparably intertwined. If one is present, the others are, too. Buddha reached the same conclusions as the 14-year-old Mother. Nothing is real, he stated, until you return to the source (Brahman, Being, etc.). Every manifestation on Earth, he argued, is an illusion because of its impermanence.

The Divine Is in Matter

Sri Aurobindo disagreed with Buddha's argument, contending that this was only one side of the equation. "Nothing can evolve out of matter," he stated, "which is not therein already contained."[3] To state the case another way: Reality is contained in matter, in the atom, and is not finished in its manifestation. The Divine has yet to reveal itself in matter. This is a supreme challenge to Buddha's philosophy, because Buddha believed that the ultimate was not to be found in matter but in Nirvana, the transcendence of matter. Sri Aurobindo argued that the transcendent or causal may be more fundamental but not less real than matter, which contains life, mind, and Supermind. He found divinity on all levels of existence:

> I found myself entering supraphysical worlds and planes with influences and an effect from them upon the material plane, so I could make no sharp divorce or irreconcilable opposition between what I have called the two ends of existence and all that lies between them. For me all is Brahman, and I find the Divine everywhere. Everyone has the right to throw away this-worldliness and choose other-worldliness only, and if he finds peace by that choice he is greatly blessed. I, personally, have not found it necessary to do this in order to have peace. In my Yoga also, I found myself moved to include both worlds in my purview—the spiritual and the material—and to try to establish the Divine Consciousness and the Divine Power in men's hearts and earthly life, not for a personal salvation only, but for a life divine here.[4]

This thought that the Divine is within matter lay at the core of Sri Aurobindo and the Mother's philosophy and their endeavor to bring Supermind to a living reality. The Mother spent the last twenty-three years of her life manifesting this new consciousness in her own body, as is chronicled in *Mother's Agenda*.[5]

At the Core of Matter

A group of Sri Aurobindo devotees met in Chicago in July 1993 at the Parliament of World Religions. After an inspired meeting one day, we decided to meet again in Baca, Colorado, in

October, at the Savitri Learning Center to see if we could make
some headway in this New Consciousness in a group or collective setting. Without any set program, we began by sitting in a
circle and focusing on what consciousness meant to us. The experiences each of us had were indeed indicative of some greater
force at work. Later, as we were meditating, I had the following
experience, which I described in my diary:

> I had gotten into a good meditative state and
> seemed to be in an extremely pleasant and sus-
> pended space. I then saw a round figure like a
> ball or sphere that had several spinning or whirl-
> ing lines going around it at an extremely rapid
> rate. Suddenly, I moved into this "ball," into its
> center. After entering, I had a momentary sensa-
> tion of moving backwards. I became absolutely
> still. I realized that my consciousness had been
> moving in meditation, but I hadn't consciously
> realized it. We are always in a consciousness that
> is moving while we're in the manifestation. I was
> now in this utter stillness without movement, but
> at the same time with a sense of incredibly rapid
> vibration. It was not really a vibration of move-
> ment but of Being itself, as though it were the
> original creative force. I *became* that consciousness.
> There was a tremendous sense of joy and free-
> dom that stayed with me the rest of the day.

The Atom

I felt as if I were inside an atom—inside the whirling and
spinning that Fritjof Capra describes from outside the atom:

> Quantum theory has shown that all these aston-
> ishing properties of atoms arise from the wave
> nature of their electrons. To begin with, the solid
> aspect of matter is the consequence of a typical
> "quantum effect" connected with the dual wave/
> particle aspect of matter, a feature of the sub-
> atomic world which has no macroscopic ana-

logue. Whenever a particle is confined to a small region of space, it reacts to this confinement by moving around, and the smaller the region of confinement is, the faster the particle moves around in it. In the atom, now, there are two competing forces. On the one hand, the electrons are bound to the nucleus by electric forces which try to keep them as close as possible. On the other hand, they respond to their confinement by whirling around, and the tighter they are bound to the nucleus, the higher their velocity will be; in fact, the confinement of electrons in an atom results in enormous velocities of about 600 miles per second! These high velocities make the atom appear as a rigid sphere, just as a fast-rotating propeller appears as a disc. It is very difficult to compress atoms any further, and thus they give matter its familiar solid aspect.[6]

Was I experiencing the Supramental Consciousness in the atom? The relativity of inside and outside is beautifully described in Verse 5 of the *Isha Upanishad*:

> That moves and That moves not;
> That is far and the same is near;
> That is within all this, and That also is
> outside all this.[7]

Sri Aurobindo commented on the single truth of existence:

> The rooted and fundamental concept of Vedanta is that there exists somewhere, could we but find it, available to experience of self-revelation, if denied to intellectual research, a single truth comprehensive and universal in the light of which the whole of existence would stand revealed and explained both in its nature and its end. This universal existence, for all its multitude of objects and its diversity of forces, is one in substance and ori-

gin; and there is an unknown quality, X or Brahman, to which it can be reduced, for from that it started and by that it still exists. This unknown quality is called Brahman.[8]

In Indian philosophy, Brahman (not to be confused with the Indian caste system) is the unknowable, the one without a second. It manifests as the Supermind or the Supramental Consciousness that brings the timeless and spaceless into time and space. This is the "real world" for Sri Aurobindo and the Mother. In this world, there is no liberation into Nirvana; ultimately, bodily death will be annulled.

Importance of Matter

Various spiritual-philosophical systems in India have evolved over the centuries based on the wisdom of the Veda, including the Upanishads, which are the true authority and source of the Vedanta philosophy. However, there have been different interpretations of the Upanishads, because of the many approaches to the Truth. None, however, gives any divine fulfillment to life on Earth except for veiled references. Indeed, before Sri Aurobindo, there was no reason to believe that the Divine could be realized in matter. Sri Aurobindo expanded on the truths of other schools and systems of thought, stating that there is a certain stage that one reaches where life on Earth seems like an illusion, as though it were not quite real, but that this is only a stage, and one can go higher.

Samadhi

The traditional yogic goal is to go into a trance state known as *samadhi*, in which there is no awareness of body or surroundings. Some yogis can become so immersed in their trance that they will not feel a hot coal placed on their skin, even though it may burn a hole in their flesh. When they come to conscious awareness from this state of ecstasy, usually hours or even days later, they cannot maintain the same level of intensity. Although they have a strong sense of reflected joy and inner well-being, this is not associated with life here on Earth. The source is somewhere else, perhaps extraterrestrial, and Earth is simply a docking station for future journeys into space.

The various major philosophical schools in India, including Buddhism, are profound, but they do not get to the heart of the matter. They do not give any significance to the global transformation of the planet. For that matter, neither does Christianity. The purpose of the descent of the Supramental Force—and the emergence of its latent power and consciousness—is to bridge this gap between Heaven and Earth. This was the mission of Sri Aurobindo and the Mother, and it is my purpose in writing this book: to show that the process is ongoing and will not stop until it is completed. (Actually, this is only the next stage in evolution, since there is no end to it.) Sri Aurobindo said the transformation was inevitable but that the how and when remained to be worked out. The Mother continued the work in her body, and we will see later what that means to us.

Mysticism

All religions have a mystical branch, or else the mysticism is incorporated into the core of the religion itself. In Hinduism, mysticism is usually implicit in the religion itself. If one has a calling, he or she will find a guru and become a disciple. Islam has its Sufis, and Christianity has its mystical branches, as does Judaism. Mysticism is nothing other than a direct experience of God. This is the intent of yoga. The experience of God will be the result of the path taken. For example, one can approach God through knowledge (*jnana*), or through love (*bhakti*), or through the will or actions (*karma*), or though service to humankind (*seva*). Integral Yoga embraces all these approaches to the Supreme in order to have an integrated being for the transformation. Personal inner experience is paramount for knowing the source. Without it we are constantly relying on our rational mind for interpretation, and that is not transforming. Scripture can only point the way.

Sat—Chit—Ananda

In Vedanta, the Supreme Consciousness or Brahman is described as *Sachchidananda*. Sanskrit is incredibly rich in philosophical and spiritual terms and has an astounding depth. Words or terms are often combined to create new concepts. In this case, *Sat* is pure existence; *chit* is pure consciousness; and *ananda* is pure bliss or joy. Thus, *Sachchidananda* is pure existence, pure consciousness, and pure bliss all rolled into one.

Sri Aurobindo added another term to *chit* called *shakti*, to create *chit-shakti*. *Shakti* (or *Sakti*) is the Divine Mother or the Mother power as worshipped in the Universal Energy made individual as a Goddess of many names and aspects. That is, *chit-shakti* is the creative force of the universe. Absolute consciousness is in its nature absolute power.

After I returned from my first trip to India in 1974, I had lost my exclusively rational way of experiencing life. There is a tremendous difference between knowing intellectually and knowing with the heart. Some have described it as "thinking with the heart," a phrase indecipherable by a rational mind. Once one has made this shift, the rational or Western approach seems very dry and impersonal. Even if one has a charismatic personality, there is still dryness. The soul is missing. Many Indians have an innate sense of this living spirituality.

Head and the Heart

The integration of the head/mind and heart/soul can happen. I discovered this in 1985 at a conference in Ashland, Oregon, a beautiful city in the southern part of the state that is famous for its Shakespearean theater company. At that time, I had done very little public speaking and developed a great deal of anxiety over a presentation I had to give. At the last minute, the night before the talk, I decided to write it out, which I had never done before. After that, I had a vision of the Mother sending Force to her children. That gave me some solace. My talk was about Sri Aurobindo, the Mother, and Integral Yoga, with a few quotes from Shakespeare's plays thrown in. It was probably the most awkward and uncomfortable thing I have ever done. As I spoke, I got extremely hot, and no matter how much water I drank, my mouth and throat were as dry as sand. I could not wait to finish, and afterwards I vowed never to speak in public again.

Then the audience split up into eight or nine discussion groups. After a while, they came back together, and one person from each group reported what that group had discussed. "When we convened," said one, "there was utter silence. No one could speak." Another one got up and said the same thing. Then it turned out, to my amazement, that *all* the groups had had the same experience. The next day, nine or ten people came up to me at different times. They were all beaming as they expressed the deep impact that my talk had had on them. One young woman said: "When you first began speaking, I had no idea what you were talking about. Then I closed my eyes and just sat quietly, and all of a sudden everything became perfectly clear. I not only understood you with my mind, but I also felt you in my heart."

I was as amazed and bewildered as everyone else. I knew for certain that it was not my presentation or my personality that had made the impact. Years later, I listened to the audiotape of my presentation: it was as bad as I had thought. So, what had happened?

I think many people there, perhaps even a majority, were ready to receive something and opened up their hearts and minds. My presentation was a focus for them, but it was really insignificant. The Mother had sent her Force to everyone who was receptive. For that to happen, I had to get out of the way and not be a dominant personality.

I have attended hundreds of talks on psychology, philosophy, and metaphysical subjects. At the end of them, I check myself to see how I feel, not necessarily what was said. Ideally, my head and my heart are resonating with a sublimating energy, and my whole body is elevated. However, this is not very typical.

Vacant Mind

In his own *sadhana*, or spiritual practice, Sri Aurobindo

achieved a vacant mind. That is, he no longer conjured up thoughts in his head, but higher thought and consciousness flowed through him. An attendant observed him sitting and simply writing page after page of his poetry and other works without any visible effort. This is a very difficult concept or process for Westerners to comprehend, although creative people do this part of the time, at least when they are inspired. But when they are not in a creative mode, they revert to their ordinary mental state. The Mother had noticed this during her student days in Paris. Some well-known impressionist painters, she said, became quite ordinary and even crude when they were not painting. There was a gap in their consciousness. When they wanted to relax, they often did stupid things and acted foolish.

Savitri

Sri Aurobindo remained in his "creative" state continually. One of his great literary works is his epic poem *Savitri*, which is 724 pages long. He continued to work on it throughout the last decades of his life, rewriting sections of it at least twelve times over the years. For each revision, he would raise his consciousness to a higher level, using this process as a means of ascension. He never rewrote or edited from the critical mind. Canto One, "The Symbolic Dawn," begins as follows:

> It was the hour before the Gods awake.
> Across the path of the divine Event
> The huge foreboding mind of Night, alone
> In her unlit temple of eternity,
> Lay stretched immobile upon Silence' marge.
> Almost one felt, opaque, impenetrable,
> In the sombre symbol of her eyeless muse
> The abysm of the unbodied Infinite;
> A fathomless zero occupied the world.[9]

What are the planes of consciousness that Sri Aurobindo was ascending? He delineated them as spiritual planes (which he called "overhead mind planes") of cosmic consciousness, "where one becomes constantly and closely aware of the Self, the One everywhere…, but it is still very much on the MIND level, although highly spiritual in its essential substance."[10]

Higher Mind

Early on, about 1970, I got a taste of an aspect of the higher mind plane. In rapid-fire succession, a deep and complex question appeared to me, followed immediately by an answer. Each question was on a different subject. This continued for a few minutes. I did not have the knowledge either to phrase the question or to answer it. This all happened so fast that I had no time to stop and take notes. When it was over, I could see that anyone who could access that state at will would have to be a genius, but I could no longer remember any of it.

Overhead Mind Planes

Sri Aurobindo divided the overhead planes into four categories in an ascending scale: (a) *the higher mind*, which is capable of luminous clarity of thought with manifold modes of expression; (b) *the illumined mind*, which transcends thought and perceives by vision; (c) *the intuitive mind*, which has spontaneous and immediate glimpses of the Truth by identifying with it; and (d) *the overmind*, which has a global awareness of being and is the originating plane of duality. The overmind is the highest of the planes in the manifest world below the Supramental. But all of these planes of cosmic consciousness are still of the "old world." The "new world" deals with matter itself, but not the matter we know, for that has been covered over with something that obscures its true state.

Illusion—Concrete Reality

On July 12, 1967, the Mother made an observation that expressed much of the transformative process of the Supermind:

> Basically, it's what gives the ordinary human consciousness the sense of reality. That's what must disappear. What we call "concrete," a "concrete reality"…yes, what truly gives you the sense of real existence—that's what must disappear and be replaced by…It's inexpressible. *(silence)*

Now I can follow.

I remember, when I came back after having BEEN those bursts—those pulsations, those bursts of creative Love [Experience of April 13, 1962], when I returned to the ordinary consciousness (while retaining the very memory of That, of the state), well, that state, which I felt to be pulsations of creative Love, is what must, is That which must replace here this consciousness of concrete reality—which is, which becomes unreal: it's like something lifeless—hard, dry, inert, lifeless. And to our ordinary consciousness (I remember how it was in the past), that's what gives you the impression, "This is concrete, this is real." Well, "this," this sensation, is what must be replaced by the phenomenon of consciousness of that Pulsation. And That *(Mother makes an intense gesture enfolding her whole face)* is at the same time all-light, all-power, all-intensity of love, and such FULLNESS! It's so full that...where That is, nothing else can exist. And when That is here, in the body, in the cells, then all you have to do is focus It on someone or something, and order is instantly restored in the person or the thing.

So, translated into ordinary words, it "heals." It heals the disease. But it doesn't heal it: it annuls it....Yes, it annuls it.

It unrealizes it.

Absolutely. I have concrete proof of it.
Any disease, any disease whatsoever.
(silence)
And the condition of all the cells (the vibrations that make up this body) is undeniably what makes the thing [healing] possible or not; that is, depending on the body's condition, it serves either as a transmitter, or on the contrary as an obstruction. Because it's not a "higher force" acting

in others THROUGH Matter: it's a direct action *(hori-zontal gesture, on a level)* from matter to matter.

What people generally call "healing power" is a very great mental or vital power that imposes itself through the resistance of Matter—but this isn't at all the same thing! It's the contagion of a vibration. And then it's irrevocable.

But it's gone in a flash. It's only a promise or an example of what will be: it WILL be like that, obviously. Obviously. When?... That's another question.[11]

Ascension—Descension

Integral Yoga is philosophically distinguished from other yogas by linking up the lowest planes of consciousness with the highest. Sri Aurobindo described this as ascension and descension. One ascends as high as possible and then brings that consciousness back into the body in the waking state. This transcends the old method of going into a trance-like state called *samadhi* without any conscious awareness later except a reflective residue. This process has been fully developed by Sri Aurobindo; now, an aspirant has only to be receptive to the descent which happens automatically. Peace is often the first descent and one feels as if one as is in a force-field when it fully establishes itself.

A Critical Step—Hierarchy or Sphere

November 24, 1926, was a significant date for Sri Aurobindo and the Mother. The highest plane in the manifestation called the Overmind, which is also known as the region of the Gods, descended into the Earth plane and was witnessed by several disciples in Pondicherry. Sri Aurobindo told the Mother to dissolve that manifestation, and that he didn't want another religion, as great as that would be. He was now ready to work for the descent of the Supermind that had been above the manifestation and beyond accessibility, as well as being asleep in matter. In more common parlance, he was ready to bring Heaven to Earth. This represented a substantial challenge to traditional thought about the hierarchical scheme of things, which had stated that to get to the fundamental reality, we have to leave Earth. Where is reality if the hierarchical ladder to the transcendent becomes connected to the "lowest" bedrock of consciousness? There is then no longer just a linear vertical upward ascent but a connecting wholeness, a circle or a sphere. One can then find God by making contact anywhere on the circle, even in matter itself. Perhaps the "real world" is right here, after all.

Image of Serpent's Tail

On September 23, 1953, the Mother was asked the following question, to which she gave her response.

> *You said that this physical world was a projection of invisible worlds. Then, why should the divine Emanations come into the physical world to transform it? They have only to do the work in the invisible planes; then the projections will be good.*

> That indeed is a serious question!... You know the image sometimes given to the universe: a serpent biting its tail? And it is taken as the symbol of the infinite, of the universe. Well, it is a fact. In the creation there is a progressive, a greater and greater materialization. But we could take another image (I am taking an approximate image): the universe is a circle or rather a sphere (but for the convenience of explanation, let us take a circle.) There is a progressive descent from the most subtle to the most material. But the most material happens to touch the point of origin of the most subtle. Then, if you understand the image, instead of going all the way round to change matter, it is much more easy to do the thing directly, for the two extremities meet—the extremely subtle and the extremely material touch, since it is a sphere. Hence, instead of doing all that (*Mother draws a circle*), it is much better to do this (*Mother touches the extreme material end of the*

circle). In fact, psychologically it is that. The rest will follow quite naturally. If that is done *(Mother touches the same extreme material end),* all the rest will get settled as a matter of course. And it is not even like this! It is precisely for the convenience of work that all has been concentrated or concretized at one point so that instead of having to spread oneself out in the infinite to change things, one can work just on the point that serves as the symbol of the whole universe. And from the occult standpoint, earth (which is nothing from the astronomical standpoint; in the immensity of the astronomical skies, earth is a thing absolutely without interest and without importance), but from the occult and spiritual point of view, earth is the concentrated symbol of the universe. For it is much more easy to work on one point than in a diluted vastness.[12]

Notes

[1]Sri Aurobindo, *Birth Centenary Library*, vol. 26: *On Himself* (Pondicherry, India: Sri Aurobindo Ashram Press, 1972), p. 98.

[2]Sujata Nahar, *Mother's Chronicles*, Book 1: *Mirra* (New York: Institute for Evolutionary Research, 1985), p. 13.

[3]Sri Aurobindo, *Birth Centenary Library*, vols. 18–19: *The Life Divine* (Pondicherry, India: Sri Aurobindo Ashram Press, 1972), p. 87.

[4]Sri Aurobindo, *On Himself*, p. 98.

[5]The Mother, *Mother's Agenda*, 13 vols., ed. by Satprem (New York: Institute for Evolutionary Research, 1979–2000).

[6]Fritjof Capra, *The Tao of Physics* (New York: Bantam Books, 1984), p. 58.

[7]Quoted here from Sri Aurobindo, *Birth Centenary Library*, vol. 12: *The Upanishads* (Pondicherry, India: Sri Aurobindo Ashram Press, 1972), p. 78, note 5.

[8]Sri Aurobindo, *The Upanishads*, p. xiii.

[9]Sri Aurobindo, *Birth Centenary Library*, vol. 28: *Savitri* (Pondicherry, India: Sri Aurobindo Ashram Press, 1972), p. 1.

[10]Sri Aurobindo, *Birth Centenary Library*, vol. 9: *The Future Poetry* (Pondicherry, India: Sri Aurobindo Ashram Press, 1972), p. 342.

[11]The Mother, *Mother's Agenda*, vol. 8: *1967*, ed. by Satprem (New York: Institute for Evolutionary Research, 1993), pp. 213–214.

[12]The Mother, *Collected Works of the Mother*, vol. 5: *Questions and Answers, 1953* (Pondicherry, India: Sri Aurobindo Ashram Press, 1976), pp. 275-276.

15

The Macrocosm

> *Every separate object in the universe is, in truth, itself the whole universe presenting a certain front or outward appearance of its movement. The microcosm is one with the macrocosm.*

> Sri Aurobindo[1]

Western civilization has lost contact with its roots of divine beingness. That is the price we have paid for intellectualization. One can see the difference immediately in any Third World country that has not succumbed to materialism. There is nothing wrong with the "good life" in itself, but it has a kind of magnetism, like gravity, that seductively pulls us in and spins a cocoon around us. Once we are entrapped by materialism, we depend more and more on it for our sustenance in all facets of our lives.

The traditional way out of this trap has been asceticism, or a kind of radical mental surgery. The philosophy has been, "If something is not working right, cut it out." There is no reason, however, why we cannot enjoy life's pleasures while at the same time having a spiritual life. Sometimes we first have to take a break from the material life of the West, as I do when I travel to India. When I return, I am more balanced in my inner and outer life.

India

I have seen in India how spirituality permeates all avenues of life, including work, business, education, and the arts, especially dance, music, painting, sculpture, architecture, poetry, and drama. People in India can see a religious play performed over and over and never tire of it, because they are *living* it. One can see the fervor in their faces.

Westerners lack that grasp of a mystical vision that is not tied to daily life. The consensus seems to be that those kinds of things may have happened in biblical times to a chosen few, but usually not today in a world of science. I believe, however, that inner spirit is being awakened in the West, and that if we had a central source of collecting people's inner experiences, we would be surprised. For example, it is only in the past few decades that we have begun to accept the validity of near-death experiences. Previously, if people spoke about this, they would be ridiculed because we couldn't conceive of an existence outside our body. Science says it's impossible.

Maya

In 1974–75, while I was completing my doctoral program at the California Institute of Integral Studies, one of my professors was lecturing on Maya, the illusion of the material world. Suddenly, he pounded on his lectern and said to us, "You can't tell me that this table isn't real!" And he was right. It *is* real, even though it could disappear at any moment—say, by fire or explosion. But the form is real (it exists as an idea somewhere), and the table can be recreated. Our bodies are real, but one day they will be gone, at least under our present form of consciousness. But our soul will survive and will assume a new body and life, until the day comes when it will be able to create any form it likes.

Matter is energy, and energy is consciousness. Imagine a body free of rational control that is able to express a divine light, power, love, and bliss. Having been in a mental prison for centuries, we are preparing for a massive breakout. Our present bodies and minds will not be adequate to fully contain and express the Supramental Consciousness in its full manifestation.

Reliance on Authority

One of our greatest obstacles to this new freedom is our reliance on authority, whether in the form of politicians, priests, gurus, or even celebrities. In fact, there is a disturbing surge of idolatrous adulation today of celebrities in all of the entertainment areas, including sports. This is a transitional stage on the way to our recognizing that each one of us has to become his or her own hero, own authority, own divinity. The Mother said that the age of the guru is over. She meant by this that we no longer have to go through an intermediary for our spiritual fulfillment. When people prayed to her, she said, she merely passed it on to the Supreme Consciousness.

Building Bridges

Integral Yoga is a series of links or bridges to all levels of consciousness, even up to the Supermind. But the path has been hewn by Sri Aurobindo and the Mother so that one does not need any special skills or training. Sri Aurobindo said that there are stages in reaching the Supermind. First there is the mind, then the purified mind, then the illumined mind, and so on. When asked if it was necessary for everyone to go through all of these stages, the Mother replied:

> It is likely that a sequence of this kind always occurs. But the duration of the stages and their importance vary considerably according to individuals.... For some the passage may be rapid enough to be hardly perceptible, while for others it may take a very long time; and according to the nature of the resistance in each one, the stress on one or another of these stages varies enormously.

> For some, it may be so rapid that it seems al-
> most instantaneous, as though it didn't exist. For
> others it may take years.[2]

A Vision

In January 1985, I was residing at the Sri Aurobindo Ashram when I awakened early one morning after having a powerful dream-experience or vision. Afterward, I recorded it in my diary:

> I was walking in a field where I passed an Indian
> woman who seemed to know me. She told me
> my wife was going to have a baby, and she asked,
> "Would you like to see it?" I said, "That's impos-
> sible. The baby is not due for two months." She
> showed me the photo of a beautiful baby lying
> on the ground. It was a very special baby with a
> glow about it, but it had a mustache. Its head was
> very unusual. It had ridges like clay that was be-
> ing molded, and the head had a transparency to
> it. Watching over the baby were seven women
> who were very attractive but detached. They were
> sitting regally behind a long table. The women
> were very similar in appearance, rather youthful
> and ageless, as though they were sisters. I believe
> they were wearing saris, but I cannot be certain. I
> said to the Indian woman, "You are in this photo,"
> and I pointed to the woman who was second from
> the left. She was noncommittal, but I took her si-
> lence to be an affirmation. She asked me if I would
> like a closer look at the baby, and then the baby
> itself was magnified. It filled the whole scene.
> Then the vision ended.

Seven Rivers—Seven Sisters

That whole day I was in a reverie. Whenever I sat down, I felt compelled to close my eyes and meditate. The vision had permeated my being and seemed to have Vedic overtones, so I consulted Sri Aurobindo's *The Secret of the Veda*. The *Rig-Veda* is a body of hymns couched in an ancient language that Sri Aurobindo translated and gave a new and meaningful interpretation. In Chapter 11, "The Seven Rivers," he wrote:

> Obviously these are the waters of the Truth and the Bliss that flow from the supreme ocean. These rivers flow not upon earth, but in heaven; they are prevented by Vritra the Besieger, the Coverer, from flowing down upon the earth-consciousness in which we mortals live till Indra, the god-mind, smites the Coverer with his flashing lightnings and cuts out a passage on the summits of that earth-consciousness down which they can flow.[3]

In the Veda, the number seven has a symbolic significance because there is a triune above and a triune below that are connected by a seventh principle. The seven rivers that flow from the supreme ocean are the waters of the Vast Truth. They are also known as the seven sisters, the seven mighty ones, the seven words, the sevenfold waters of the Truth, the seven strands of all being, and the seven streams or currents or forms of movement of the one conscious existence.

Agni—Divine Spark

The seven sisters are linked with the Earth-plane through the birth of Agni, who is symbolic of the Divine Fire or Spark within and the Divine Force and Will that will manifest all the latent divine possibilities in people. As Sri Aurobindo wrote:

> The gods discovered Agni visible in the waters, in the working of the sisters.... The gods gave body to Agni in his birth.... The child of the waters, the mighty and most strong Agni.[4]

Agni is the divine, immortal Conscious-Force that has assumed ordinary will and knowledge. The birth of the child of the waters symbolizes the manifestation of the Supermind on the mortal plane. Sri Aurobindo said of the waters:

They lead to the Truth, they are themselves the
source of all Truth, they flow in the unobstructed
and shoreless Vast as well as here upon the earth.[5]

Mother-Child or Child-Mother

These waters are symbols of the streams of consciousness
that flow here on Earth. The waters are more diluted here than
at their Superconscient source because the human mind analyzes
and dissects knowledge, which leads away from wholeness and
toward disunity. Because of this, we experience only a reflected
light, love, joy, and power. We need a representative who is seated
within every human being and can give birth to these powers in
their fullness. As is written in the *Rig-Veda*, I.95.4:

> Which of you has awakened
> to the knowledge of this secret thing,
> that it is the Child
> who gives birth to his own mothers

The child is the representative of the mothers or seven sisters on the Earth-plane, who manifest their streams of consciousness so that they can be embodied. At this stage of evolution, it
is the Supermind that is to be embodied here and is the connecting link of the upper and lower worlds.

Seven Streams of Consciousness

The birth of the mothers is symbolic of the flow of the seven
waters to Earth, the seven streams of consciousness, one of which
is the Supramental. The other six streams are existence, consciousness, and bliss on the Superconscient plane, and life, mind, and
matter on the Earth plane.

Just as the child gives birth to the mothers, as well as the
other way around, so the waters that flow downward also flow
upward to the source of mental clarity and the streams of divine sweetness. The waters become universal, transformed
into what Sri Aurobindo called "masses of the vast and infinite consciousness."[6]

Divination

After I looked at *The Secret of the Veda*, I consulted *Savitri* as a means of divination. A profound book can be consulted by concentrating for a moment on a question or problem and then opening the book at random. The passage that I found was in the Canto entitled "The Birth and Childhood of the Flame":

> In this high signal moment of the gods
> Answering earth's yearning and her cry for bliss
> A greatness from our other countries came.
> A silence in the noise of earthly things
> Immutably revealed the secret Word,
> A mightier influx filled the oblivious clay:
> A lamp was lit, a sacred image made.
> A mediating ray has touched the earth
> Bridging the gulf between man's mind and God's;
> Translating heaven into a human shape
> Its brightness linked our transience to the Unknown.
> A spirit of its celestial source aware
> Descended into earth's imperfect mould
> And wept not fallen to mortality,
> But looked on all with large and tranquil eyes.[7]

Vastness

After reading this passage I meditated, and my consciousness moved into a tremendous vastness of freedom and joy. I casually "drifted" from one place to another, but there were no forms anywhere. In Sri Aurobindo's vision, the Vast is the plane of Truth-Consciousness. This is the macrocosm, as opposed to the microcosm, which is found in the interior of the atom. Both are the same Supreme Consciousness, but in different manifestations. The feeling from each is similar, but the Vast is one of extreme expansiveness, as if my consciousness were moving through eternity, while the interior of the atom has an extreme intensity and vibrancy. It is incredibly alive, but does not move about. Both states give a sense of freedom and joy.

Microcosm—Macrocosm

There is a new relationship being formed between the macrocosm and the microcosm. Previously, the microcosm was represented by the soul or psychic being. The soul is described in the *Katha Upanishad* as "the Purusha, the Spirit within, who is no larger than the finger of a man."[8] Now, due to the advent of the Supermind, the microcosm also includes the supreme consciousness in the atom, in matter itself. All seven rivers flow from the Superconscient to the Inconscient, and Spirit is housed in the body.

Notes

[1] Sri Aurobindo, *Birth Centenary Library*, vol. 12: *The Upanishads* (Pondicherry, India: Sri Aurobindo Ashram Press, 1972), p. 73.

[2] The Mother, *Collected Works of the Mother*, vol. 8: *Questions and Answers, 1956* (Pondicherry, India: Sri Aurobindo Ashram Press, 1976), pp. 171–172.

[3] Sri Aurobindo, *Birth Centenary Library*, vol. 10: *The Secret of the Veda* (Pondicherry, India: Sri Aurobindo Ashram Press, 1972), p. 108.

[4] Sri Aurobindo, *The Secret of the Veda*, pp. 110–111

[5] Sri Aurobindo, *The Secret of the Veda*, p. 112.

[6] Sri Aurobindo, *The Secret of the Veda*, p. 115.

[7] Sri Aurobindo, *Birth Centenary Library*, vol. 28: *Savitri* (Pondicherry, India: Sri Aurobindo Ashram Press, 1972), p. 353.

[8] Sri Aurobindo, *The Upanishads*, p. 265.

16

Supramental Consciousness

The manifestation of the Supramental upon earth is no more a promise but a living fact, a reality.

It is at work here, and one day will come when the most blind, the most unconscious, even the most unwilling shall be obliged to recognize it.

—The Mother
(April 24, 1956)[1]

In these early stages of this unprecedented transformative action upon Earth, we are witnessing a leap into the future. It is expected to continue for centuries as the Supreme manifests more and more in matter to ultimately bring a divine life on Earth and a conquest of death. We are fortunate to be living at this time. As the Mother said, "There is truly an opportunity on earth that is offered only once in thousands of years, a conscious help, with the necessary Power."[2]

The Supermind is not mental; it is beyond mind and is the transcendental Truth-Consciousness-Force that is now active on Earth. Very few historical data exist about it except what has been given to us by Sri Aurobindo and the Mother. Otherwise, there are only a few oblique references to it in the Vedas and Upanishads. Some of the mysteries of the atom have been discovered by science, but, to my knowledge, no religious or spiritual groups have explored the Supramental. But the Supramental influence is global and continues to press down on matter, humanity, institutions, and governments to bring about the transformation. On a more personal level, pressure on people from the Supramental Force is bringing up long-suppressed feelings that either immobilize the individuals or cause them to behave erratically until they obtain some inner clarity.

The Supramental realization is the perfect union of what comes from above with what comes from below. In 1969, the Mother discussed this point with Satprem:

> [SATPREM:] This is the strange contradiction of that Supramental, which seems to combine or integrate immobility and extreme swiftness, perhaps so extreme in its vibration that it is perceived as immobile....

> [THE MOTHER:] It's a state that seems to be completely immobile.... I don't know what it is. It isn't immobility, it isn't eternity.... I don't know, but it is something—it's something which is...yes, it's Power, Light, and really Love.[3]

Receptivity

If we can experience profound beauty, perhaps even on a cellular level, our receptivity to the unseen expands. We become more porous, less dense. Dissatisfaction with life can motivate us to experience and embody a truly new and remarkable conscious power—one that transcends the mind and yet is right here in matter itself. Science can help us to understand the contradictions in matter—for example, seeing electrons both as waves *and* particles. The Mother said that "the fourth dimension of the physicists is only the scientific transcription of an occult knowledge."[4] Science itself can be a type of yoga. As the Mother said, "the sciences that are practiced sincerely, honestly, exclusively with a will to know are difficult paths—yet such sure paths for the total realization."[5]

Why is the Supramental transformation happening now? Because we are at the stage in our evolution when the mind has been fully developed, and the next stage is beyond mind to Absolute consciousness (which paradoxically is also in matter, too). This means that eventually pure Existence, pure Consciousness-Force, and pure *Ananda* will be established in life itself. The aspects of this triune consciousness that are gradually manifesting are Truth, Power, Consciousness, and Love. Sri Aurobindo and the Mother laid the groundwork for this manifestation. It is our task, and our good fortune, to open up to the process, much as we open to beauty. We do not have to be supermen or superwomen to do this. There are no barriers of gender, age, race, education, wealth, or position aside from what we ourselves impose as restrictions.

Where Is God?

One of the limitations we have to overcome in Western civilization is the division of spirit and matter that has been inculcated in us. We have been taught that God is worshipped primarily in a holy place on certain days of the week, that God is outside us somewhere "up there," and that we have to pray for God's intervention in our lives. God and life are placed in separate mental compartments. It is time for us to open to new possibilities that include something other than meditation, isolation, retreats, vegetarianism, gurus, and the rest. We may include some or all of these in our spiritual quest, but they should not be our primary focus. Our spiritual path is a personal choice. Now there is no such thing as a "spiritual or religious life." *All* life is now infused with Spirit, and we have only to be receptive to it.

Global Change

When something new comes into existence, the mind tends to panic. Our security blanket is gone. For example, the stock market can have unprecedented rises and falls, baffling "experts"—especially those without an historical perspective—who try to make sense of the astronomical fluctuations. The same lack of historical perspective can apply to the evolution of consciousness. Many things do not make sense. For instance, random violence is everywhere, strange diseases are appearing or reappearing throughout the world, and falsehoods are being exposed at every level of society.

However, we are now in the midst of a global change in consciousness that is affecting every facet of our lives. It is not history repeating itself or even reinventing itself. It is nothing short of timelessness and spacelessness presenting themselves in time and space—that is, in our very bodies and cells. The repercussions of this paradoxical process stretch our imagination to the utmost.

Unprecedented Opportunity

Meanwhile, our opportunities for progress are unlimited if we can open up to the new consciousness. The process of opening up is so simple that people tend to want to complicate it by continuing their old ways and habits. If we can open to the beauty of a rose, a loved one, a painting, or music, we can certainly open to the Supramental force that is active in the world today. But our habits get in the way. Actually, we are composed of a *mass* of habits—mental, vital, physical, and cellular—all of which have to be released to some extent.

Mother's Agenda

Surprisingly enough, there are many valuable records concerning this process of transformation. The records appear in thirteen volumes of some six thousand pages, called *Mother's Agenda*, in which the Mother described many of her experiences between 1951 and 1973.[6] Twice a week during most of those years, she met with Satprem and his companion, Sujata, to relate her experiences with the Supramental transformation. Each session lasted for less than an hour, during which the Mother related her experiences with the new consciousness. She was remarkable in her ability to express the inexpressible, but even she had difficulties at times, because no language had been devised for her extraordinary explorations into her own body and cells.

Has to be Expressed

In 1960, she said to Satprem, "I saw this Secret—I saw that the Supreme only becomes perfect in terrestrial matter, on earth…, a kind of accuracy or exactitude right down to the atom."[7] But this perfection has to be expressed *on Earth*. If a masterpiece from a Rembrandt, Van Gogh, or Bach is never physically *expressed*, but remains locked within the consciousness of the artist, can it ever reach perfection? I think not. It has to be articulated in a material form.

Similarly, each of us is a partial expression of God's ultimate masterpiece. But clearly, we are not finished products. The march of evolution to the next stage will lead to our fulfillment. No doubt, the process will occur in stages, because the body has to learn to adapt to this new vibration. The Supramental power is unlimited, so its force is self-regulated—that is, it gives us what we can handle. During my own spiritual awakening, I had jolts of energy that were electrifying and magnificent, but lasted all night, so that I could not sleep. It was extremely intense, but subsided after a day or two.

It is a grave mistake to be too ambitious by trying to move quickly, for this can cause the body to become ill. I suspect that many illnesses today are misdiagnosed because there is no known model for what is occurring. The Mother developed a model of transformation through her own *sadhana* (spiritual practice) in her body. She related many of her experiences to give us markers or guideposts for this new path of transformation. Similarly, others who have had transformative experiences should follow the Mother's example by making their experiences widely known.

Cosmic Order

One may well ask: Why wasn't this spirit in matter known before by the spiritual masters over the past three thousand years? The answer is that if knowledge is released too soon, or out of cosmic order, the entire evolutionary process is thrown out of balance. Previously, two options in consciousness were available to people: (a) grin and bear life, make the most of it, and hope for improvements in the hereafter; or (b) join an esoteric order and, through a long religious discipline, achieve a state of superlative transcendence—a state of bliss sometimes called Samadhi, Nirvana, or Satori. This process would absolve one of Karma, allowing one to escape the endless rounds of birth, death, and rebirth. Neither option, however, is satisfactory. The former guarantees countless sufferings. The latter negates the meaning of life on Earth, serving no purpose other than individual escape.

Same Supreme—Above and Below

We now have another option, taking us into an entirely different dimension: a conjunction of the Supreme above and the Supreme below. The former, which the Vedantins call *Sachchidananda*, resides in the formless eternal transcendent. The latter, which Sri Aurobindo called the Inconscient, was formerly asleep in matter. The joining of these two realms completes the circle and reconciles opposites, unifies consciousness, and brings the eternal into mortality.

Prelude to the Supermind

In the first decade of the twentieth century, before they met, Sri Aurobindo and the Mother both had similar but independent knowledge of this possible conjunction. It was their mission to make this a reality. At first, Sri Aurobindo took the lead in integrating the upper and lower hemispheres by making a series of ascents and descents into the universal mind planes, climbing higher and higher until he was at the Supermind.

The descent of the overhead mind planes—including the Higher Mind, the Illumined Mind, the Intuitive Mind, and the Overmind—was completed on November 24, 1926. The next stage was to bring the Supermind down to Earth. The Mother said about the distinction between the Overmind and the Supermind:

> Above the mind there are several levels of conscious being, among which the really divine world is what Sri Aurobindo has called the Supermind, the world of the Truth. But in between is what he has distinguished as the Overmind, the world of the cosmic Gods. Now, it is this Overmind that has up to the present governed our world: it is the highest that man has been able to attain in illumined consciousness. It has been taken for the Supreme Divine, and all those who have reached it have never for a moment doubted that they have touched the true Spirit. For its splendors are so great to the ordinary human consciousness that it is absolutely dazzled into believing that here at last is the crowning reality. And yet the fact is that the Overmind is far below the true Divine. It is not the authentic home of the Truth. It is only the domain of the *formateurs*, all those creative powers and deities to whom men have bowed down since the beginning of history. And the reason why the true Divine has not manifested and transformed the earth-nature is precisely that the Overmind has been mistaken for the Supermind. The cosmic Gods do not wholly live in the Truth-Consciousness: they are only in touch with it and represent, each of them, an aspect of its glories.
>
> No doubt, the Supermind has also acted in the history of the world, but always through the Overmind. It is the direct descent of the Supramental Consciousness and Power that alone can utterly re-create life in terms of the Spirit. For in the Overmind there is already the play of possibilities, which marks the beginning of this lower triple world of Mind, Life, and Matter in which we have our existence.[8]

The next stage, the descent of the Supermind, commenced and apparently was close to manifestation in 1939, when Hitler launched World War II, diverting the efforts of Sri Aurobindo and the Mother from an occult battle to a physical war.

The Grand Opening

In 1950, Sri Aurobindo left his body to continue his work in the subtle physical realm. The Mother carried on the work alone, running the ashram, ministering to 750 or more ashramites, and pursuing her inner work, much of which is detailed in *Mother's Agenda*. On February 29, 1960, she made the following announcement regarding the descent on February 29, 1956.

> This evening the Divine Presence, complete and material, was there present amongst you. I had a form of living gold, bigger than the universe, and I was facing a huge and massive golden door which separated the world from the Divine.
>
> As I looked at the door, I knew and willed, in a single movement of consciousness, that "THE TIME HAS COME," and lifting with both hands a mighty golden hammer, I struck one blow, one single blow on the door, and the door was shattered to pieces.
>
> Then the Supramental Light and Force and Consciousness rushed down upon earth in an uninterrupted flow.[9]

This was the grand opening of a new episode of life on the planet; one with potential for a divine life in the body. There were no newspaper headlines or media dissemination. Only a very few disciples felt anything, but the mission of Sri Aurobindo and the Mother had been completed.

Actually, this descent was only a partial manifestation into the subtle physical realm, which is a plane of consciousness next to our physical realm. On July 24, 1959, there was a partial descent into the physical, or matter itself.

Descent into Matter

On January 4, 1969, after there had been a full descent of the Supermind into matter, the Mother said:

> On the first [of January], something really strange took place.... It was something very material, I mean it was very external—very outward—and luminous, with a golden light. It was very strong, powerful. But its character was a smiling benevolence, a peaceful joy....
>
> I feel it's the formation that's going to permeate and express itself—permeate and express itself—in the bodies...which will be the bodies of the Supramental.
>
> Or maybe...maybe the Superman? I don't know. The intermediary between the two. Maybe the Superman: it was very human, but a human of divine proportions, you understand.
>
> A human without weaknesses and shadows: it was all luminous—all light and smile and...sweetness at the same time.[10]

This was the decisive moment, the conscious merger of spirit and matter, when Heaven came down to Earth. When the two extremes joined, the merger was complete. Now the manifestation of the Supermind had to be worked out in life on Earth, where there had been resistance for millennia.

My Path

It has taken me thirty years to put all of the pieces together, at least up to this moment. When I was first exposed to Integral Yoga in 1969, I had no idea what lay ahead. I was starting from my own personal quest to find meaning in life among all the absurdity, injustice, and suffering. I brought questions about these matters with me to ask the Mother when I first went to India in 1973. She died shortly before I reached Pondicherry. Nevertheless, when I pleaded with her to fill me with consciousness, I felt wave after wave of bliss flowing through me, day after day, for weeks on end. Each time I returned to India after that, I tried to assimilate the consciousness there. Over the years, the gap between my mental and spiritual consciousness has closed, to the point where I now feel that I can move quite easily back and forth. However, for many people a trip of this magnitude is not desirable, feasible, or even necessary. But one can accelerate one's growth considerably.

Churning Process

The Supramental consciousness has been working incessantly since its first global manifestation in 1956. Nowadays, one does not have to look very hard to see the Force at work. All relationships between people, governments, and organizations are being pressured by the Force to clear the path for Truth Consciousness. This churning process ultimately brings up people's dark sides; hence the proliferation of senseless violence, road rage, rudeness, and impatience.

Resistance

The first of the thirteen volumes of *Mother's Agenda* started to appear in English translation from the French in 1979. Before that, the concept of the Supermind had been explored extensively by Sri Aurobindo, but it had not been fully worked out in the body or on a collective level. Furthermore, the idea of the Supermind was generally looked upon by people familiar with Sri Aurobindo's philosophy as a utopia that only the Mother could enter, or, at best, as something for future generations. It was fine to talk about the Supermind as a concept, but that's as far as it went. This attitude, which was a manifestation of the defeatist physical mind, impeded—and still impedes—the continuation of the Mother's work.

Equality

One characteristic of the Supermind is perfect equality. Our physical mind is the mind of habits and incessant repetition. What has given us our routines in life, teaching us to define ourselves, now has to open to new possibilities. The physical mind gives us fixity in nature, anchoring us to the Earth. In the transition to Supramental Consciousness, we need a new kind of anchor. This is what the Mother was attempting in her body *sadhana*, and this is what I myself was attempting, without any conscious plan, when I tried to feel as great here in America, in the workaday world, as I had felt in India. However, after a while, the blissful consciousness partially dissipated. Thus, I decided to return to India every two or three years to recharge my spiritual batteries. Unfortunately, it was never the same after my first visit, for there was still some inexplicable link missing. I kept returning to India to find that missing link.

Knowledge

Aside from perfect equality, another characteristic of the Supermind is absolute knowledge. The ability to know every detail at every moment throughout the world and the universe is simply unimaginable. But this is the essence of Oneness and explains the apparent relatedness of unrelated events. There is an incredible network of connection in the universe, whose implications become increasingly important in personal and global transformations. *Nothing* is trivial or unimportant. Everything we think, feel, or do has an impact somewhere in the world because of this network of connections.

Contagion

What one person accomplishes, especially in a breakthrough in consciousness, makes it easier for others to accomplish. I remember when Roger Bannister broke the four-minute mile in 1954. Miler after miler had attempted it, but couldn't quite cross over the seemingly invisible time barrier. However, once Bannister broke the record, many others did, too.

Sri Aurobindo wrote in the 1920s about this concept—which the Mother called "contagion." Counting on it to spread her work of bodily transformation, she said that what she did would make it easier for others to do. However, where she spent years struggling to transform some part of herself, we may be able to do the same thing in a much shorter time.

Sheldrake

Biologist Rupert Sheldrake has experimented with and

written extensively about this contagion, which he calls "morphic resonance," defined as "the influence of previous structures of activity on subsequent similar structures of activity organized by morphic fields."[11] Sheldrake goes on to say:

> Through morphic resonance, formative causal influences pass through or across both space and time, and these influences are assumed not to fall off with distance in space or time, but they come only from the past. The greater the degree of similarity, the greater the influence of morphic resonance. In general, morphic units closely resemble themselves in the past and are subject to self-resonance from their own past states.[12]

In other words, when a new habit is formed within a species and reaches a certain critical mass, that behavior "leaps" across time and space to other members of the species without any physical contact. Sheldrake has conducted a number of experiments to demonstrate this theory and also has documented cases from nature. For example, in Great Britain the bird species known as blue tits spontaneously spread the habit of opening milk bottles delivered to doorsteps early in the morning. These birds do not usually wander more than a few miles from their breeding place, and yet the milk-bottle practice spread throughout Great Britain and into continental Europe over several decades. In Holland during World War II, the delivery of milk bottles to private homes was discontinued, so the birds went without this source of food. However, when deliveries resumed after the war, the blue tits quickly resumed their attacks on the bottles.[13]

Obverse Side

Everything in life is important, and so it is often the little habitual things that block us. Contagion has an obverse side. One small dark vibration in our body can spread like a cancer cell. Conversely, one small gain can lead to a magnificent triumph. In other words, at this time in our evolution, we can make momentous strides moving into and assimilating the new consciousness. Similarly, we can also go off the deep end more easily. It is a time to be vigilant, but it is also a time to take advantage of the opportunity for accelerated growth in consciousness. One of the Mother's *sutras*, or aphorisms, which she stated in 1957, was:

> It is the Supreme Lord who has ineluctably decreed the place you occupy in the universal concert, but whatever be this place, you have equally the same right as all others to ascend the supreme summits right to the supramental realization.[14]

Erasing Karma

A definitive realization of our psychic being can erase our karma, causing us to become free souls. The Supramental Consciousness also has the capacity to free us of our karma. This is logical, since we are being freed both from our past deeds and from the encumbrances from birth (atavism) that we inherited as we move through this churning toward a divine harmony.

Oneness

The principal and identifying characteristic of the Supermind is unity or oneness. We are all of one consciousness, but express our uniqueness in multiple ways. This oneness is now expressing itself in matter itself. As resistance throughout the world disintegrates and the Supermind is able to permeate deeper into matter, harmony will begin to prevail—a harmony that comes from Oneness *but not uniformity*. Our uniqueness will be preserved, but it will be a glorified uniqueness.

The Earth is a symbol of the universe, and what is accomplished here will reverberate elsewhere. The relationship between the Earth and the rest of the universe is similar to the relationship between a single cell or small cluster of cells and the trillions of cells in the rest of the body—about which I will have more to say in the next chapter.

310 GOD SHALL GROW UP

Notes

[1]The Mother, *Mother's Agenda*, vol. 1: *1951–1960*, edited by Satprem (New York: Institute for Evolutionary Research, 1979), p. 75.

[2]The Mother, *Mother's Agenda*, vol. 1, p. 245.

[3]Satprem, *Mother or the Mutation of Death* (New York: Institute for Evolutionary Research, 1976), pp. 70–71.

[4]The Mother, *Mother's Agenda*, vol. 1, p. 223.

[5]The Mother, *Mother's Agenda*, vol. 1, p. 209.

[6]The Mother, *Mother's Agenda*, 13 vols., edited by Satprem (New York: Institute for Evolutionary Research, 1979–2000).

[7]The Mother, *Mother's Agenda*, vol. 1, p. 366.

[8]The Mother, *Collected Works of The Mother*, vol. 3: *Questions and Answers* (Pondicherry, India: Sri Aurobindo Ashram Press, 1976), p. 173.

[9]The Mother, *Mother's Agenda*, vol. 1, p. 69.

[10]The Mother, *Mother's Agenda*, vol. 10: *1969*, edited by Satprem (New York: Institute for Evolutionary Research, 1998), pp. 18–20.

[11]Rupert Sheldrake, *The Presence of the Past* (New York: Vintage Books, 1989), p. 371.

[12]Sheldrake, *The Presence of the Past*, p. 371.

[13]Sheldrake, *The Presence of the Past*, pp. 177–178.

[14]The Mother, *Mother's Agenda*, vol. 1, p. 119.

17

Spirit in Matter

*A progressively perfect real-
ization in the body is the aim
of human evolution.*

—*Sri Aurobindo*[1]

We are quite ignorant of the true nature of matter so long as we rely on our mind and senses. While our body appears to us as solid and inert, this is a perception of false matter. Our entire worldview is based on ignorance of the true reality of things. Matter is real, not an illusion, but something false has been added to it, and that is what we perceive. Science has demonstrated that matter is really energy in motion. But energy in its essence is actually consciousness that is an extension of the Supreme.

The Mother made the following observations in 1968 about cellular composition:

> The cells have an inner composition or structure, which corresponds to the structure of the uni-verse…. Each cell is composed of different radi-

ances, with a wholly luminous center, and the
connection is established between light and
light…. Each cell is a world in miniature corresponding to the whole…. That is precisely what
the transformation of the body is: the physical
cells not only become conscious, but receptive to
the true Consciousness-Force; that is, they allow
the working of this higher Consciousness. That
is the work of transformation.[2]

The conscious transformative process that the Mother was
going through—and that is still unconsciously operative in the
world today for most of humanity—is a monumental shift from
the false to the true reality. When I returned from my first trip to
Pondicherry, in 1974, I was unconsciously attempting to bridge
this gap in the body. Just as our perception of beauty comes in
gradations, so our process of transformation also comes in stages.
Our body has to learn to adapt, for it cannot absorb the higher
energies all at once. This is one of the reasons why the process
has to extend over a period of years.

Body Holds the Key

Our body is so much a part of us that we never look at it for
answers in our spiritual quest. The Mother remarked about the
importance of the body:

The body is something very, very simple
and very childlike, and it has that experience so imperatively, you understand, it
doesn't need to "seek"; it just has to stop
its activity for a minute and…it's there.
So then, it wonders why people haven't
been aware of that since the beginning? It
wonders, "Why, why have they sought all
kinds of things—religions, gods…all
kinds of things—when it's so simple!" So
simple, for the body it's so simple, so self-
evident.

All those constructions—religions,

philosophies...all those constructions— are a need of the mind to "play the game." It wants to play the game well. While the body is so simple, so simple, so obvious! So obvious, so simple: "Why," it wonders, "Why, why have they been seeking all kinds of complications...when it's so simple?" The very fact of saying, "The Divine is deep within you"...(it remembers its own experience, you understand) is so complicated, while it's so simple!

It can't explain, can't express, there are no words, but it has a sort of conscious perception of...(*Mother makes a slight twisting gesture with the tips of her fingers*) what distorts and veils. And that's what has become reality for all human consciousnesses.

It's hard to express.

For the body it's become such an obvious fact.... It wonders how one can think otherwise, feel otherwise? It's so obvious. [3]

Purification of the Cells

The cell is the smallest independent unit of living substance that requires purification. It is a different kind of purification from the purification of our mental and emotional beings whereby we have to establish some measure of equality and peace.

Mantra

Our body and cells are heavily influenced by our thoughts, which can create poor health or illness. Our sensations, thoughts, and emotions create a type of covering over our cells that causes opacity. All physical bodies have this. To bring light into the cells—or rather, to let the cells radiate their essence of light is the desired state. The preparatory stage is a gradual process. I know of no single method to achieve it. The Mother used a process called *Japa* ("repeating a mantra"), which she considered essential for her own pioneering efforts, saying that it had the power to calm everything. After a while, she noticed that the cells themselves spontaneously repeated the mantra:

> *Om*
> *Namo*
> *Bhagavate*

The Mother translated and commented on this as follows:

> *The first word represents:*
> *the supreme invocation*
> *the invocation to the Supreme.*
> *The second word represents:*
> *total self-giving;*
> *perfect surrender.*
> *The third word represents:*
> *the aspiration,*
> *what the manifestation must*
> *become—Divine.*[4]

The Mother said about this mantra that "the slightest mental activity lessens the power; there must be a thrust of the whole being, with as little thought as possible."[5]

When I use this mantra on occasion, I visualize a golden light stationed above my head, which then sweeps down through my body and out the bottom of my feet—all in a few seconds. It is like taking a divine shower. While I am doing this, I recite the mantra, starting with *Om* at the top of my head and finishing with *Bhagavate* at my feet. Then I repeat the process several times until I feel permeated with divine consciousness.

Supramental Ship

The Mother described her experience of the transition between two worlds as passing from false to true matter.[6] She symbolically represented the Supramental work being carried out as an immense ship, as big as a city, in which people destined for the Supramental life were being trained. Although she described this world in symbolic terms, she noted that it actually exists on another plane.[7]

In the Mother's vision, the immense ship has just arrived at the shore of the Supramental world, and the first batches of people destined to become future inhabitants are about to disembark at the wharf. Those ready to go ashore are screened. Some, however, are not of a uniform color, but have dull gray patches on them that resemble the Earth's substance. These people cannot go ashore and have to stay on the ship for more training—that is, purification of matter. The decision is based exclusively on the substance constituting their bodies—that is, on whether or not they are made of the Supramental substance. In no way is the criterion moral or psychological.

The Mother later said that this ship was only a stage in the work:

> This physical body is capable of a progressive development; the physical substance progresses through each individual formation, and one day it will be able to build a bridge between physical life as we know it and the supramental life that is to manifest.[8]

I believe that this stage has been completed and that Supramental Consciousness and matter have now been connected. My point in relating this vision was to place emphasis on the necessity of our purifying our cells. Because the Force bypasses the mind and goes directly into the body, some people may be going through this purification unconsciously.

Purification in Death Valley

One warm spring day in March 1986, I learned for the first time how effective the purifying process can be. Surama and I were staying at the Furnace Creek Inn in Death Valley, where the unique landscape of the desert is spectacular. The dry heat and the grandeur of the vista allowed us to open up. That night, I had a dream, which I recorded in my diary:

> I seem to be outside the Sri Aurobindo Ashram in Pondicherry. Although the buildings and people look familiar, there is nothing quite like it there. To gain access inside, I am told by someone, whom I do not recognize, to stand at a certain spot. As I stand there, a light (either silver or golden—I am not sure which) comes from overhead down through my body and out my feet. As I look down, the light has turned grayish, almost brackish, as it leaves my body. I do not know what to make of this, other than that my body seems to be purified, and I am allowed entry. There are many people mingling inside in a courtyard with open stairs alongside a building. Everyone is of a different nature than we see on Earth—luminous and joyful. On the stairway, there is an attractive woman who stands out. She is neither clothed nor naked, but has glittering sequins or pieces of paper on her body. She has a particularly joyful, vital presence. As I walk up the stairs, I meet a man who appears to know me, but I do not recognize him. He says he lives on the avenues in San Francisco.

A few years later, around 1992, I met Rev. Joseph Martinez, who had his residence and spiritual healing center between 8th and 9th avenues in San Francisco. I believe he was the man I saw in the dream. I did not ask him about this, as I did not make the connection until after he passed away in 1995.

My dream, which I later realized was an experience of cell purification, came spontaneously without any effort or knowledge on my part, and I believe something similar can happen for others. The Mother's stated objective was to make it easier for others who followed her. We are all in the same boat.

Opacity in Matter

"It's a certain opacity in Matter, of the substance," the Mother said, "which prevents it from being able to manifest the Consciousness."[9] The very cells of our bodies have to be prepared to receive the Supramental vibration. By necessity, this must be a gradual process, so that the body will be capable of receiving and containing the higher vibration. When I awoke from my dream, I felt cleansed and fantastic, but it was many years before I noticed a decisive change in my body. The conversion is rapid, but the preparation is long.

Nervous System

Another preliminary stage is the transformation of our nervous system. Our nerves can be very difficult to control and, as we all know, are very sensitive to any stimuli. The Mother's nervous system was a formidable obstacle for her in 1968. As the pioneer for Supramental Consciousness, she took months—and in some cases, years—to work through a particular transformation in her own body. After she removed the barriers, the rest of us could progress much more quickly.

A few years ago, my own nerves became extremely sensitive—something I had never experienced before. That lasted about a week and then subsided, at which point I went into a deep calm within my body. I was able to talk effortlessly with people, whereas conversation had previously exhausted me.

For years, the Mother went through one bodily difficulty after another in order to make her body more and more receptive to the Supramental Consciousness. Nevertheless, she said that her body was no different from anyone else's and was made up of the same substances.

The Web

One bodily difficulty that the Mother had was her encounter with the covering that is around each cell. This covering, which she called the "web," is what separates false from true matter. The Mother said about this:

The body is being given an education: it's being taught how to will—the true way of being and willing. And over the entire material creation (*gesture covering and enveloping the earth*), there is a tissue—which we might call "catastrophic"—a tissue of bad will. That is to say, a sort of web, yes, a defeatist web—defeatist, catastrophic—where you botch what you wanted to do, where there are all possible accidents, all possible bad wills. Like a web. And the body is being taught to get out of it.

It's as if mingled with the Force that realizes and expresses itself; it's like something mingling with the material creation. And the body is being taught to break free from it. But it's difficult, very difficult.

It's the cause of diseases, the cause of accidents—it's the cause of all destructive things.

And this web is there constantly, all the time, like this (*same covering gesture*).

It's very tightly mingled [with the body].*It's not clearly separated yet.[10]

Physical Mind

This web encases the cells with layers of mind. The most obstinate layer that the Mother encountered was the physical mind, the mind of habits and routines. It is this mind that is incessantly repeating, "Did I lock the door? Did I turn the heat off? Did I feed the cat?" It is such repetition that keeps us trapped in our false matter, our illusions. The Mother eventually found that this physical mind was essential for stabilizing the new consciousness in the transformed body.

To get a better idea of the impact of this physical mind on our consciousness, think of all the things you tend to resist: accepting the new and giving up the old. New ideas, new ventures, new routines. Old judgments, old preferences, old fears. The list is endless. We not only struggle with these impediments within ourselves, but are constantly bombarded by them in our own environment.

That

The Mother was getting closer and closer to the purpose of life on Earth—or rather, the experience of that purpose in matter. It is not possible to identify or delineate the Supreme either in or out of its manifestation. The Supreme cannot be comprehended by the mind, which "knows" by dividing, dissecting, and analyzing. The Supreme, on the other hand, is whole, knows by unity, and encompasses the spaceless and the timeless. The Mother referred to the Supreme as "That" (*Tat* in Sanskrit). The manifest and the unmanifest worlds exist simultaneously, one over the other, although we have been familiar only with the former. To the Mother, the unmanifest world was becoming known in the manifest. This is the Supermind, or Supramental Consciousness. Oneness can be experienced in substance as well as in the mind. "That" permeates matter.

Power as Protection

The ultimate effect of this is beyond our wildest imagination. Presently, some indications of that effect are registered in time and space. The Supermind, at least at this stage in the Earth's evolution, is extraordinarily powerful. This power is likely to be the first aspect of the Supermind to manifest, since the new beings will need the utmost in protection. The Mother has described this Supramental power as a warm, radiating, dense golden light. In my diary, I described my own experience of it in these words:

> In my meditation, I had a very clear vision of myself walking down a city street. Ahead of me were three menacing young men. They approached me, and one lifted up his arm as if to strike me. At that moment, a golden light appeared (it seemed to emanate from me) and flooded the scene. It was thick and rich (like 24K gold) and vibrating with incredible power (moving and not moving). At the same time, it was

320 GOD SHALL GROW UP

transparent. The scene ended there with my as-
sailant frozen in space with his arm extended,
unable to move. The power was not threatening,
but had a quality of love to it. Everyone there
appeared to be transformed by the peace of that
force.

The initial utility of Supramental power serves as our protection in the world and gives us a hint of the benevolent stu-
pendous force of matter. The Supermind has a direct will on
matter. Time and space are no longer barriers in the material
world. Eventually, one should be able to move through space by
a projection of will to one location or many. The division between subject and object will no longer apply. "I am here; you
are there" will become "I am here; you are here." Life and death
will merge so that one will be neither on this side (life) nor that
side (death), but a third state will prevail. Past, present, and future will become a convention of convenience rather than a bind-
ing law of physics.

Life and Death

This is the natural consequence of the merger of consciousness of the time-bound and the eternal. Death, too, is in the process of change. The conquest of death is the central theme of Sri
Aurobindo's epic poem *Savitri*. In the *Agenda*, the Mother explored and talked extensively about her experiences moving to
the realm of death and back to life. The barrier between the two
diminished for her.

Eventually, a few people will be able to have life at will—
that is, they will decide when to leave their material body. The
problem the Mother faced, and that we are all facing today, is
the necessity of extending physical life long enough to have the
necessary experiences to transform our consciousness and body.
Science appears to be making progress in the aging process, so
we may have some cellular method within the next decade available to us to extend life.

Her Legacy

There are yogic disciplines for people to move in consciousness from one place to another. The Mother had this ability, but she was compelled to remain in her body for the bodily transformation she was undergoing. She could not keep her consciousness separated from her body. She said that she knew every yogic trick in the book, but she had to endure every discomfort and pain while in her body. Her transformation had to take place in her physical body. That is her legacy to us. As a result of her accomplishments, we have an opportunity to move more quickly and easily into the new consciousness.

Fixed in the Body

The key to the entire transformative process is to fix the Supramental Force in our body so that there is one mass of Supramental vibration throughout every part of us. The vibration becomes part of our body permanently, day and night, awake or asleep. We may become momentarily annoyed or irritated or even depressed, but the vibration is still there. *It is fixed in matter.* No longer do we have to go out of our body into an unconscious state of reverie to find spirit. That state is continual in our body. It feels like a constant adrenaline rush, or even a bit like a fever, but one that makes you feel alive. As the vibration intensifies, it also feels like a burning sensation, but it is not unpleasant. There is a joy in the body that emits a continual faint smile.

This consciousness in the body does not have to be instructed. It knows what to do and when to do it. The movement is progressive—that is, it self-regulates according to the body's capacity to receive the Force. In order to receive and contain the Force, we must attain some equanimity in our mental, physical, and vital beings. We allow the Force to take over the transformative process, so that we do nothing more than stay out of the way. The Force may decide to exert its influence on or transmit its consciousness to others, but there is never any motivation for egotistical gains. In fact, the Force cannot operate in that sphere. If there is any egotistical attempt in that domain, the Force will withdraw. No special training or knowledge is needed for the

Force to act. Once the Supramental Force has been fixed in the body and cells, it becomes self-sufficient. Looking at if from the direction of the cell (and the atom), we see the light of God revealing itself. It was there all along, but asleep. A mighty blow has awakened spirit in matter.

When the San Francisco Giants baseball team had its first season in its new stadium, Pacific Bell Park, located on the bay, I went to watch a game with the St. Louis Cardinals. I knew it would be a long day, but I didn't give it any thought. I left home at 4:00 P.M. to take the ferry from Oakland, planning to return home about midnight. On the return trip, I noticed that I still had a lot of energy. Rather than sitting down, I was pacing back and forth on the boat. It occurred to me later that my body had self-regulated the energy for the long day in the crowd. I realized that when I had awakened that morning, I had done thirty modified pushups when I normally can only do fifteen, at best. Apparently, my body consciousness had anticipated the need for additional energy.

Vibration

When we deal with the invisible realm, we are always talking about vibration. It is vibration that created the universe. We are a mass of vibrations, which course throughout our body. Acupuncturists allow our bodies to heal by restoring their blocked vibrations.

If the human body could tolerate an ultra-high vibration, it would disappear, at least to most eyes. The new being would be invisible to most people because their focus has been conditioned to be on inert matter, and they are blinded to new ways of being. They have to expand their visual limits.

New Sight

Very likely, the first sense to change in Supramental Consciousness will be sight. Just as 3-D glasses turn two dimensions into three at the movies, so Supramental Consciousness will add an extra dimension to our vision, allowing us to see into infinite space. Objects in the foreground will not obstruct objects in the background. We will be able to see around everything, which will be exhilarating. Furthermore, we will be able to see physical events at a distance as they are happening. This will not be a type of clairvoyance, but rather a new way of seeing, whether our eyes are open or shut. I myself have already experienced both distance-vision and seeing around objects to infinity, so I know they are possible.

New Breathing

Each of our other senses will also be transformed into new and direct forms of perception, as will other bodily functions. For example, as I discovered from experience one morning a few years ago, breathing can come from a source other than our lungs. Initially, we will inhale through our subtle physical body and then exhale through our entire physical body. This "exhaling" will feel and appear like light in all of our cells. It will be an Ananda in the cells that produces waves of ecstasy with each exhalation. The process will be repeated over and over, just like our normal breathing today. It is already possible, but the euphoria is so intense that one would have difficulty functioning in everyday life. But at some point, when the entire physical organism and the environment are sufficiency prepared, there will be a transfer of authority to the Supramental Being, and Supramental breathing will be as easy and as natural as the conventional breathing that it replaces. As Sri Aurobindo wrote in *Savitri:*

> A divine force shall flow through tissue and cell
> And take the charge of breath and speech and act
> And all the thoughts shall be a glow of suns
> And every feeling a celestial thrill.[11]

Psychic Being as the Medium

The Mother pondered the new being, or at least the next stage in the Supramental process. With her experience of the Supramental personality or superman consciousness on January 1, 1969, she realized that this would be the intermediary being who would take material form. The medium for this form will be the psychic being that each of us is forming over innumerable lifetimes. Each psychic being preserves its uniqueness and yet has the same fundamental creative source, the Supreme, which only becomes perfect in matter. The question remains how and when that psychic being will manifest in our material world. It seems that our existing physical body must go through an extensive adaptive process (kneading of matter) to make it receptive while our new being is created in another dimension of consciousness. And it may well be that it is a combination of these two processes, or a merging of the two, that will give material form to the psychic being.

Individual and Collective Together

My own perception is that it is human resistance more than anything else that is delaying the manifestation of the process. The individual and collective transformations must be linked. It is likely, even probable, that a few people will start the process and that consciousness will be transmitted to others who are receptive and ready to collaborate. No one person can do it, no matter how evolved, knowledgeable, or powerful he or she may be. The transformation will require a representative sample of personality types to be effective and complete. The Lord plays in the universe in innumerable forms, not in just one or a few. Each of us can be His masterpiece expressed in a Supramental body.

A Vision

In July 1990, I saw my own "new body," radiant and full of light in the subtle world. The vision lasted for only a few seconds so I did not have time to observe any details. But tears of joy flowed after the vision. On March 24, 1972, The Mother related her own similar experience:

> For the first time, early this morning, I saw myself: my body. I don't know whether it's the supramental body or…(what shall I say?) a transitional body, but I had a completely new body, in the sense that it was sexless: it was neither

woman nor man.

It was very white. But that could be because I have white skin, I don't know.

It was very slender (*gesture*). Really lovely, a truly harmonious form.[12]

Notes

*The words in brackets were added by Satprem. At the end of this paragraph, he has the following footnote: "This 'web' is what separates our false matter from the true world 'like a lining of ours,' the place where Mother did not see previously."

[1]Sri Aurobindo, *Birth Centenary Library*, vol. 12: *The Upanishads* (Pondicherry, India: Sri Aurobindo Ashram Press, 1972), p. 89.

[2]The Mother, *Collected Works of the Mother*, vol. 12: *On Education* (Pondicherry, India: Sri Aurobindo Ashram Press, 1976), pp. 345–346.

[3]The Mother, *Mother's Agenda*, vol. 9: *1968*, edited by Satprem (New York: Institute for Evolutionary Research, 1995), pp. 345–346.

[4]The Mother, *Mother's Agenda*, vol. 6: *1965*, edited by Satprem (New York: Institute for Evolutionary Research, 1989), p. 29.

[5]The Mother, *Mother's Agenda*, vol. 6, p. 30.

[6]The Mother, *Mother's Agenda*, vol. 1: *1951–1960*, edited by Satprem (New York: Institute for Evolutionary Research, 1979), p. 141.

[7]The Mother, *Mother's Agenda*, vol. 1, p. 137.

[8]The Mother, *Mother's Agenda*, vol. 1, p. 251.

[9]The Mother, *Mother's Agenda*, vol. 9, p. 263.

[10]The Mother, *Mother's Agenda*, vol. 9, pp. 245–246.

[11]Sri Aurobindo, *Birth Centenary Library*, vol. 29: *Savitri* (Pondicherry, India: Sri Aurobindo Ashram Press, 1972), p. 710.

[12]The Mother, *Mother's Agenda*, vol. 13: *1972–1973*, edited by Satprem (New York: Institute for Evolutionary Research, 1983), p. 96.

18

A Simple Aspiration

Imagine the Supreme Himself coming and saying, "Listen now, I'm here to tell you that this is the way it is, get ready."

—The Mother[1]

I related earlier the vision I once had of a luminous Earth surrounded by pulsating colors. Here is the Mother's description of a similar vision, which she had in 1963:

> I was shown a glorious earth, lit with an inner light. So instead of a burning sun, it was a Light that allowed Life to exist—you understand, it was the Physical itself that had become luminous. I saw that, I remember VERY DISTINCTLY seeing it.[2]

We can begin to see now that all the centuries of pain and suffering have had a purpose. It is the only way to knead matter to make it receptive to the Supramental. Death itself has created

328 God Shall Grow Up

intensity in the cells—an intensity that would not have been there otherwise.

We have learned from and participated in our universe through the play of opposites. We have learned the difference between life and death, fear and courage, love and hate. The manifestation of Supramental Consciousness allows us to know and experience the joy of unity, the conjunction of opposites, but with a difference. Something else emerges beyond good and evil. Perfection and imperfection are there side by side. We have focused on imperfection. When Rainbow, the homeless hippie poet, made a slight shift in his consciousness, his perfection emerged, instantly visible for others to see.

Transitional Period

Oneness is the key, with enormous diversity within it. We have the opportunity to participate in life with a new harmony, and this consciousness will not only bring peace to us but to the Earth as well. Meanwhile, we have to withstand the accelerated chaos, violence, and falsehood that is surfacing today. Sri Aurobindo said that all governments would be under the direct influence of the Supramental by 1967. But Grace does not mean that everything will run smoothly. If we have a larger perspective, a global outlook, we can be aware of what the transformation is leading to. We have witnessed the breakup of the Soviet Union.

The adverse forces are unleashing their fury in the world because they know their time of rule is up. The Mother remarked about this:

> The world as it is today is in its greater part under the influence of the adverse forces. We call them adverse because they do not want the divine life; they oppose the divine life. They want things to remain as they are, because it is their field and their power in the world. They know very well that they will lose all power and all influence the moment the Divine manifests. So they

are fighting openly and completely against the Divine, and we have to tear away from them bit by bit, little by little, all the things they have conquered in the outer life.[3]

New Reality

Reality is not what we have been led to believe. Our minds and senses deceive us. A new reality is emerging. The preparation is long because we have to be ready to receive the Supramental and contain it in our bodies. No longer do we have to go out of our body into an altered state of consciousness. The preparation that establishes peace in our bodies is gradual, but the transformation itself is sudden.

Keep It Simple

The most difficult part of this entire process is to know how simple it is. Our mind continually wants to complicate matters and figure things out. This is a circular process that only leads to confusion. We cannot understand the Divine manifesting in matter any more than we can understand God. As the Mother said, "NOBODY can comprehend to what extent the Lord is intermingled, is present and active in all things."[4] All we can do is to collaborate, lend our good will, aspire, surrender ourselves, and have faith. This can be most difficult for those with a high degree of mental development, who want to figure things out, those who lack faith, and those who have no aspiration for a higher consciousness.

Women Will Lead

In general, this transformative period will be a time when women will come to the front because they have the qualities that are ideally suited for the transformation. Men will have to nurture those feminine qualities within themselves. Women know how and when to surrender, which is essential for the process. They know how to share power, so it will be women who will help lead us to the future. They have an innate sense of beauty. Their mistake in the present age is to imitate the masculine qualities and to reject the feminine ones. The new emphasis on beauty will not be to create sex appeal but to express the radiance of the Divine.

Offering

Everything is offered to the Divine. A most intimate dialogue is initiated and maintained, which is a karma yoga whereby we offer the Divine all of our thoughts, feelings, and problems. The Mother herself was faced with the difficulty of pioneering the transformation of her own body. At every step of the way, she offered herself to the Lord, saying, "Here it is, Lord. You do it." She once remarked about this fundamental process:

> Struggling, giving itself headaches— phew!…Absolutely useless, absolutely useless. It leads nowhere, except to more confusion.
>
> You find yourself facing a so-called problem: "What am I to say? What am I to do? How should I act?…" There is nothing to do! Nothing but to say to the Lord, "You see, here's the situation." That's all. And then keep very still. And spontaneously, without thinking about it, without reflecting, without calculating, without doing anything, anything whatsoever, without the slightest effort…you do what must be done. But it's the Lord who does it, it's no longer you. He does it, He arranges the circumstances, He arranges the people, He puts the words in your mouth or under your pen—He does it all, all, all, all, and you have nothing more to do, nothing but let yourself live in bliss.
>
> I am beginning to be convinced that people don't really want it.[5]

When the Mother said this, Satprem said to her: "But it's the spadework beforehand, clearing the way for it, that's hard, that's difficult."

"You don't even need to do that!" the Mother replied. "He does it for you."

"But there's a constant invasion," Satprem insisted, "the old consciousness, the old thoughts." To this, the Mother said:

> Yes, out of habit it all tries to start up again. But all you need to say is, "Look, Lord; see, see how it is." That's all. "Look at this, Lord, look at that, look at this idiot here…" and it's over. Immediately. And the change comes automatically, *mon petit*, without the slightest effort. Simply…simply be sincere, in other words, TRULY want the right thing. One is quite conscious of being powerless, utterly incompetent: more and more, I feel that this amalgam of matter, of cells and all the rest, is just pitiful! Pitiful. I don't know, under certain conditions people may feel powerful, wonderful, luminous, competent…but as far as I am concerned, that's because they have no idea what they're really like! When you really see what you're made of…it's nothing, really nothing. But it's capable of anything, provided…provided you let the Lord do it.[6]

All Life Is Spiritual

The age we are in now is not meant to be for creating another religion or philosophy, or even a spiritual practice with a set of rules and established order of discipline. There is to be *no* "spiritual life," because *all life* is to be spiritual. Every act is to be consecrated.

Faith

Faith is a very necessary quality to nourish in this process. The more faith we have, the more open and receptive we are. The idea that "faith can move mountains" is very appropriate today because it is our perception of matter itself being moved to another dimension. Since space-time has already been integrated with eternity, the movement is actually only a shift in our consciousness. The mountain only *appears* to move.

The power of faith to cure illness is well recognized by physicians, who call it the "placebo effect." A significant percentage of people experience healing simply by taking a sugar pill. They have put their faith in the pill, doctors, science, and the whole medical establishment. Faith can take us out of limiting lifelong habits, opening us to a new dawn of light.

Time to Choose

Sri Aurobindo wrote extensively about the entire process of the Supramental, of which we are only now at the first stage. It will likely take centuries before the process is completed. If we can realize our psychic being, as I described in an earlier chapter, we will be prepared for the Supramental manifestation. The higher spiritual or cosmic planes, which Sri Aurobindo described as a series of ascents and descents, bringing consciousness down onto the Earth plane, have now been completed. The descent of peace, power, light, and bliss will occur spontaneously when we are prepared to receive them without any effort on our part. Everything is right here, right now! The lower and higher parts of the circle were joined by those ascents and descents. The Supreme above in the Superconscient has joined with the Supreme below in the Inconscient. The Supramental has manifested in matter, and we have only to submit to the process. This is our challenge and our choice.

We can choose to participate by making a simple aspiration. The level of participation is up to us—that is, how quickly and how far we wish to progress. The transformation is happening now on a global basis, but largely at an unconscious level. People are having experiences in their bodies without understanding or even realizing it, because the process is not mental. Nevertheless, a few know that something is afoot. The process is direct: matter to matter. Those who are most prepared will be able to receive and contain the Supramental Consciousness. Now is the time to choose. Judgment Day is here, but *we* are the judges.

There is no exclusiveness in this process. No one book or individual has all the truth. Transformation is both an individual and a collective process, to which each person has something unique to contribute. No one can have exclusive possession of the Truth, because the Truth is Oneness, containing everything, both in matter and in consciousness.

The Mother said about the descent and process of the Supermind:

> Sri Aurobindo [described] what was to be done to enter into contact with the Supermind and prepare the ground for its manifestation; but now that it has entered the earth-atmosphere, I don't see why a single, precise procedure should be inflicted upon it in its manifestation. If it chooses to directly illuminate an instrument which it finds suitable or ready or adaptable, I don't see why it should not do so....
>
> I think that all possibilities are predictable and that all sincere aspiration and complete consecration will have a response, and that the processes, means, transitions, transformations will be innumerable in nature—not at all that things will happen only in a particular way and not otherwise.
>
> In fact, anything, everything that is ready to receive even a particle or a particular aspect of the supramental consciousness and light must *automatically* receive it. And the effects of this consciousness and light will be innumerable, for they will certainly be adapted to the possibilities, the capacity of each one according to the sincerity of his aspiration.
>
> The more total the consecration and the intenser the aspiration, the more integral and intense can be the result. But the effect of the supramental action will be countless in its manifestations —multiple, innumerable, infinitely varied, not necessarily following a precise line which is the same for all. That is impossible. For it is contrary to the very nature of the supramental consciousness....

But that does not mean that anybody at all, at any moment and in any way, is suddenly going to become a supramental genius. That is not to be expected.

I was going to say, if one only noticed that one was a little less stupid than before, that would already be something![7]

Another error is eclecticism, or wanting to take a little of this and a little of that to make a spiritual system. That only muddles everything. Obviously, there will be a strong tendency to codify the Yoga of Transformation, trying to systematize its methods, but that only makes a bigger box. We want no box at all. There are no longer any limitations. But each person has to find his or her own way. There are a million paths to the Truth. Sincerity is the key and the safety net. We have to want to know our own truth of being with an ever-increasing aspiration, or flame in the heart. We must increase our sincerity and faith, and be more and more receptive to the Divine Force. Our freedom must be preserved in our journey. That is, each of us has to decide if and when to surrender to the Divine.

Contagion

The seed has been planted to take root in all those who are ready. I have discussed under the concept of contagion how the realization of Supramental Consciousness by one person is spread to others. The consciousness of the illumined cell is transmitted to other receptive cells. This process is happening now all over the Earth and is ongoing. This was the Mother's gift to us. She described it as a kind of contagion or imitation:

There are two things.... One, for instance, which I have often observed: an illness is triggered, or a disorder is triggered, and there is a kind of...it isn't a contagion (how can I explain it?), it would almost be like an "imitation," but that's not quite it. Let's say that a certain number of cells give way; for some reason or other (there are countless reasons), they submit to the disorder—obey the disorder—and a particular point becomes "ill" according to the ordinary view of illness. But that intrusion of Disorder makes itself felt everywhere, it has repercussions everywhere: wherever there is a weaker point which doesn't resist the attack so well, it manifests. Take someone who is in the habit of getting headaches, or toothaches, or a cough, or neuralgic pains, whatever, a host of little things of that sort that come and go, increase and decrease. But if there is an attack of Disorder somewhere, a serious attack, all those little troubles reappear instantly, here, there, there.... It's a fact I have observed. And the opposite movement follows the same pattern: if you are able to bring to the attacked spot the true Vibration—the Vibration of Order and Harmony—and you stop the Disorder...all the other things are put back in order, as if automatically.

And that doesn't happen through contagion, you see; it isn't that, for instance, the blood carries the illness here or there, that's not it: it is...almost like a spirit of imitation.

But the truth is that the Harmony that keeps everything together has been attacked, it has given way, and so everything is disrupted (each thing in its own way and according to its own habit).

I am speaking here of the body's cells, but it's the same thing with external events, even with world events. It's even remarkable with regard to earthquakes, volcanic eruptions, etc.: it would seem that the entire earth is like the body; that is to say, if one point gives way and manifests Disorder, all the sensitive points suffer the same effect.

From the human standpoint, in a crowd, it's extraordinarily precise: the contagion of a vibration—especially vibrations of disorder (but the others, too).

It is an absolutely concrete demonstration of Oneness. It's very interesting.

It is something I have observed on the level of the body's cells hundreds and hundreds of times. And then, you no longer have at all that mental impression of one "disorder added to another, which makes the problem more difficult"— that's not it at all, it's…if you get to the center, all the rest will be naturally restored to order. And that's a fact: if order is restored at the center of disorder, everything follows naturally, without your paying it any special attention.

From the human standpoint, from the standpoint of revolutions, from the standpoint of fights, from the standpoint of wars, it's extraordinarily accurate and precise.

An absolutely concrete demonstration of Oneness.

And it is this knowledge of Oneness that gives you the key.

People wonder how, for instance, the action of one man or of one thought can restore order— this is how. Not that you have to think of all the troubled spots, no: you have to get to the center. And everything will be restored to order, automatically.[8]

America

One of the places in the world that will be especially receptive to this Oneness and change in consciousness, according to the Mother, is the United States, which has a unique role to play in the Supramental transformation. Below are some of the Mother's comments that relate to the receptiveness of Americans to the Yoga of Transformation:

The Old World is an OLD world in the true sense of the word. India is much, much older, but more alive. Yet now it strikes me as so very rotten! They went rotten. You know what happens when a rotten apple is put next to a good one: England came and stayed much too long. It made things go quite rotten. Very, very rotten; it's difficult to heal. Otherwise, what's not rotten is truly good.

But there is a place where something is awakening, a small something like what little children and animals have, going like this (*Mother imitates a baby bird poking its beak out of the nest and peering around*), peep-peep-peep, oh, alert and eager to know: America. They have a carapace as hard as an automobile's—it has to be hammered open, but underneath there's something that wants to know...and knows nothing, nothing, is totally ignorant—but oh, it wants to know! And this can be touched. They may be the first to awaken.

A few in India, but a more widespread movement in America.[9]

In a conversation with Satprem, the Mother noted how open Westerners in general are to change:

[SATPREM:] Yet you get the feeling that with the kind of sincerity Westerners have, they would progress very quickly once they understood.

[THE MOTHER:] That's more or less what Sri Aurobindo was saying.

[SATPREM:] Because they're sincere.

[THE MOTHER:] Yes, they have a sincerity, on one level, which is not the same as spiritual sincerity. They have a material sincerity, a material HONESTY, and with that, once they understood, they would progress very quickly. But I think it will be primarily a question of individuals, not something general.[10]

At one point, the Mother noted how Americans' childlike innocence makes them so open-minded:

The Americans are more open, because they have remained more childlike—they think they know everything on a material level, but they also know that there are things they don't know.[11]

It is the very youthfulness of Americans, according to the Mother, that gives them the spirit of adventure.

They're young and still feel they want to learn— they blunder, they make a mess of many things, but there remains the need to learn.

I have the feeling that's where the center of transformation will be. The European countries are old.

They've lost the enthusiasm that makes you act without thinking about consequences. They're constantly weighing the consequences of everything they do. In America there's an aspiration. That's where the push will be.[12]

Despite the American preference for speed, however, the Mother observes that the transformation there will not be quick:

One of the things in the offing is the conversion of America, the United States, but it will take time.[13]

Joy of Progress

It is time to choose. Will we collaborate or not? The transformation will go on with or without us, but it may be very painful if we do not collaborate. Furthermore, we will miss the joy of progress. We are indeed fortunate to be on Earth at this time. Eternal hope is materializing into a reality that is present and available to us all. As Sri Aurobindo wrote in *Savitri*:

Nature shall live to manifest secret God,
The Spirit shall take up the human play,
This earthly life becomes the life divine.[14]

Sowing the Seed

As the Mother said :

> ... for the transformation of the body and eventu-
> ally of the earth, by the transforming action of
> the Supramental, would be accomplished if I
> could sow a seed of this Supramental substance
> in the human species and which will then ensure
> its continuity on earth... Even if it be only a thou-
> sandth infinitesimal part of what I carry, it will
> be sufficient to perpetuate this movement.[15]

And the work continues.

Notes

[1]The Mother, *Mother's Agenda*, vol. 2: *1961*, edited by Satprem (New York: Institute for Evolutionary Research, 1981), p. 352.

[2]The Mother, *Mother's Agenda*, vol. 4: *1963*, edited by Satprem (New York: Institute for Evolutionary Research, 1987), p. 243.

[3]The Mother, *The Synthesis of Yoga: The Mother's Talks*, edited by Shyam Sundar (Pondicherry: All India Press, 1989), p. 54.

[4]The Mother, *Mother's Agenda*, vol. 3: *1962*, edited by Satprem (New York: Institute for Evolutionary Research, 1982), p. 266.

[5]The Mother, *Mother's Agenda*, vol. 3, p. 377.

[6]The Mother, *Mother's Agenda*, vol. 3, p. 377.

[7]The Mother, *Synthesis of Yoga*, pp. 211–212.

[8]The Mother, *Mother's Agenda*, vol. 5: *1964*, edited by Satprem (New York: Institute for Evolutionary Research, 1988), pp. 212–213.

[9]The Mother, *Mother's Agenda*, vol. 3, p. 260.

[10]The Mother, *Mother's Agenda*, vol. 3, p. 268.

[11]The Mother, *Mother's Agenda*, vol. 4, pp. 289–290.

[12]The Mother, *Mother's Agenda*, vol. 12: *1971*, edited by Satprem (New York: Institute for Evolutionary Research, 1982), p. 37.

[13]The Mother, *Mother's Agenda*, vol. 12, p. 335.

[14]Sri Aurobindo, *Birth Centenary Library*, vol. 29: *Savitri* (Pondicherry, India: Sri Aurobindo Ashram Press, 1972), p. 711.

[15]Mona Sarkar, *The Supreme* (Pondicherry, India: Sri Aurobindo Ashram Press, 2001), p. 53.

About the Author
Wayne Bloomquist, Ph.D.

Dr. Bloomquist was first exposed to the teachings of Sri Aurobindo by Dr. Haridas Chaudhuri in 1969 at the Cultural Integration Fellowship (CIF) in San Francisco, and has made extended visits to the Sri Aurobindo Ashram in Pondicherry, India, since 1973. He received his Ph.D. in East-West Psychology from the California Institute of Integral Studies (CIIS) in 1976. From 1989 to 1996, he was the president of the Sri Aurobindo Association, for which, with his wife, Surama, he was the national book distributor in the United States.

Dr. Bloomquist has also been a board member of the CIF and CIIS, and was president of the CIIS Alumni Association. He has lectured at both institutions, as well as at the Cellular Evolution Workshop (Atlanta), the East-West Center (Los Angeles), the Phoenicia Pathworks (New York), the Savitri Learning Center (Baca Grande, Colorado), and the School for Natural Order (Baker, Nevada).

Over the years, Dr. Bloomquist has organized and hosted numerous conferences on spirituality, including "Spirit and the Flame" for the Cultural Integration Fellowship (1985); "Cellular Evolution: Transformation of the Body" for the Sri Aurobindo Association (1995); and "Divine Life in the Process of Evolution" at the Sri Aurobindo Ashram in Pondicherry (1998).

Dr. Bloomquist is the author of "Creativity and the Psychic Being," a chapter in a book devoted to Sri Aurobindo's foremost disciple, Nolini Kanta Gupta. He is also the editor of two compilations of writings by the Mother, *Search for the Soul* (1990) and *the Soul and Its Powers* (1992), both published by Lotus Light Publications.

Glossary of Terms

Agni: The divine fire or spark within that will manifest the latent divine possibilities within individuals.

Ananda: The bliss of pure conscious existence with love and beauty as its powers.

Aspiration: A call to the Divine for perfect delight of spirit.

Asura: Ignorant egoistic hostile beings in revolt against the Divine.

AUM (OM): Supreme invocation to the absolute.

Avatar: Incarnation of the Divine in human form.

Bhagavad Gita: A holy scripture that presents an episode of the great Indian epic, the Mahabharata, in which Krishna reveals to Arjuna, his disciple, the divine wisdom of the ages.

Brahman: The Supreme, Absolute, Eternal, Lord, or Self that is both mutable and immutable, active and inactive, and with and without qualities.

Central Being: Comprised of the Soul (spark of the Divine), psychic being, and the Jivatman.

Chit-Shakti: The creative force of the universe; the Consciousness-Force.

Consciousness: The self-aware force of existence that creates the universe by its motion or movement of energy.

Consciousness-Force: A universal energy that is a power of the Cosmic Spirit working out the cosmic and individual truth of things; the Divine Mother-Energy.

Contagion: Influence of structures of activity on subsequent similar structures of activity.

Darshan: Seeing God in one's guru, or the spiritually great, by an inner communication.

Delight: Ananda, bliss.

Divine, the: The Supreme Being and the Supreme Truth that has three aspects: Individual, Cosmic, and Transcendent.

Ego: The identification of our existence with our outer self, causing ignorance of our inner divine presence.

Evolution: Progressive unfolding of Spirit in the individual from its involved state of consciousness.

Inconscience: An inverse reproduction of the supreme Superconscience that is in a vast involved trance.

Integral Yoga: A total union with the Divine in the individual, universal, and transcendent parts of our being. Also called Purna Yoga.

Japa: Repetition of a mantra.

Jivatman: The Spirit or Eternal Self that is unborn but presides over the living human being from birth to birth; the true individual.

Karma: The principle of action in the universe with its stream of cause and effect. It should not, however, be understood as the fundamental cause of existence, which is the Supermind.

Kundalini: The sleeping divine power at the base of the spine.

Lila: A play of the Divine Being; a cosmic game.

Maya: Phenomenal consciousness; unreality; the original creative illusion.

Mysticism: Fundamental union with God.

Nirvana: Extinction of ego-limitations; dissolution of the external existence into some indefinable absolute.

Occultism: The knowledge and right use of the hidden forces of nature.

Overmind, the: The highest of the planes below the Supramental; global awareness.

Physical Mind, the: The part of the mind that is concerned only with physical things.

Prakriti: Energy or substance apart from consciousness (Purusha).

Psychic Being: The soul developing in evolution.

Purna: *See Integral Yoga.*

Purusha: The true being or basic consciousness in whatever plane it manifests; Spirit.

Realization: Reception in consciousness and establishment there of fundamental truths of the Divine.

Sachchidananda: The One, or God, with a triple aspect: existence (*Sat*), consciousness (*Chit*), and Ananda (*Bliss*).

Sadhana: Practice of yoga.

Samadhi: A trance or going inside consciousness away from outer objects.

Samsara: Wheel of continuous birth and rebirth sustained by karma.

Sankhya: One of six orthodox schools of philosophy in India, which teaches the two eternal realities of Spirit (Purusha) and Substance (Prakriti).

Sanskrit: A sacred language that expresses the truth of the seer-sages of ancient India.

Shakti: Power of the Lord.

Soul: Unformed essence of the Divine; spark.

Subtle Physical, the: The plane that is closest to the physical but has a freedom, plasticity, intensity, power, and color not found on our Earth-plane.

Supermind, the: Truth-Consciousness; a vast self-existence of the Brahman. The Supermind is infinite wisdom and infinite will totally free of all ignorance. Its fundamental character is knowledge by identity. It is the sole effective agent to transform humanity.

Supramental, the: Truth-Consciousness.

Surrender: Giving oneself to the Divine.

Sutra: Aphorism.

Tapasya: Spiritual effort.

TAT: The Absolute; That.

Transformation: An infusion of higher consciousness into the mind, the body, and the vital being.

Truth-Consciousness: An ordering self-knowledge, present everywhere, by which the One manifests the harmonies of its infinite potential in multiplicity.

Upanishads: Treatises in poetry and prose on spiritual and philosophical subjects.

Veda: Collections of illuminating hymns to the gods and goddesses of inner and outer nature.

Vedanta: A philosophy and spiritual discipline that presents the ultimate wisdom of the Vedas.

Vital, the: The life-nature made up of desires, sensations, feelings, passions, and energies of action.

Yoga: Union with the Divine through the practice of knowledge (jnana), through love (bhakti), or through actions of the will (karma).

Bibliography

Aurobindo, Sri. *Birth Centenary Library*, vol. 1: *Bande Mataram*. Pondicherry, India: Sri Aurobindo Ashram Press, 1972.

Aurobindo, Sri. *Birth Centenary Library*, vol. 5: *Collected Poems*. Pondicherry, India: Sri Aurobindo Ashram Press, 1972.

Aurobindo, Sri. *Birth Centenary Library*, vol. 9: *The Future Poetry*. Pondicherry, India: Sri Aurobindo Ashram Press, 1972.

Aurobindo, Sri. *Birth Centenary Library*, vol. 10: *The Secret of the Veda*. Pondicherry, India: Sri Aurobindo Ashram Press, 1972.

Aurobindo, Sri. *Birth Centenary Library*, vol. 12: *The Upanishads: Texts, Translations, and Commentaries*. Pondicherry, India: Sri Aurobindo Ashram Press, 1972.

Aurobindo, Sri. *Birth Centenary Library*, vol. 15: *Social and Political Thought*. Pondicherry, India: Sri Aurobindo Ashram Press, 1972.

Aurobindo, Sri. *Birth Centenary Library*, vol. 16: *The Supramental Manifestation*. Pondicherry, India: Sri Aurobindo Ashram Press, 1972.

Aurobindo, Sri. *Birth Centenary Library*, vol. 17: *The Hour of God*. Pondicherry, India: Sri Aurobindo Ashram Press, 1972.

Aurobindo, Sri. *Birth Centenary Library*, vols. 18–19: *The Life Divine*. Pondicherry, India: Sri Aurobindo Ashram Press, 1972.

Aurobindo, Sri. *Birth Centenary Library*, vols. 20–21: *The Synthesis of Yoga*. Pondicherry, India: Sri Aurobindo Ashram Press, 1972.

Aurobindo, Sri. *Birth Centenary Library*, vols. 23–24: *Letters on Yoga*. Pondicherry, India: Sri Aurobindo Ashram Press, 1972.

Aurobindo, Sri. *Birth Centenary Library*, vol. 26: *On Himself*. Pondicherry, India: Sri Aurobindo Ashram Press, 1972.

Aurobindo, Sri. *Birth Centenary Library*, vol. 27: *Supplement*. Pondicherry, India: Sri Aurobindo Ashram Press, 1972.

Aurobindo, Sri. *Birth Centenary Library*, vols. 28–29: *Savitri*. Pondicherry, India: Sri Aurobindo Ashram Press, 1972.

Aurobindo, Sri. "Some Personal Notes by Sri Aurobindo." *Mother India: Monthly Review of Culture*, 23, no. 2 (March 1971).

Aurobindo, Sri. *Sri Aurobindo in Baroda*. Compiled and edited by Roshan and Apurva. Pondicherry, India: Sri Aurobindo Ashram, 1993.

Aurobindo, Sri. *Tales of Prison Life*. Translated by Sisirkumar Ghose. Calcutta, India: Sri Aurobindo Pathamandir, 1979.

Baker, Kenneth. "Book Review." *San Francisco Chronicle*, November 28, 1999.

Capra, Fritjof. *The Tao of Physics*. New York: Bantam, 1984.

Donne, John. "Divine Poems." In *Tudor Poetry and Prose*, edited by J. William Hebel et al. New York: Appleton-Century-Crofts, 1953.

Drabble, Margaret, ed. *The Oxford Companion to English Literature*, 5th ed. New York: Oxford University Press, 1985.

Engman, Robert. "Sculpture." In *The Creative Experience*, edited by Stanley Rosner and Lawrence E. Abt. New York: Dell, 1970.

Frank, Anne. *The Diary of a Young Girl*. New York: Doubleday, 1995.

Gupta, Mahendranath. *The Gospel of Sri Ramakrishna*. Translated by Swami Nikhilananda. Madras: Sri Aurobindo Math, 1974.

Gupta, Nolini Kanta. *Collected Works*, vol. 6: *Sweet Mother*. Calcutta: Nolini Kanta Gupta Birth Centenary Celebrations Committee, 1989.

Head, Joseph, and Cranston, Sylvia. *Reincarnation: The Phoenix Fire Mystery*. Pasadena, CA: Theosophical University Press, 1998.

Heehs, Peter. *Sri Aurobindo: A Brief Biography*. New Delhi: Oxford University Press, 1989.

Iyengar, K. R. Srinivasa. *On The Mother: The Chronicle of a Manifestation and Ministry*, vols. 1–2. Pondicherry, India: Sri Aurobindo International Centre of Education, 1978.

Joshi, Kireet. *Sri Aurobindo and The Mother: Glimpses of Their Experiments, Experiences, and Realisations*. Delhi: The Mother's Institute of Research, 1996.

Joyce, James. *A Portrait of the Artist as a Young Man*. New York: Viking, 1963.

Jussara. "Interview." *Auroville Today*, October 1997, p. 3.

Keats, John. "Ode on a Grecian Urn." In *John Keats: Complete Poems*, edited by Jack Stillinger. Cambridge: Harvard University Press, 1982.

Kelly, John. "Interview with John Kelly." *Collaboration*, 10, no. 2 (Spring-Summer 1984), 16–18.

Koestler, Arthur. *The Act of Creation: A Study of the Conscious and Unconscious in Science and Art*. New York: Dell, 1964.

Korstange, Jeanne. "Sri Aurobindo and The Mother on Beauty." *Collaboration*, 13, no. 1 (Fall 1986), 3.

Lidchi-Grassi, Maggi. *The Light That Shone into the Dark Abyss*. Pondicherry: Sri Aurobindo Ashram Press, 1994.

MacIver, Rod. "Gordon Orions and David Abrams, *On Red-Winged Blackbirds and on Beauty*." *Heron Dance*, 24 (1999), 32–33.

Maheshwar, ed. *Bhagavad Gita in the Light of Sri Aurobindo*. Pondicherry, India: Sri Aurobindo Ashram Trust, 1985.

Marvell, Andrew. "To His Coy Mistress." In *Love Poems*, edited by Peter Washington. New York: Knopf, 1993.

May, Rollo. *My Quest for Beauty*. Dallas: Saybrook, 1985.

Miller, Henry. "Reflections on Writing." In *The Creative Process: A Symposium*, edited by Brewster Ghiselin. New York: Mentor, 1952.

Mother, The. "Art." *Bulletin of the Sri Aurobindo International Centre of Education*, February 1961, p. 126.

Mother, The. *Collected Works of The Mother*, vol. 1: *Prayers and Meditations*. Pondicherry, India: Sri Aurobindo Ashram Press, 1979.

Mother, The. *Collected Works of The Mother*, vol. 2: *Words of Long Ago*. Pondicherry, India: Sri Aurobindo Ashram Press, 1978.

Mother, The. *Collected Works of The Mother*, vols. 3–9: *Questions and Answers*. Pondicherry, India: Sri Aurobindo Ashram Press, 1972–79.

Mother, The. *Collected Works of The Mother*, vol. 11: *Notes on the Way*. Pondicherry, India: Sri Aurobindo Ashram Press, 1980.

Mother, The. *Collected Works of The Mother*, vol. 12: *On Education*. Pondicherry, India: Sri Aurobindo Ashram Press, 1978.

Mother, The. *Collected Works of The Mother*, vols. 13–15: *Words of The Mother*. Pondicherry: Sri Aurobindo Ashram Press, 1980.

Mother, The. *Collected Works of The Mother*, vol. 16: *Some Answers from The Mother*. Pondicherry, India: Sri Aurobindo Ashram Press, 1987.

Mother, The. *Flowers and Their Messages*. Auroville, India: Auropress Trust, 1973.

Mother, The. *Glimpses of The Mother's Life*, vols. 1–2. Compiled by Nilima Das, edited by K. D. Sethna. Pondicherry, India: Sri Aurobindo Ashram, 1978–80.

Mother, The. *Mother's Agenda*, (Agenda of the Supramental Action Upon Earth), 13 vols. Edited by Satprem. New York: Institute for Evolutionary Research, 1979–2000.

Mother, The. *On Women*. Compiled by Vijay from the writings of Sri Aurobindo and The Mother. Pondicherry, India: Sri Aurobindo Society, 1978.

Mother, The. "Questions and Answers on Thoughts and Aphorisms." *Bulletin of the Sri Aurobindo International Centre of Education*, February and August 1961.

Mother, The. "Sri Aurobindo—His Life and Work." *Bulletin of the Sri Aurobindo International Centre of Education*, August 1962.

Mother, The. *The Synthesis of Yoga: The Mother's Talks*. Edited by Shyam Sundar. Pondicherry: All India Press, 1989.

Mother, The. *Words of The Mother*. Pondicherry, India: Sri Aurobindo Ashram, 1949.

Nahar, Sujata. *Mother's Chronicles*, Book 1: *Mirra*. New York: Institute for Evolutionary Research, 1985.

Nietzsche, Friedrich. "Composition of *Thus Spake Zarathustra*." In *The Creative Process: A Symposium*, edited by Brewster Ghiselin. New York: Mentor, 1952.

Plato. *The Republic*. Translated by H. D. P. Lee. Baltimore: Penguin, 1953.

Poddar, Vijay, ed. *Sri Aurobindo and The Mother on India*. Pondicherry: Sri Aurobindo Society, 1973.

Purani, A. B. *On Art: Addresses and Writings*. Nargol, India: Nava Sarjan Society, 1965.

Purani, A. B. *Sri Aurobindo: Some Aspects of His Vision*, 2nd ed. Bombay, India: Bharatiya Vidya Bhavan, 1977.

Ram, N. Sri. "Thoughts for Aspirants." *For the Love of Life*, 12 (April 1986), 38.

Rodman, Selden. "Poetry." In *The Creative Experience*, edited by Stanley Rosner and Lawrence E. Abt. New York: Dell, 1970.

Ronsard, Pierre de. "Corinna in Vendôme." In *Love Poems*, edited by Peter Washington. New York: Knopf, 1993.

Sastry, T. V. Kapali. *Sadhana*. Pondicherry, India: Dipti Publications, 1976.

Satprem. *Mother or the Mutation of Death*. New York: Institute for Evolutionary Research, 1976.

Sheldrake, Rupert. *The Presence of the Past*. New York: Vintage, 1989.

Stevenson, Ian. *Twenty Cases Suggestive of Reincarnation*. New York: American Society for Psychical Research, 1966.

Terkel, Studs. "Interview." *San Francisco Chronicle*, May 29, 1977.

Van Vrekhem, Georges. *Beyond the Human Species: The Life and Work of Sri Aurobindo and The Mother*. St. Paul, MN: Paragon House, 1997.

Order Form

God Shall Grow Up

Body, Soul & Earth Evolving Together

Please send me the following:

Quantity:	Item	Price:
_____	God Shall Grow Up	$16.95 ea.

Subtotal . . . .   _____

Shipping ($4.95 per book within USA . . . . . .   _____

TOTAL . . . .   _____

Customer Information (please print)

Name: _____

Mailing Address: _____

City: _____State: _____ Zip: _____

Phone_____

Fax: _____Email: _____

Date: _____

Make checks payable to: Pondy Publishing

BOOK ORDERING INFORMATION
Pondy Publishing
2868 Vista Blvd. #124
PMB #200
Sparks, NV 89434